Preface

Aims and scope of the book

The aim of this book is to provide comprehensive coverage of the principles and practice of Business Administration in both the private and public sectors. Because of the wide ranging nature of the subject it will also be found suitable for university, college and professional courses in Business Organisation, Business Studies, Introduction to Management, Business Environment as well as Business Administration.

It provides full coverage of the appropriate syllabuses for the following professional examinations:

Association of Accounting Technicians
Institute of Administrative Management
Chartered Institute of Management Accountants
Chartered Association of Certified Accountants
Chartered Institute of Bankers
Chartered Institute of Secretaries and Administrators
Institute of Purchasing and Supply
Chartered Institute of Public Finance and Accounting

It will also be found suitable for a variety of courses at universities and colleges including:

Access courses
BTEC Higher National
Certificate and Diploma in Management Studies
National Examination Board in Supervisory Management
Diploma, Degree and Post-Experience Courses

Approach

The book has been written in a standardised format with chapter objectives, headed paragraphs, end of chapter summaries and review questions at the end of each chapter.

To gain genuine understanding of any technical subject constant reinforcement of knowledge and practice in answering problems is vital. Special attention has been given to this and, at suitable stages, the book includes several Assessment and Revision sections. These contain:

- ❐   assignments for individual or group activity;
- ❐   mini-cases with tasks to be accomplished;
- ❐   examination questions (with and without answers);
- ❐   suggestions for further reading.

Note for lecturers

This book is suitable both for topic based teaching or student centred learning using the questions without answers, assignments and cases provided in the Assessment and Revision sections.

A Lecturers' Supplement is available free to lecturers adopting this book as a course text (apply to the publishers on college-headed paper giving course details). The supplement contains:

- ❐   guidance notes on the cases;
- ❐   answers to the questions in the book;
- ❐   OHP masters of key diagrams from the book.

Terry Lucey
July 1994

Contents

1   *Business administration: an overview*

Objectives

After you have studied this chapter you will:

❏ *Be able to define Business Administration.*

❏ *Know how various subjects and disciplines contribute to the study of Business Administration.*

❏ *Have been introduced to themes developed throughout the book including: the management of change, human relations, decision making, international influences and Information Technology.*

❏ *Understand the scope and development of subject matter throughout the book.*

Introduction

This short chapter provides an outline of the scope, principles and objectives of Business Administration and serves as an introduction to the book as a whole. In addition it introduces themes which are developed throughout the book.

In general the book moves from broad external factors, for example the influence of the European Union on organisations, progressively through to more detailed internal matters, for example, form design for the office in the last chapter. Knowledge is thus developed in a logical sequence which greatly assists understanding.

Business administration defined

There does not appear to be a single universally accepted definition of Business Administration but for the purposes of this book it can be defined as:

The study of the influences on organisations, how they are structured and managed and how they operate. It includes study of the nature and roles of management, especially the key tasks of planning, control and decision-making, and of the importance of information and communications. The principles of business administration apply to all types of organisations; Public or Private Sector, Profit or Non-Profit seeking.

It will be apparent from the above definition that business administration is a wide ranging field of study. It draws upon relevant principles and techniques from many sources and disciplines, typical of which are the following:

Subject/Discipline	Typical examples of relevance to the Study of Business Administration
Economics	to help understand demand, competition pricing and the environment.
Behavioural Science	the motivation of individuals, group working, leadership.
Politics	the role of the State, Government policies, the European Union.
Finance	sources of capital, the Stock Exchange, financial control.
Management theory	principles of responsibility and authority, delegation, coordination.
Mathematics and Statistics	forecasting, decision making, setting control levels.
Technology	information processing, communications, networks, machine control.
Law	Health and Safety legislation, contract law, company law.

At appropriate points in the text sufficient subject/disciplinary material is introduced to be able to deal with the particular business administration topic being covered.

Themes developed throughout the book

Numerous themes are progressively developed in this book. They include: change and the management of change, the importance of human factors in organisation, international influences, decision-making and the impact of Information Technology.

These themes are briefly introduced below and then dealt with in detail in the chapters which follow.

Change and the management of change

Enormous change has taken place and is still continuing, within organisations, in the UK economy and in the world economy. Change takes many forms; for example, increased competition, new products and technologies, privatisation, changes in working patterns, contracting out services in the Public Sector and many, many others. Long-term stability seems to be a thing of the past.

To deal with change organisations must be flexible and adaptable. This may mean new products or methods, new structures, new ways of working and so on. Only one thing is known for certain; organisations which do not adapt will not survive. Adaptation requires management action.

Importance of human factors

People are all important in organisations. Well motivated people working effectively are the key to organisational success. In the early part of this century the Scientific Management movement tended to treat people merely as factors of production, almost as adjuncts to machines. This attitude persisted until quite recent times but nowadays it is realised that people respond positively to increased responsibility and being trusted. Hence the current trends in 'empowering' people, pushing decisions down to the lowest possible level, and encouraging team work.

International influences

The growth in international trade, better communications, technology transfers, the activities of multi-national companies, the European Union and many other factors mean that the UK economy is ever more closely inter-related with the world economy. This may cause a transfer of ownership, (e.g. Rover sold to BMW) it may be the effect on the London Stock Exchange of movements in New York, Tokyo or Frankfurt or it may be a UK manufacturer having to compete with low cost manufacture in China or Taiwan.

Decision making

Decision-making means choosing between alternatives. It is a key function of management, indeed it could be said to be the primary function. Decision making takes place at all levels but naturally the scope and importance of the decisions vary. Decision making always relates to the future and is based on information about numerous factors including; financial, social, psychological, political and other considerations.

Information Technology (IT)

IT is a general term for the application of micro-electronics, computers and networks in information processing and transfer. Low cost, high power IT equipment is widely used in offices, factories, shops and elsewhere and is changing not only how work is done but where it is done and is even having an impact on the way organisations are structured. For example the middle management level in many organisations is fast disappearing partly due to the use of computers to carry out tasks which previously required management intervention. Examples include; credit scoring in banks, stock control in retailing and so on. Special emphasis is given throughout the book to information and communications.

Figure 1.1 shows the progressive development of subject matter in the subsequent chapters of this book. It is recommended that the diagram is examined with care because it provides a logical framework for a study programme.

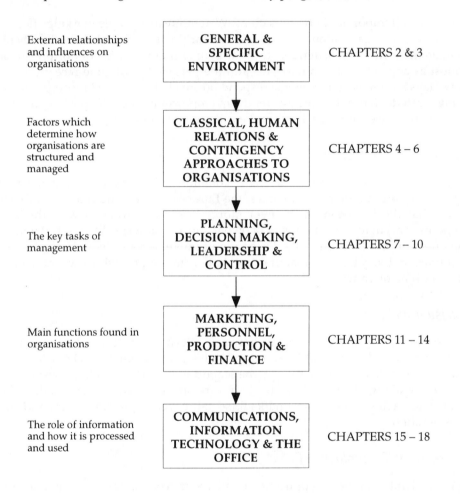

Figure 1.1: Development of subject matter

Key point summary

❑   Business Administration can be defined as the study of the influences on organisations, their structures and management and how they operate. It applies to all types of organisations.

❏ Numerous subjects are of relevance to Business Administration including; economics, law, behavioural science, finance, management theory etc.

❏ The book develops various themes including; the management of change, human relations, international influences, decision-making and IT.

❏ The main sequence of subject development is; the Environment, Organisations, Management principles, Functions, and Information and Communications.

Self review questions

1. *Define Business Administration.*

2. *Give five subjects or disciplines which the study of Business Administration draws upon.*

3. *Name four themes which are developed throughout the book.*

4. *List the broad sequence of subject matter covered in the book.*

2 The business environment: introduction and general factors

Objectives

After you have studied this Chapter you will:

☐ *Understand that organisations are open systems which must interact with their environment.*

☐ *Be able to distinguish between an organisation's general and specific environment.*

☐ *Understand the general economic framework within which organisations work.*

☐ *Know the main Government influences on organisations.*

☐ *Be able to describe the impact of the European Union.*

☐ *Understand how cultural and demographic factors influence organisations.*

☐ *Know how the Law influences all aspects of an organisation's operations.*

Organisations and the external environment

All organisations exist within an external environment. They are influenced by their environment and, in turn, they cause changes in the environment. Because of this, Systems Theory classes organisations as 'open systems'. This means they receive inputs and influences from their environment, transform or deal with these inputs in some way and pass outputs back to the environment. Fig 2.1 shows the organisation as an open system and gives examples of inputs and outputs for two typical open systems; a manufacturing firm and a college.

Interaction with the environment is vital and is the way that organisations adapt to change and respond to demand. The adaptation can take many forms. It may mean changes in the goods or services supplied, the way they are processed or the way the organisation is structured. An important managerial task especially at senior levels, is constantly to monitor the environment for development and trends which will have an impact on the organisation. Inward looking organisations which ignore environmental trends are doomed to failure.

The environment interacts with and influences the organisation in an ever changing variety of ways; some welcome and some less so. Examples include; opportunities to grow because of new markets or developments in technology, threats from new competitors and substitute products, difficulties caused by supply problems and so on.

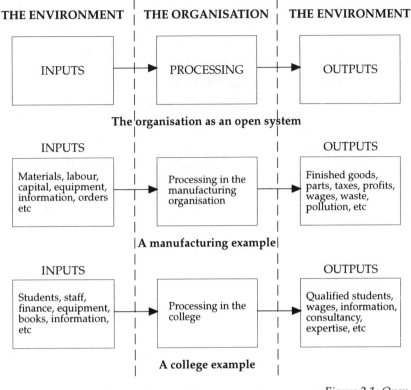

THE ENVIRONMENT | THE ORGANISATION | THE ENVIRONMENT

INPUTS → PROCESSING → OUTPUTS

The organisation as an open system

INPUTS | | OUTPUTS

Materials, labour, capital, equipment, information, orders etc → Processing in the manufacturing organisation → Finished goods, parts, taxes, profits, wages, waste, pollution, etc

A manufacturing example

INPUTS | | OUTPUTS

Students, staff, finance, equipment, books, information, etc → Processing in the college → Qualified students, wages, information, consultancy, expertise, etc

A college example

Figure 2.1: Open systems

What is an organisation's environment?

In a literal sense the environment can be thought of as everything external to the organisation but this meaning is too general and vague. For our purposes, the relevant environment of an organisation comprises those elements and influences with which it has some significant connection or relationship. The relationships and connections may be indirect and subtle e.g. the increasing importance to the general public of 'green' issues or they be direct and immediate, e.g. a reduction in selling price by a competitor. The relevant influences in the environment may be classified in numerous ways and Fig 2.2 shows the major environmental influences separated into those connected with the general environment and those in the specific environment although there is often no true dividing line between the two.

As will be seen from Fig 2.2 the influences in the specific environment are those which are closest and most immediate e.g. the relationship of an organisation with its customers whereas the general environment comprises less direct factors; for example, the type of economy in which the organisation operates.

Figure 2.2: The general and specific environments

The influences which make up an organisation's specific and general environment can be rearranged geographically as shown in Fig 2.3.

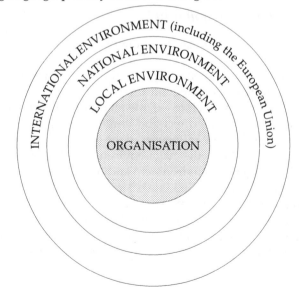

Figure 2.3: Geographical environments

Naturally, there is a tendency for the organisation's local environment to be of more specific and immediate concern but national and international factors frequently have a direct impact.

> For example, the cessation of links with Iraq in 1990 due to the invasion of Kuwait had an immediate effect on UK firms working on Iraqi contracts causing redundancies and financial loses.
>
> The outbreak of civil war in what was Yugoslavia naturally halted tourism causing the collapse of travel firms specialising in holidays in that part of the World.

Descriptions of the major influences in the general environment are given below; those for the specific environment are dealt with in the next chapter.

The general environment

The distinction between the specific and general environment of an organisation is ever changing. What is considered a general, indirect influence today can become more specific and immediate tomorrow. As a rule, organisations can influence their specific environment more than the general environment and local factors more than national and international ones. However, size is important. Large organisations, particularly what are called multi-nationals can exert influence on national and even international politics and economics.

Multi-nationals are large corporations which operate from bases in a number of countries and which are co-ordinated by a global strategy. Many multi-nationals are American; for example, IBM, General Motors, EXXON and so on but there are European and UK examples; including Unilever, Shell, BP etc. whilst the Japanese and Asian growth continues with organisations such as Nissan, Sony, Mitsubishi and many others.

For convenience, the elements of the general environment, as shown in Fig 2.2, are described separately below but they should not be thought of as self contained, watertight compartments. They interact with each other and, singly and jointly, influence the organisation. The environment is diverse, complex and, for most organisations, ever changing. It is these characteristics which caused the System Theorists Emery and Trist, to coin the term 'turbulent environment' to describe an environment whose very nature is changing due to political, social and economic influences. In such circumstances adaptability and flexibility are all important.

General environment – the economic framework

The economic framework within which the organisation operates can be considered to have two levels. Firstly, there are general economic principles which underpin all business activity and secondly, the organisation of the economy itself.

Clearly this book is not the place to describe all the principles of economics and students without some economics background are recommended to study a good economics text. However, it is worth summarising some of the more important principles:

The general economic problem is of finite resources and infinite wants.

People are assumed to be rational and to be utility maximisers (where utility means the satisfaction people gain from goods and services).

The quantity demanded of a good changes in relation to its price. In general, if the price is increased, less will be demanded. (This is known as the First Law of Demand).

There is diminishing marginal utility. As more units of a commodity are consumed in a period the utility obtained from each successive unit declines.

The principle of diminishing returns. Where more and more variable factors are added to a fixed factor, output at first increases, then slows down and eventually declines. For example, if more labour, materials and machines were introduced into a factory, output would initially increase but increasing inputs would eventually cause output to fall.

Economies of scale. If an item is produced in large numbers there is likely to be greater efficiency and lower costs per unit. This is because size enables better equipment to be used and more division of labour. Division of Labour means that people carry out a narrow task and become more specialised and proficient. However, note that research evidence suggests that these ideas cannot be pursued too far. Increasing size brings managerial, organisational and communication difficulties and excessive specialisation also has problems. These points are developed later in the book.

Opportunity cost. The true cost of an action is the benefit foregone of the alternative. Thus the true cost of a stretch of new motorway is the Hospital that could have been built instead.

The economy

Organisations are greatly influenced by the type of economic system in which they exist. The two theoretical extremes are the planned (or command) economy and the free market (or capitalist) economy.

In a planned economy, agencies of government make all key economic decisions; what types and quantities of goods will be produced, where the goods will be produced, the prices at which goods will be sold, how they will be produced and distributed and so on. In addition, all economic resources (land, buildings, transport etc) are in public ownership. It is difficult to give an example of a pure planned economy but the Soviet Union and the Eastern bloc countries were effectively planned economics up until the mid 1980's since when, of course, there have been major changes.

In a free market economy economic decisions are not centralised. Market forces or the profit motive determine prices, production levels, the type of goods produced, how they are produced and so on. Transactions between consumers and suppliers are guided by competition and self interest and a feature of such economies is the private ownership of the means of production.

The UK, along with most industrialised countries is a mixed economy where free enterprise is combined with state involvement. State involvement includes public ownership, legal regulation, various forms of planning and direction, overall demand management and direct employment by the State. Nowadays all political parties accept the notion of a mixed economy which, ideally, should combine the benefits to be gained from market forces, for example, enterprise, efficiency, competition, with sufficient State intervention to control exploitation and excesses which could occur from unregulated self interest.

It is normal to analyse the economy into three main groups:

Primary	These are the extractive industries e.g. mining, fishing, agriculture.
Secondary	All forms of manufacture and construction.
Service	All forms of services: public, personal and commercial.

In the UK, like most developed countries, the proportion of people employed in the service sector has been increasing relative to the other two sectors. For example, in 1960, 48% of the working population were employed in the service sector but by 1990 this had risen to 69%. (Source: Department of Employment Gazette).

The size of organisation in the economy varies widely. In the UK, as in most developed countries, a relatively small number of large organisations are responsible for most economic activity. This is particularly pronounced in sectors such as transport, chemicals, refining, manufacturing, utilities (gas, water, electricity) and so on. In other sectors, such as retailing, building, agriculture etc. smaller organisations have a more important role but even in such sectors there is a tendency for large firms to dominate; for example, Marks and Spencers, Sainsburys, Tescos and so on in retailing, Tarmac, Wimpeys and others in constructions.

As a consequence, the actions of large organisations regarding prices, production, employment and investment have a major effect on the economy. This applies particularly to multi-nationals operating in the UK and recognition of this importance is demonstrated by the efforts of National and Local Government to attract investment by multi-nationals.

General environment – government influence

The influence of the modern state extends into every aspect of the economy. Despite the well publicised disagreements between the main UK political parties over the 'right' amount of State intervention in the economy, in practice it is likely that State involvement will remain substantial in spite of successive privatisations. In general, the State seeks to create secure and stable conditions for economic growth without sharp fluctuations between boom and recession. This ideal is, of course, difficult to achieve and there are sharp divisions between political parties about the best ways to bring about such conditions.

Whilst it would be impossible to catalogue all aspects of State involvement, examples of major areas are shown in Fig 2.4 grouped into the four categories suggested by Grove; the Government as *regulator, promoter, entrepreneur* and *planner.*

Government as regulator	Government as promoter
examples:	examples:
❒ consumer protection	❒ provision of training and education
❒ regulation of wages and hours of work	❒ provision of finance, grants and subsidiaries
❒ control of monopolies	❒ protection of domestic industry through tariffs and quotas
❒ control of utilities eg OFTEL, National Rivers Authority	❒ promotion of research
Government as entrepreneur	**Government as planner**
examples:	examples:
❒ public sector employment	❒ fiscal policies relating to indirect and direct taxation
❒ public corporations	❒ monetary policies relating to money supply and interest rates
❒ purchases of materials and services	❒ regional planning

Figure 2.4: State involvement with the economy

One traditional way of dividing the economy is into the public and private sectors. The public sector is that part of the economy over which the State has direct control whereas the private sector is that part where market forces provide the goods and services. However, this simple division does not adequately describe the complexities of modern economies and implies a separateness that does not exist.

For example, many parts of the public sector sell goods and services in the market place sometimes in competition with the private sector. Examples include nationalised industries such as British Rail, the Post Office and British Coal.

Trading, profits and competition are being encouraged elsewhere in the public sector.

For example: schools are being urged to compete for pupils and are being provided with operating budgets – the National Health Service is being made into an internal market with hospitals providing prices of treatments so that competitive choices can be made and so on.

Conversely many of the activities of firms in the private sector are subject to direct State control and regulation, a few examples being; trading standards, safety, hours and conditions of work, advertising, noise and pollution controls, building and planning regulations and so on. The organisation has to consider not only the direct and indirect influence of the national Government on its environment but also the growing influence of the European Union.

General environment – European Union (EU)

The European Union[1] comprises 12 European countries with a combined population of some 350 million people. The establishment of the EU meant setting up a customs union and a common market. A custom union means that tariffs between members are abolished and the levy of a common external tariff to the rest of the world. The objective of the common market is, eventually, to treat the organisation of the economies of the member states as if they were one country with free movement of labour, capital and enterprise. So far only in agriculture, through the Common Agricultural Policy, has there been a truly common policy. However the establishment of the Single Market in 1992 committed the member states to move towards much greater harmonisation.

The elimination of trade restrictions to achieve the Single Market covers the following areas:

(a) Free movement of capital.

(b) Harmonisation of national Laws on trade marks and patents to protect industrial property.

(c) European wide standards to ensure the free marketing of products across the community.

(d) The opening up of public and government contracts to all EU members on an equal basis.

(e) Greater and more equal competition in air routes, shipping, telecommunications and information technology.

(f) Professional qualifications from one country will be acceptable across the community.

There are, of course, still many problems to be solved before a true Single Market exists; a major one being fiscal harmonisation. This means that taxes, both direct and indirect should be roughly equivalent across the EU. Indirect taxes are taxes such as VAT and excise duties and direct taxes are income tax and taxes on companies, known in the UK as Corporation Tax. As an indication of the discrepancies which exist, the excise duty on a bottle of spirits is 12p in Greece and 735p in Denmark and VAT rates vary across the Community from 12% to 36%.

1   *From November 1993 the group of 12 European Countries is called the EUROPEAN UNION. Previous names were the European Economic Community (EEC), European Community (EU) or, popularly, the Common Market.*

Another longer term objective of the EU is to have a single currency for the entire community which would mean that there would have to be a central monetary authority to issue and control it. In effect, this would mean that the UK's monetary policy would be controlled in Brussels rather than by the UK government.

The objective of a single currency is proving to be politically divisive in many countries of the EU, not least the UK. The UK government joined the Exchange Rate Mechanism (ERM) in 1990, but were forced to leave it abruptly in September 1992. The ERM is a system where the value of national currencies is kept within defined ranges against other EU currencies and its operation is a necessary prelude to the establishment of a single currency. Because of the strains that have occurred in the ERM it is likely that it will be many years before there is a single currency throughout the EU, if it ever occurs at all.

How the EU works

The EU is a Law making body and thus has a direct effect on the sovereignty of the UK and the other member states. The Council of Ministers (consisting of 12 members, one minister from each country) frames the major policies and decisions of the community and initiates what is known as Secondary Legislation. Secondary Legislation takes three forms:

(a) Regulations. These apply to the population of the community and automatically form part of the Law of member states. Where there is a conflict between a Regulation and an existing national law, the Regulation takes precedence.

(b) Directives. These are binding instructions to member states which the individual states must implement. As an example, the UK Companies Act implemented the EU's fourth directive on the disclosure of information by small companies.

(c) Decisions. These are directly binding but relate to specific organisations or individuals, not to the population generally.

The EU is the world's largest market and its relationship with member states deepens as each year passes. Accordingly no organisation can afford to ignore EU influences especially those who trade or have links with Europe and the rest of the world.

General environment – social cultural and demographic influences

Clearly this heading is an enormous one and the influences concerned are all pervasive although often indirect and long term. The attitudes, numbers, social organisation and level of education of the population are ultimately the key influences in the environment although the effects are not always readily foreseen. Figure 2.5 provides a summary of the major social and other characteristics which are briefly developed below.

Cultural influences	Social influences
examples:	examples:
❐ leisure patterns	❐ social structure and mobility
❐ patterns of communication, and the Media	❐ family patterns
❐ ideologies and belief systems eg religion	❐ level of industrialisation
❐ personal values and norms – attitudes to the environment, economic growth, science and technology etc	❐ crime and alienation
	❐ emigration and immigration
Demographic influences	**Educational and training influences**
examples:	examples:
❐ size and rate of population growth	❐ levels of literacy and numeracy in population
❐ birth and death rates	❐ structure of the educational system
❐ age and sex discrimination	❐ amount of technical/vocational training
❐ geographic distribution	❐ numbers in further/higher education
❐ amount of urban and regional concentration	

Figure 2.5: Social and other influences in the environment

Although Fig 2.5 shows a four way division this is for convenience only because the various influences are inextricably linked and inter-mingled and this must be borne in mind whilst studying the following paragraphs.

Cultural influences

Culture is a highly complex subject and comprises the ideas and attitudes through which individuals perceive and interpret the world, the values, norms and beliefs which people have, the customs they follow and so on.

These values and attitudes are not static but change over time, sometimes surprisingly rapidly. As an example, when their standard of living rises, peoples' attitudes and priorities change. They often become less concerned about material possessions and become more interested in a cleaner environment, greater job satisfaction, increased leisure and so on. During the 1980's the Government tried to encourage an enterprise culture and increased self reliance, especially in matters such as pensions, health provision and education. They were, in effect, trying to change peoples' attitude to the Welfare State. The extent to which underlying attitudes actually changed is, of course, arguable.

Although the idea of cultural influence appears rather nebulous, the cumulative total of cultural differences between countries is readily apparent. Contrast, for example, the attitudes and beliefs of the UK population with say, the Germans and also with people in a developing country. Cultural differences also exist within the same country; one region compared to another, the countryside and the city and so on.

Demographic influences

Changes in the size of population, its age structure and its distribution are key elements in environmental change. Because the numbers already born are known, it is possible to predict changes in population and population structures with reasonable accuracy, although it is much more difficult to predict the effects of these changes. For example, two known demographic trends which are likely to have significant effects on the UK economy in the 1990's and into the 21st century are the increase in the number of people of pensionable age and the decrease in the number of 15–29 year olds. At the end of the 1980's there were 13 million 15–29 year olds but by 2000 this will decline to 10.8 million. This will mean, for example, that there will be less pressure on schools and colleges, a decline in purchasing power for the group, a shortage of young recruits into employment and so on. Organisation which rely on a continuing intake of young people are already feeling the effects; an example being the difficulties encountered by the National Health Service in maintaining the flow of student nurses.

Conversely, the increase in elderly people will place more pressure on Social and Health Services, change expenditure patterns (and thus production and marketing plans) and have many other effects.

Population location

The location and movements of population also affect the economy. In the 19th and early 20th century there was a general movement from the countryside to towns and cities. Now there are different changes; city centres are decaying and becoming less pleasant to live in and increased affluence and mobility are enabling people to live in pleasant surroundings. There is also population drift between regions. In spite of problems caused by housing there is a continuing net movement of people into the relatively prosperous South East of England from other parts of the UK.

The greater use of Information Technology (computers, faxes etc) and of data transmission is affecting not only how work is done but where it is done. In America it is estimated that over 9m people now work at home using computers and data links. Tofler has coined the phrase 'electronic cottage industries' to describe this trend which is also apparent in the UK.

In the UK, British Telecom (BT) use the term teleworking and define this as:

Working in a location that is remote from an employer or from the normally expected place of work either on a full-time or part-time basis. The work generally involves the electronic processing of information, the results of which are communicated remotely to the employer, usually by a 'telecommunications link'.

The Henley Centre for Forecasting think that up to 15% of all work days will be accounted for by teleworking.

Various benefits have been claimed for teleworking both for the employee and employer. These can be summarised thus:

Benefits to the employee:

- ☐ Reduced travelling.
- ☐ Better choice of area in which to live.
- ☐ Suitability for parents with young children, disabled people.
- ☐ Flexibility of working.
- ☐ Possibly greater responsibility.

Benefits to the employer:

- ☐ Increased productivity.
- ☐ Reduced costs e.g. smaller offices.
- ☐ Wider pool of potential employees.

Naturally there are problems associated with teleworking which include; possible lower status for the employee, security problems, extra costs associated with equipment, rentals etc. On balance it seems likely that teleworking will increase, especially for part-time workers.

To summarise; the movement and concentration of population affects the economy in numerous ways including; housing, transport needs, the provision of services, marketing, labour supply, the impact on the environment and so on.

Social influences

The family has been the most important social unit throughout history but in recent years there have been profound changes. The typical arrangement today is a nuclear family consisting of just parent(s) and children which should be contrasted with the traditional pattern of an extended family where there was a close network of support and assistance from grandparents, aunts, uncles and so on. The structure of society is also influenced by the increasing number of divorces and one parent families, the changing role of women in society – especially the higher number of women working outside the home – and greater social and geographical mobility.

One visible change in UK society over recent decades is the growth of ethnic minorities; mainly West Indian, Indian and Pakistani. This is not so much because of overall numbers (approximately 6% of the population) but because of high concentrations in certain areas, especially inner cities. In the past, immigration has caused political and social tensions but has now effectively ceased except for special cases.

Although for most people the quality of life has improved over the past few decades many problems and tensions remain. Crime has increased and there are widening gaps between the 'haves' and the 'have nots', the employed and unemployed, the North and the South. There is growing alienation of the disadvantaged sections of the community which is expressed by a general rejection of, and non-participation in, conventional society.

Educational and training influences

Education is of great influence in a society not only because of the knowledge and qualifications we may or may not gain but also because it helps to form attitudes and social values.

Despite a tendency for more pupils to attend fee paying schools nearly 90% of all UK pupils are still educated in the State sector. This sector is therefore of critical importance and is undergoing substantial change e.g. in 1989 the National Curriculum was introduced and is being progressively implemented, state schools are being allowed to 'opt out' of local authority control, City Technology colleges are being established to cater for more able pupils and so on. It is, of course, too early to judge the success or otherwise of these developments. They have been implemented to try to cure what are seen as problems in UK education, for example, poor standards of literacy and numeracy, lack of knowledge of technology and so on.

Beyond school level, problems still exist. UK participation rates in further and higher education are much lower than in countries such as Japan, Germany and USA. As an example 80% of German managers are graduates compared with fewer than 50% in the UK. Also, the degrees of German managers are more vocationally oriented with engineering and other technical subjects predominating.

It is not only at the degree level that problems exist, it is also at the skilled technician level. A typical Japanese or German worker receives far more on the job training than their UK counterpart, especially in the application and use of high technology equipment. In Germany about 85% of all school leavers who do not go into higher education enter a three year apprenticeship. This combines on the job training with attendance at a vocational college. There have been various attempts to improve the UK training position; for example the Industrial Training Act, Youth Training Schemes and so on but with little real success. In comparison with most of our main competitors, the UK labour force is under trained and lacks essential skills. Regrettably these deficiencies have existed for many, many years and were first commented on in Victorian times.

General environment – legal influences

The Law exerts not only general influence on an organisation it also forms part of the organisation's specific environment. The Law regulates the activities of organisations by providing a known framework of rules within which they operate. Some aspects of law constrain the organisation e.g. consumer legislation, some direct the organisation e.g. health and safety rules, some protect the organisation e.g. patent and trademark protection, and some parts of the Law are an enabling medium e.g. contract Laws enable an organisation to acquire assets and sell their products safely. The Law also provide ways of resolving the conflicts and differences which arise from time to time.

The Law pervades most facets of personal and organisational life and whilst this may be deplored by some it is clear that one of the characteristics of a stable society is the existence of a known legal framework which is applied impartially and consistently.

Some of the more important areas in which the Law affects organisations are:

EMPLOYMENT: e.g. legislation relating to minimum wages, hours of work, union recognition, redundancy, trade disputes.

ENVIRONMENT: e.g. legislation relating to waste disposal and pollution, noise, planning and zoning.

OPERATIONS: e.g. legislation relating to health and safety, product safety, hours of work, transport routing.

MARKETING: e.g. legislation relating to consumer protection, product/pricing, descriptions, weights and measures, misleading advertising.

PUBLIC INTEREST: e.g. legislation relating to mergers and monopolies, cartels, price fixing, insider trading.

FINANCE: e.g. legislation relating to tax collection by organisations for the State (i.e. PAYE income tax and VAT) corporation tax payments, financial statistics, records and statements.

ORGANISATION: e.g. legislation relating to rights, obligations and characteristics of different business organisations (companies, public corporations, trusts etc) rights and duties of directors, local government law and so on.

General environment – green issues

There is general acceptance that green issues will influence political debate and public awareness for the foreseeable future. Issues such as air and water pollution, forest and habitat destruction, global warming, acid rain, depletion of the ozone layer and others have directed attention to what many believe is the main problem facing the world; namely the degradation of the natural environment.

All political parties accept the importance of environmental issues although, as is to be expected, their approaches differ. In 1990 the Government announced the appointment in each Government department of a Minister responsible for environmental matters and whilst it is too early to assess their effectiveness it does demonstrate recognition of public concern.

Environmental awareness is causing many changes in behaviour both by individuals, organisations and government. As examples; government have reduced taxation on unleaded petrol, introduced regulations about carbon dioxide emissions and water cleanliness, manufacturers stress in their advertising the cleanliness and non-polluting nature of their products (catalytic converters for car, biodegradable detergents and so on), individuals are opting for organic food, recycling paper and glass, creating pressure groups on environmental matters and so on. It is of significance that issues that were decided solely on financial and social considerations just a decade ago are now being challenged on environmental grounds. Two major examples being nuclear power generation and motorway construction.

In Europe, especially in Germany, Green Parties have been politically successful and Green candidates have been elected. Whilst this has not happened yet in the UK, the Green Party did poll 20% of the vote in the 1989 elections to the European Parliament although their support has waned considerably since then although it can be argued that the main political parties have been greatly influenced by that success. As an example the Government published in 1993 what they considered to be seven deadly environmental sins:

- Emissions of carbon dioxide from burning coal, oil and gas;
- Worsening local air pollution, caused mainly by increasing emissions from road transport;
- The rising demand for water, threatening to dry out streams;
- Water pollution caused by farming, sewage, industry and acid rain;
- Loss of countryside to roads, homes and other development;
- Damage to habitats and loss of wildlife. Each year about 1 per cent of the 5,600 Sites of Special Scientific Interest suffer damage which may be irreversible;
- Rising demand for sand, gravel and rock quarries and pits which harm wildlife, landscapes and communities.

General environment – international influences

All economics of the world are inter-related so that international influences are important to all, especially to small and medium sized economies, such as Britain.

The markets for some commodities can only realistically be considered on an international basis; oil being the prime example. No one country can control the price and unforeseen rises and falls can have devastating effects on some economies, even including oil rich countries; for example, Mexico and Nigeria. Also the world market for manufacturing goods is becoming more competitive and volatile, especially with the massive growth in output of nations such as Japan, Korea, Taiwan and China.

Apart from import and export problems international influence is also exerted by the growing activity of multi-nationals operating in the UK. Although countries generally welcome inward investment by multi-nationals their activities can produce more uncertainty and volatility in the host country's economy and a reduction in control by national governments.

To suit the multi-national company, manufacturing and supply can be transferred rapidly from one country to another, profit may be withdrawn from the host company and taxes avoided by the use of transfer pricing. Transfer prices are prices charged from one subsidiary to another subsidiary of the same multi-national operating in another country. The prices are set to suit the needs of the multi-national and are adjusted so as to move profits from countries with high taxes to those with low taxes. Of course, multi-nationals also produce many benefits for the host country. Jobs are provided and wealth created by the increased activity. Contact with multi-nationals may also increase knowledge of more up-to-date technology and methods with obvious benefits to home industries. An example is the increasing use of so called lean production methods copied by UK and American manufacturers from Japanese implants. Lean production methods are Japanese invented production systems which are; flexible, quality based, use many robots and where production is integrated with deliveries.

Another part of the economy which is strongly influenced by international factors is the financial market. Modern technology and instantaneous worldwide communications mean that stock exchanges are linked across the world and UK share prices, exchange rates, interest rates, money supply and so on are as much affected by what happens in Tokyo, Frankfurt and New York as they are by what is happening in the British economy.

Key point summary

☐ Organisations must interact with their environment and adapt to change.

☐ An organisation's environment can be broadly divided into general or indirect factors, and more specific ones.

☐ Organisations work within general economic principles (i.e. utility maximising, economies of scale, opportunity cost etc) and the framework of the economy.

☐ The Government acts as regulator, promoter, entrepreneur and planner.

☐ The European Union is the UK's largest market and is a major influence to be considered by all organisations.

☐ The EU is a Law making body where the key decisions are framed by the Council of Ministers.

☐ Cultural and demographic factors exert fundamental influences on organisations albeit in a long-term, indirect way.

☐ Information technology and communication links are influencing not only how people work but where they live.

☐ Great changes are taking place in social and family structures and in education, all of which affects the general environment.

☐ The Law affects all aspects of the environment including; organisation structures, health and safety, pollution, taxation, employment and so on.

❒ Green issues, environmental degradation, the use of scarce resources are becoming dominant influences.

❒ International factors including the activities of multi-nationals are of increasing importance in the modern world.

Self review questions

1. *What is an open system?*

2. *Distinguish between an organisation's general and specific environments.*

3. *What are multi-nationals?*

4. *Give six important principles of economics.*

5. *Distinguish between a planned and a free market economy.*

6. *In what ways does Grove categorise State involvement in the economy?*

7. *What is the European Union (EU)?*

8. *What are EU Regulations, Directives and Decisions?*

9. *What demographic changes will take place over the next 10-20 years?*

10. *Contrast nuclear and extended families.*

11. *Give five ways in which The Law affects organisations.*

12. *Give examples of five environmental problems as specified by the UK Government.*

13. *Give four important international influences on the UK economy.*

3 The business environment: specific features

Objectives

After you have studied this chapter you will:

❏ *Understand that some environmental factors have a direct, often day-to-day influence on the organisation.*

❏ *Be able to define marketing and understand its primary role.*

❏ *Know the main types of market ranging from Perfect Competition to Monopoly.*

❏ *Know that Personnel Management deals with recruitment, selection, training, industrial relations.*

❏ *Be able to describe the various sources of finance available to an organisation.*

❏ *Understand the influence of technology on operations, communications, jobs.*

❏ *Know the importance of, and difficulties associated with, suppliers and materials.*

❏ *Understand the effect of various forms of competition on the organisation.*

Specific environment

The specific environment comprises those influences with which the organisation has direct contact, often on a day-to-day basis. The influences are more immediate and may well be local, although they need not be. The major elements in an organisation's specific environment are shown in Figure 3.1.

In the same way as the factors in the general environment, they are described separately below for convenience only. In practice they may influence the organisation jointly, in various combinations.

Figure 3.1: The organisation's specific environment

Specific environment: customers and markets

All organisation exist to meet the needs of their customers or clients. This applies as much to non-trading organisations such as schools, hospitals, local government etc. as it does to trading organisations such as Fords, Harrods or British Rail. To be able to satisfy needs, the needs must first be identified so all organisations must practise marketing; even Government departments!

Marketing has been variously described but a useful definition is:

> the process responsible for identifying, anticipating and satisfying customer requirements profitably (for trading organisations) or effectively (for non-trading organisations).

This means that, ideally, the whole organisation should be seen from the customer's point of view. Marketing is thus a vital management function and is described in more detail later.

Types of market

The type of market in which the organisation trades has a major influence on prices, types of products, output volumes and other key decisions. Fig 3.2 summarises the main market types according to the number of producers, type of product and ease of entry.

Market type	Number of producers	Product	Entry to market
Perfect competition	Many	Homogeneous	Unrestricted
Monopolistic competition	Many	Differentiated	Unrestricted
Pure oligopoly	Few	Homogeneous	Restricted
Differentiated oligopoly	Few	Differentiated	Restricted
Monopoly	Few	–	Restricted

Figure 3.2: Market types

A firm in *pure* or *perfect competition* is a price taker and cannot affect price because this is set by the market. Although perfect competition in its classical form does not exist many facets of perfect competition appear in markets dealing with raw materials or agricultural products. In such industries there are often wide swings in prices, production and incomes so that governments often intervene with subsidies, quotas and other devices to create a more orderly market and to safeguard incomes.

The position in *monopolistic competition* is similar except that the products are differentiated. Thus the organisation has some control over price and competition takes place through advertising, packaging and service as well as price. The retail trade shows many of these characteristics.

Oligopoly is where there are only a few sellers of commodity or service. Oligopolists may produce virtually identical goods or services or there may be product differentiation, which is often created by brand advertising. There are numerous sectors in the UK which are dominated by a few large firms. For example, detergents are dominated by Proctor and Gamble and Unilever, banking is dominated by the big five High Street Banks, cross channel ferries are dominated by P & O, STENA and Brittany Ferries and so on. Although producers do have control over prices there is rarely any price competition between oligopolists. More usually, competition takes the form of image or brand advertising, product improvements and service innovations.

Monopoly means that there is only one producer of a commodity or service. In the UK there are a number of nationalised industries which are State monopolies. Examples include British Rail, the Post Office and British Coal. In the private sector, monopolies, or effective monopolies, also exist. For example, Tate and Lyle have a virtual monopoly of the cane sugar market as does British Telecom with domestic telephone services.

Where there is a monopoly, in theory, producers have complete control over prices or output and hence profit levels. In practice however, monopolists choose not to maximise profits because they fear either that government may intervene and curtail their activities or the large profits may cause competitors to enter the market and challenge their monopoly. Alternatively where the monopolies have been created by privatisation, for example the Water and Electricity Boards, British Telecom, a Regulator is appointed to oversee pricing and service.

Specific environment: personnel and unions

All organisations employ people so every organisation needs direct links with the environment to ensure that it is able to recruit personnel with the required skills. As a consequence, the numbers, ages, level of education and training, experience and attitudes of people available for employment are of critical importance to organisations.

The growth in the size of organisations and the complexities of modern economics have led to the development of a specialist function called *Personnel Management.* Personnel Management is that part of management which is concerned with people at work and their relationships. It includes the activities connected with recruitment, selection, training, pay administration and industrial relations. Most larger organisations have specialist personnel managers but in many small and medium sized organisations, personnel matters are dealt with by managers who also have other duties. The function of personnel management is dealt with in more detail later in the book.

Over the last 20 years there has been a general loss of jobs in the primary sector (agricultural, mining and fishing) and de-industrialisation has caused the loss of 3 million jobs in manufacturing since 1960. During this period there have been job gains in the service sector particularly in financial services, catering and the professions. More women are now employed and there is more part-time working. Indeed there is evidence that some UK firms are following Japanese and American practice by having a smaller core of permanent, fully trained workers supported by part-time employees whose numbers can be quickly adjusted to meet changing demands.

The role and power of Trade Unions has changed drastically over the years. This is due not only to Government attitudes and legislation but also due to the decline of many traditional industries which were heavily unionised. Examples include,ship-building, coal mining, engineering and so on. The existence of high unemployment through most of the 1980's, especially in the regions, has also weakened Trade Union influence. Since 1980, Government legislation has imposed greater restrictions on striking, picketing, closed shops, leadership elections and so on. The Unions see these restrictions as being politically motivated whereas the Government see them as contributing to economic stability and protecting the freedom of the individuals. Whatever one's views on this, it is clear that organisations have to recognise the changed nature and influence of Unions in their environment.

Specific environment: finance

Every organisation needs money to invest or to spend. The sources of funds for organisations vary greatly depending on the type of organisation. Commercial companies may raise funds from their shareholders or from other investors by way of loans. Alternatively, they may retain profits instead of paying them as dividends. Charities raise most of their funds from donations or through grants. A local council will receive funds direct from Council Tax and rate payers plus grants from Central Government and so on.

The availability and cost of finance is constantly changing. High interest rates makes borrowing more expensive and government spending policies will influence the amounts available to the various central Government departments (Health, Social Security etc) to nationalised industries, to Local Government and so on. The level of economic activity (boom or recession) greatly influences the amount spent by the public, the amount saved and what money is spent on (luxuries or food, for example). The volatility of the finance market is increased by the linkages which exist between the world money markets especially, between Tokyo, New York, Frankfurt and London.

Commercial companies do not generally have access to Government funds. Consequently the finance they need over and above the amount generated internally, must be raised from the market. Funds may be required for short term or long term purposes and the length of time for which the money is required largely determines the particular source that will be approached. Fig 3.3 provides a summary of the types of finance required and typical external sources but it should be realised that the categories shown are far from watertight.

Although many external sources are shown it must be emphasised that funds generated internally within the company, i.e. retained profits, depreciation etc are by far the most important source of company finance, accounting for about 70% of all funds available.

Time scale of finance	Short term (say up to 3 years)	Medium term (say 3–8 years)	Long term (say 8 years +)	Permanent
Typical uses:	Stocks, working capital	Vehicles, plant and machinery	Buildings, major plant, re-equipment	Permanent capital for acquisitions, expansion etc
Typical sources:	Clearing banks Factoring companies Leasing companies Finance houses	Clearing banks Leasing companies Government agencies Merchant banks	Clearing banks Merchant banks Government agencies Pension funds Insurance companies	Merchant banks Government agencies Pension funds Insurance companies Stock Exchange

Figure 3.3: External sources and uses of finance

The financial structure of most commercial organisations is complex and is largely determined by their legal status. Apart from the smallest organisations, most are *limited liability companies.* Limited liability is a vitally important concept because it enables someone to buy shares in a company without being liable to lose more than they have paid or promised to pay into the company. A person who buys shares in a company becomes a part owner of that company and is entitled to receive dividends from the company, which are effectively a share of the profits. There are two main types of shares:

Ordinary or equity shares

These are the risk capital of the business. Holders are not guaranteed any dividend but the shares usually carry voting rights so that ordinary shareholders, in principle, have ultimate control over the company.

Preference shares

These are less risky shares which have a prior claim in the distribution of profits and repayment of capital if the company is wound up. They usually have the right to a stated percentage dividend which must be paid before any dividends are paid on the ordinary shares. The dividends paid to preference shareholders can never be more than the stated percentage even if profits are high. Dividends on ordinary shares are not restricted in this way and may be high if profits are high but may be non-existent if profits are low.

In addition to raising money through share capital, companies also raise money by loans which are usually secured against the assets of the company. One particular form of a loan is a *debenture.* Debentures are loans to the company which carry a fixed rate of interest which must be paid before shareholders receive anything. Debenture holders are not owners of the company and the debentures may be bought and sold on the capital markets.

Specific environment: technology

Technology can be described as the application of machines, equipment, methods and skills to create and use materials, processes and products. Technology refers not only to machinery and physical items but also to the way they are used and the theories governing their application. Research studies have shown that technology exerts a strong influence on the structure of organisations, the relationship between departments, the style of management and the way work is organised. This influence appears to be stronger in smaller organisations but as they grow, it is size itself which becomes the more dominant influence.

The term *new technology* is frequently encountered. Although this is ill defined it can be taken to mean the application of micro-electronics to telecommunications, manufacture, information, processing, administration and so on. New technology is found in an ever increasing variety of applications. Examples include; in retailing, electronic point of sales systems (EPOS) provide instant information on cash flows, stock levels and sales; in manufacturing, robotics and computer aided design and manufacturing (CAD/CAM) have revolutionised manufacturing methods; in offices, word processing systems, computer based data processing, electronic mail systems, fax machines and others have increased efficiency, reduced response times and improved quality.

Another important influence of technology is on the number and types of jobs. Research by Daniels showed that the introduction of new technology in manufacturing produced some job losses, mainly in lower-skill jobs. However the job losses were small in relation to losses caused by other factors such as declining markets. In the service sector the reverse has happened and employment has increased. As an example, Banks have used the productivity and flexibility of new technology as a basis for providing new forms of customer service and total employment in Banks has risen.

In general, research indicates that the introduction of new technology has improved the quality of jobs although deskilling has taken place for a minority of workers, particularly in manufacturing. The effect of this is that the demand for unskilled workers has reduced whilst that for skilled labour has risen. This helps to explain the paradox of job vacancies which cannot be filled even though there is high unemployment. Whatever the effect on jobs caused by its introduction there seems little doubt that if the UK does not introduce new technology in line with other industrialised nations there will be severe job losses through declining competitiveness.

Specific environment: suppliers and materials

A major interaction with the environment concerns the various materials and services an organisation buys from its suppliers. Bought in services and materials constitute a large proportion of costs, especially for organisations such as manufacturing companies, retailers, wholesalers and so on. Consequently, the *purchasing function* is an important one in all organisations. This is particularly so in manufacturing where it has developed into what is called *materials management*. This is an approach which considers all aspects of materials planning, control, purchase, storage and usage.

The availability and price of some commodities can fluctuate sharply due to both national and international factors. For example, the Gulf crisis in 1990 upset the world oil market, trade disputes may affect the availability of components or disrupt their delivery, fluctuations in the Brazilian coffee harvest affects the world price of coffee and so on. Organisation that are particularly dependent on uninterrupted flows of materials seek to minimise problems by a variety of methods. These include; forward purchasing of materials, stockpiling where necessary, special arrangements with suppliers and even the acquisition of raw material suppliers or manufacturers of components, (this latter process is known as *vertical integration*).

An organisation can build up a close relationship with a single supplier but there may be greater security in having several sources. The choice of supplier is always important and reliability, quality and delivery must all be considered as well as price. The role of quality in international competition is becoming increasingly recognised.

As an example, the UK Government through the British Standards Institute have established British Standard 5750. This is only awarded to companies who are able to show that quality is built into every stage of the production process and whose employees have a genuine commitment to quality issues. The government has said that it will only give contracts to firms which possess BS 5750 and it is expected that this attitude will spread throughout industry and even to the general consumer.

By virtue of their purchasing power some organisations have considerable influence over their suppliers and can demand special discounts or preferential treatment over supplies. As an example, in an attempt to match the buying power and influence of the large supermarket chains independent foodstores have banded together for bulk purchasing and formed associations such as Spar, VG and Mace.

As is to be expected the Japanese have greatly influenced modern approaches to supplying operations. Their general approach can be summarised as:

☐ Standardise parts and materials, wherever possible.

☐ Develop long-term relationships with fewer suppliers.

☐ Keep stock levels as low as possible.

☐ Integrate deliveries with production requirements.

Many western manufacturing organisations have adopted these principles successfully and there is evidence that similar ideas are beginning to be adopted outside manufacturing. For example:

St James Hospital in Leeds in conjunction with consultants from Lucas, have reviewed their purchasing operations. Traditionally these were complex, involving over 1600 companies supplying nearly 15,000 products per year.

After review both suppliers and products were rationalised. As an example, 26 types of surgical gloves were originally ordered at up to £1 per pair, most have been replaced by 20p alternatives. The object of the exercise is to buy 80% of supplies from a maximum of 30 suppliers rather than from more than 100 and to eliminate excess stocks.

Specific environment: competition

In market economies where choice is possible, all organisations face some form of competition. There is the obvious type of competition where manufacturers compete against one another to sell their products. Cadburys compete against Rowntrees and others to sell their confectionery, Fords compete against Rover, Fiat, Nissan and others to sell their cars and so on.

There are also other, less obvious, forms of competition. For example, charities compete with one another for donations, a football club trying to attract spectators for a match has to compete with alternative forms of entertainment available at the same time, a local authority trying to recruit school leavers is in competition with other local employers and so on. Commercial competition tends to increase when it is relatively easy to enter the same product market. For example, in most cities new wine bars, restaurants and shops constantly appear creating increased competition for existing businesses. This makes for a highly volatile, competitive market where failures are frequent. The threat posed by potential entrants is reduced if there are barriers to entry. These may be; financial, brand loyalty, patent rights and so on. For example, new owners wishing to enter steel manufacture, oil refining or mass car manufacture would find the initial costs daunting, a firm wishing to make films would find existing brand loyalties to Kodak, Agfa and others difficult to overcome and so on.

Organisations naturally try to minimise the adverse effects of competition even though their efforts are not necessarily in the interests of consumers. As already pointed out when a few firms dominate a market (oligopoly) they tend not to compete on price as they fear that genuine price competition will diminish industry total profits.

As an example, consider the cross channel ferry market which is dominated by a few firms who currently charge virtually identical prices. Their position will soon be challenged by the Channel Tunnel but the operating company for the Tunnel have already said that they will charge similar prices to the ferry companies. Thus, although all the firms would claim it is a competitive market care is taken to avoid any competition in what most would regard as the most crucial area; that of price.

Conclusion – the organisation and the environment

Thus in summary an organisation relates to the environment in three main ways:

(a) The organisation draws as inputs resources of all types from the environment (e.g. equipment, finance, materials, personnel etc) and produces outputs of goods and services which go back into the environment.

(b) The organisation has to take account of the demands, rights and claims of the individuals and groups with which it interacts. These are known as stakeholders and include; suppliers, shareholders, customers, employees, the Government and so on.

(c) The environment is the source of exploitable opportunities e.g. new markets, inventions, new technology, improved materials etc. and also the source of threats to the organisation. These include; competing products, new competitors, changes in legislation, natural disasters, wars, political unrest and so on.

Key point summary

❑ Because organisations exist to satisfy needs, the needs must first be identified hence all organisations must practise marketing.

❑ In perfectly competitive markets there are many producers, in an oligopoly there are only a few whereas in a true monopoly there is only one.

❑ Personnel management deals with recruitment, selection, training, wages and pension, administration and industrial relations.

❑ Finance may derive from loans, share capital and internally generated funds.

❑ Limited liability means that an investors liability is limited to the amount paid or due on the shares.

❑ New technology is the application of micro-electronics to communications, manufacture, information processing, and administration.

❑ Purchasing has developed into materials management which encompasses materials planning, control, purchase, storage and usage.

❑ The Japanese approach to supplying is to standardise, develop long-term relationships with suppliers, eliminate stocks and integrate deliveries with production.

❑ All commercial organisations face competition which may be direct or indirect.

Self review questions

1. *What is marketing?*
2. *Contrast monopolistic, oligopolistic and perfect competition.*
3. *What is personnel management?*
4. *From what sources can an organisation raise finance?*
5. *What is limited liability?*
6. *What is meant by 'new technology'?*
7. *What is materials management?*
8. *What is competition in the market place?*

Assessment and revision section

Assignments

1. Over the last decade the UK has been successful in attracting a considerable amount of inward investment i.e. investment by foreign countries in the UK. Find examples of inward investment in the UK by Japan, Germany and the USA. What advantages do you think this brings to the UK? Are there any disadvantages?

2. The age at which people marry and have children is increasing. Analyse the likely effects of these trends on the UK economy.

3. In 1995 the European Union plans to increase in size to include 16 member countries with the admission of Sweden, Norway, Finland and Austria. Investigate the likely advantages and disadvantages to the UK of this enlargement.

4. Find three examples each of Primary, Secondary and Tertiary Industries. How have the relative importance of these sectors changed over the past 10 years in terms of proportions of Gross Domestic Product and numbers employed?

5. A large industrial company is contemplating building a new distribution warehouse close to the junction of the M4 and M25 motorways. Investigate the main environmental regulations and legislation with which the development will have to comply.

6. Find an industry which is dominated by a few oligopolists. Analyse how the firms compete with each other. Can you find any evidence of collusion between the firms even though they are competitors? Why do you think the industry is dominated by only a small number of firms?

Examination questions with answers

A1 (a) Using examples, distinguish between legislation and delegated legislation.
   (b) Describe the main sources of law that might affect the conduct of a business organisation undertaking business in the European Community.

CIMA Business Environment and Information Technology

A2 What impact would you expect the Single European Market to have on the various activities of business organisations in both the public and private sectors.

IAM Europe - Institutions and Issues

A3 Show how aspects of market structure, specifically the number and size distribution of sellers, the height of entry barriers, potential substitutes and the power of suppliers and buyers, can influence market conduct and performance.

ACCA Managerial Economics

A4 The directors of a successful private company are considering whether to convert their company into a public company.
Requirements
(a) Explain how a public company may be created.
(b) Explain how forming a public company affects the functions and duties of the board of directors.

CIMA Business Environment and Information Technology

A5 Describe and illustrate some of the requirements for the effective local management of international operations.

ACCA Effective Management

A6 You are required to
(a) State the basic objectives of governmental economic policy;
(b) Discuss the practicability of achieving these aims by relying mainly on monetary policy.

CIMA Economics

Examination questions without answers

B1 (a) Explain what is meant by deindustrialisation.
(b) Examine the consequences of deindustrialisation for the size distribution of firms.

ACCA Effective Management

B2 (a) Contrast the essential features of a market economy with those of a planned economy.
(b) Describe the economic problems that the countries of the former Soviet Union may experience as they move to a market economy.

CIMA Economics

B3 Performance Indicators which local authorities are required to collect and publish under the citizen's charter have been issued by the Audit Commission and were implemented in April 1993.
    What are the main aims and objectives of this measure?
    Give examples of some of the key indicators included in this first list.

IAM Public Sector Management in the UK

B4 Explain briefly how stock markets work and assess their usefulness to business as a source of long-term capital.

CIMA Economics

B5 The ultimate aim of European integration is to create a people's Europe or a business persons' Europe. Discuss

IAM Europe - Institutions and Issues

B6 (a) Why is the level of business investment important in the economy?
    (b) How might governments encourage a higher level of business investment?

CIMA Economics

Additional reading

The Economist Guide to the European Community, D.Leonard, Century Business Publications.

Economics, R.Powell, DP Publications.

Business Law, K.R.Abbott and N.Pendlebury, DP Publications.

Understanding the UK Economy, P.Curwen, MacMillan.

The Business and Marketing Environment, A.Palmer and I.Worthington, McGraw Hill.

4   Organisations: scientific management and the classical school

Objectives

After you have studied this chapter you will:

❑   *Be able to define an organisation.*

❑   *Understand the main influences which have contributed to our knowledge of organisations.*

❑   *Be able to explain the main principles of Taylorism or Scientific Management.*

❑   *Understand the benefits and drawbacks of Scientific Management.*

❑   *Know the contribution made by the Classical School.*

❑   *Understand Fayol's approach to management.*

❑   *Be able to define bureaucracy.*

❑   *Understand the main Classical principles*

What are organisations?

An organisation is a group created and maintained to achieve specific objectives. It may be a hospital with objectives dealing with health care, it may be a local authority with objectives concerned with providing services to the local community, it might be a commercial company with objectives including earning profits, providing a return for shareholders and so on.

Modern economies consist of countless organisations so their efficiency and performance is of critical importance. As a consequence the types of organisations, their structures, methods of management used, the relationships with other organisations and so on have been extensively studied and researched.

There is no universally accepted definition of an organisation but the following are examples from well known management writers.

> 'Organisations are systems of interdependent human beings'   *Pugh*
>
> 'Organisations are intricate human strategies designed to achieve certain objectives'   *Argyris*
>
> 'An organisation is a system of cooperative human activities.'   *Barnard*

Although there will probably never be a universally accepted definition, the following features describing organisations would be accepted by most people;

> Organisations are:
>
> (a) Goal orientated, i.e. people with a purpose.
>
> (b) Social systems, i.e. people working in groups.
>
> (c) Technical systems, i.e. people using knowledge, techniques and machines.
>
> (d) The integration of structured activities, i.e. people coordinating their efforts.

Note particularly, the emphasis in definitions on 'people' and that organisations are more than just groups of people. There may be a group of people in a disco or a club but they do not have a structure or a common purpose nor do they coordinate with each other. They are a group but not an organisation.

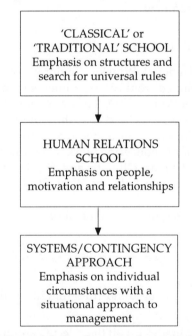

Figure 4.1: Development of organisational and management theories

Influences on organisations

The modern view of organisations describe them in terms of open systems, their responses to external and internal influences and the way they achieve their objectives. However, this is a view which has evolved from earlier ideas which have had, and still have, considerable influence on the structure and operation of today's organisations. Figure 4.1 shows in broad chronological sequence the three main schools of thought which have contributed to an understanding of the nature of organisations and their management.

Traditional or classical schools

Traditional organisational theory is based on contributions from a number of sources including scientific management (from Taylor, Gantt, Gilbreth and others), administrative management theorists (Fayol, Urwick, Brech and others) and from academics, notably Weber who, unlike the other contributors to the classical view of organisations, was not a practising manager, but an academic sociologist.

Whilst not completely ignoring the behavioural aspects of organisations, the traditional emphasis was on the structure of organisations, the management of structure and detailed analysis and control of production methods. All organisations were treated similarly and there was a search for universal principles which could be applied to any organisation and, on the whole, took a relatively mechanistic view of organisations with a tendency to treat them as *closed systems,* i.e. systems which do not interact with their environment.

Scientific management or 'Taylorism'

At the turn of the century Frederick Winslow Taylor introduced the concept of *scientific management.* This developed from his experiments in improving labour-productivity at the Bethlehem Steel Works, USA. He was committed to improving the efficiency of working methods and realised that this could only be done by detailed analysis, timing and the elimination of unnecessary movement, that is the substitution of fact for opinion. Taylor's pioneering work was refined and developed by other workers such as Frank and Lilian Gilbreth and H. Gantt and their approach has evolved into the technique known today as Work Study which is used throughout the world.

Scientific management has four main principles:

(a) Develop the best or ideal method of doing a task and determine 'scientifically' a standard.

(b) Select the best man for the task and train him in the best way to achieve the task.

(c) Combine the scientific method with the selected and trained men.

(d) Take all responsibility for planning and preparing work away from the worker and give it to management. The worker's only responsibility is for the actual job performance.

Scientific management was based on strong, financial incentives but undoubtedly the most far reaching principle was that management should take over work organisation. This reduced the scope for individual workers and this fragmentation of work effect – or *deskilling* – still has strong repercussions today, nearly a century later.

A number of recent managerial developments, for example, job enrichment and group assembly methods have been designed to counteract the frustrations caused by the legacy of the worst aspects of scientific management.

Scientific management was applied to lower level routine and repetitive tasks and said nothing about higher level planning and decision making in the organisation. Taylor's heavy emphasis on financial incentives, rationality and the need for close supervision of 'unwilling' workers has had strong and lasting influences on management thinking and practice. The attitudes and approaches adopted by the Scientific Management movement are still clearly discernible today in many organisations.

Benefits and drawbacks of scientific management

The major benefits and drawbacks of Taylorism can be summarised as follows:

Benefits:
- ❐ Improved working methods resulted in enormous gains in productivity.
- ❐ The measurement and analysis of tasks provided factual information on which to base improvements in methods and equipment.
- ❐ It provided a rational basis for piecework and incentive schemes which became more widely used.
- ❐ There were considerable improvements in working conditions.
- ❐ Management became more involved with production activities and were thus encouraged to show positive leadership.

Drawbacks:
- ❐ Jobs became more boring and repetitive.
- ❐ Planning, design and control became divorced from performance thus de-skilling tasks.
- ❐ Workers become virtual adjuncts to machines with management having a monopoly of knowledge and control.
- ❐ De-skilling, excessive specialisation, repetition and so on cause workers to become alienated and frustrated. This has become an increasing problem with generally rising education standards and personal expectations.

Classical school – departmental approaches

A number of earlier management thinkers notably Fayol, Urwick, Brech and others developed a top down view of organisations which contrasted with the factory floor emphasis of Taylor. Fayol and others described organisations based upon the grouping of various activities into departments. They looked at organisation as a large machine and tried to develop universal laws or principles which governed the machine's activities.

The general problem addressed by them was; how are tasks organised into individual jobs, how are jobs organised into administrative units and how are these combined into departments? The result of this analysis was the structuring of departments within an organisation; each department containing a set of tasks to be performed by the people in that department.

As an example a common departmental organisation on a functional basis might have the following divisions:

❑ Finance – activities associated with providing funds and ensuring their effective use.

❑ Production – the provision and maintenance of equipment to convert raw materials into finished products and the control of the production process.

❑ Marketing – including sales, distribution, promotion.

❑ Supply – the procurement of raw materials and other inputs for production and administration.

❑ Personnel – providing and training the people for the organisation.

❑ Research and Development – the development of new products and processes and the modification of existing products and processes.

Of the classical management thinkers Henri Fayol was the first and undoubtedly the most influential.

Henri Fayol

Fayol was a successful French industrialist (1841 – 1925) who also thought deeply about the management and structure of organisations. Fayol's original definition of management has become a classic and has served as the basis of more modern ones.

Fayol's definition of management:

'To manage is to forecast and plan, to organise, to command, to co-ordinate and to control'.

Some modern variations are:

'Managing is an operational process initially best dissected by analysing the managerial functions (of): planning, organising, staffing, directing and leading and controlling'.

or

'(Management is) a social process entailing responsibility for the effective and economical planning and regulation of the operations of the organisation in the fulfilment of a given purpose or task involving

(a) Judgement and decision in determining plans and in using data to control performance and progress against plans and,

(b) The guidance, integration, motivation and supervision of the personnel compromising the enterprise and carrying out its operations'

There are common themes throughout these definitions and it should be noted how more modern attitudes to people at work are reflected in the change of Fayol's original phrase, 'to command' into 'directing and leading' and 'guidance, integrating and motivating'.

Fayol's principles of management

Based on his experience Fayol derived fourteen general principles of management which had served him well in his career. These are shown in Figure 4.2 together with a brief explanation of each.

Fayol's General Principles formed the basis of later works by writers such as Urwick and Brech. These writers amended and refined Fayol's ideas but still adopted a largely prescriptive approach with an emphasis on the structural nature of organisations.

A contemporary of Fayol's, Max Weber (1864–1920), a German Sociologist, also studied formal organisation structures and developed a concept which he termed *bureaucracy* which remains of fundamental importance.

Bureaucracy and organisations

Although the term bureaucracy has popularly acquired the sense of inefficiency, officialdom and 'red tape' it was first coined by Weber to describe a particular organisational form which exists to some extent in every large scale enterprise whether in the private or public sector.

In Weber's view the bureaucratic organisation was a logical, rational organisation which was technically superior to all other forms.

The key elements in the 'ideal' bureaucratic type of organisation were as follows:

(a) A well defined hierarchy of legitimate authority.

(b) A division of labour based on functional specialisation.

(c) A clear statement of the rights and duties of personnel.

(d) Rules and procedures in writing should exist to deal with all decisions and situations.

(e) Promotion and selection based on technical competence.

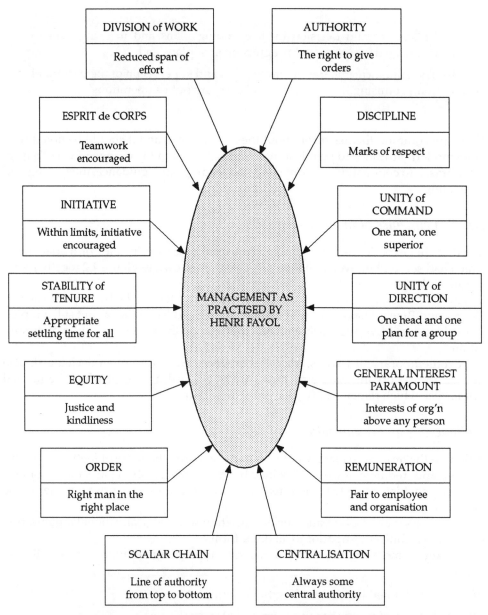

Figure 4.2: Fayol's principles of management

In Weber's view a depersonalised form of organisation, such as outlined above, would minimise the effect of human unpredictability. Weber concentrated on the structural aspects of organisations and in consequence took a rather mechanistic and impersonal standpoint.

A number of problems and weaknesses have identified with the bureaucratic model of which the following are the most important.

- ❏ Adaptability and change are made more difficult because of standardised rules, procedures and types of decisions.
- ❏ Rules tend to become important in their own right rather than as a means of promoting efficiency.

However, in spite of these and other deficiences, as organisations grow in size and/or complexity the need increases for some form of systematic organisation, which experience shows inevitably incorporates a number of Weber's bureaucratic elements.

The main traditional 'principles'

The traditional approach to organisational problems and structures sought to discover or prescribe basic principles which could universally apply to any organisation. Although it is generally recognised today that there are few, if any, principles which can be applied equally to all organisations, the principles developed from the classical approach have, for generations, had strong and pervasive influences on management thinking and consequently on the structure of organisations. The main organisational principles developed from the traditional or classical movement are as follows:

- ❏ The scalar or hierarchical principle;
- ❏ Span of control;
- ❏ Unity of command;
- ❏ Specialisation and division of labour;
- ❏ The principle of correspondence.

Each of these principles is discussed in the following paragraphs.

The scalar or hierarchical system

Hierarchy appears to be a natural order of nature which applies to organisations. This was recognised by classical organisation theory in the statement of the scalar principle which refers to the vertical division of authority and responsibility within the organisation. This states that there should be a flow of authority and responsibility, in an unbroken chain, from the top to the bottom of the organisation.

This flow reflects the hierarchical nature of the organisation and the way that duties have been assigned to the sub-units of the organisation, i.e. the departments and sections. The vertical flow of authority is known as *line authority* and the managers who exercise it are known as *line managers*.

Span of control

The span of control or span of supervision, means the number of subordinates a supervisor can supervise effectively.

At higher levels the span should be small but at lower levels, where activities are more repetitive, the span may be larger. Various numbers of subordinates were specified as appropriate, ranging from 3 to 6 but it must be recognised that these numbers are quite arbitrary. Implicit in the span of control concept is the need for a superior to co-ordinate the activities of subordinates which would be generally recognised as a primary management function.

Unity of command

Essentially this is a restatement of the hierarchical, scalar principle and means that a subordinate should receive orders from only one superior, i.e. one person, one boss. The vertical, downward flow of authority, as espoused by classical organisational theory, has a militaristic appearance in relation to modern, complex organisations where technological, financial, legal and other implications make it necessary to diffuse authority across the hierarchy as well as vertically downwards.

Specialisation and division of labour

Division of labour means that work is sub-divided into small tasks or areas. By working at their narrow task people gain more skill and proficiency and become specialists. The classical school were by no means the first to recognise the gains in efficiency that could be made, from specialisation. Indeed, it is arguable that this is a process which has been evident throughout history, but they were extremely influential in emphasising its importance in organisations.

Specialisation applies not only to production workers on the shop floor but to every level in the organisation, including management. In modern organisations there are very few people indeed who are not specialists in some form or another.

The principle of correspondence

This states that authority should be commensurate with responsibility.

Authority is the right to give an instruction or to carry out a task and responsibility is the obligation to carry out the task satisfactorily.

The classical theorists saw authority solely in terms of formal authority, i.e. that specified and imposed by the organisation. This makes for status conscious, authoritarian organisations where upward communication is reduced and personal initiative is stifled.

Nowadays it is recognised that authority is more likely to be acceptable to subordinates when superiors are respected personally and technically. Military style authority is replaced by the concept of teamwork in which the superior works with, rather than being placed over, subordinates.

Classical theories in retrospect

Although the classical theorists did not ignore people and their needs their concentration undoubtedly was on structures, authority and control. The search for universal principles produced too much emphasis on what ought to be and thus investigations into actual behaviour, its causes and consequences, were limited.

In spite of many modern criticisms, a number of the classical principles have become almost universally adopted. Examples include; the scalar chain of authority, the matching of authority and responsibility, clear definition of jobs and so on. Others such as unity of command, style of leadership and so on may well have suited earlier, paternalistic organisations but appear to have little place in modern society.

The contribution of the classical theorists can be summarised thus:

❑ they introduced the idea that management was a suitable subject for intellectual analysis.

❑ they provided a foundation of ideas on which subsequent theorists have built.

❑ criticism of their work has stimulated empirical studies of actual organisational behaviour.

Modern view on organisations have become markedly less rigid than the classical approach. Perhaps the following quotation from William Ouchi, author of *Theory Z*, represents the ultimate expression of the modern viewpoint:

'My ideal of a completely efficient and perfectly integrated organisation is one that has no organisational chart, no divisions, no visible structure at all. In a sense, a basketball team that plays well fits this description, although on a small scale. The problem facing a basketball team is huge in its complexity and the speed with which problems occur is great. Yet an effective team solves these problems with no formal reporting relationships and a minimum of specialisation of positions and tasks'.

Key point summary

❑ Organisations have been variously described but there is general agreement that they combine both social and technical systems in which efforts are co-ordinated to achieve specified objectives.

❏   The main theoretical approaches to organisations include: Scientific management, the departmental approach, the human relations school and the systems/contingency school.

❏   Scientific management was a production orientated rational approach to organisations pioneered by Taylor.

❏   Fayol and others adopted a 'top-down' view of organisations.

❏   Line relationships are those in the direct chain of command.

❏   Bureaucracy, as defined by Weber, was an ideal, rational view of organisations with clearly defined tasks and relationships.

❏   The main traditional principles of organisations include the scalar principle, unity of command, span of control and specialisation.

Self review questions

1.   *What is an organisation?*

2.   *What are the three main schools that have contributed to our understanding of organisations?*

3.   *What is Scientific management?*

4.   *What was the approach to organisations adopted by Fayol and others?*

5.   *What is Fayol's definition of management?*

6.   *What are the features of Weber's bureaucratic form of organisation?*

7.   *What are the main traditional 'principles' of management applied to organisations?*

8.   *What is the consequence of task specialisation?*

5 Organisations: human relations and the contingency approach

Objectives

After you have studied this chapter you will:

❐ *Understand the contribution of the Human Relations School to organisation theory.*

❐ *Appreciate the importance of motivation in organisations.*

❐ *Be able to describe Maslow's hierarchy of needs.*

❐ *Understand McGregor's Theory X and Theory Y.*

❐ *Be able to distinguish between motivators and hygiene factors.*

❐ *Understand the reasoning behind the contingency approach to organisations.*

❐ *Be able to describe the features of key studies such as those conducted by Lawrence and Lorsch, Burns and Stalker and Woodward.*

Human relations school

The problems of organisations have also been studied from a human relations or behavioural viewpoint which to some extent was a reaction against the more mechanistic and impersonal bias of the classical school. The undoubted pioneers in this area were Mayo, Roethlisberger and Dickson who conducted the famous 'Hawthorne Experiments' at the Hawthorne, Illinois plant of Western Electric.

Initially the studies were carried out to see the effects of productivity of such factors as heat, lighting, fatigue and layout. As such these studies were in the tradition of the scientific management movement, at least initially. But as the study progressed it became clear that efficiency was being influenced by factors beyond the physical working environment and as a result of the emphasis of the study changed to an examination of the motives and attitudes of individual workers, the characteristics of the work group and the relationship of the individual to the group. The research found that worker performance could be favourably influenced by social factors in the work environment and by changes in attitudes of supervisors.

The Hawthorne studies clearly showed that people do not pursue financial ends blindly nor can their behaviour be predicted and governed in the way that Taylor and colleagues assumed, i.e. virtually as adjuncts to machines with predictable responses. Although the methodology of the Hawthorne Experiments has been criticised in recent years the study remains a major landmark in the study of organisations from a behavioural viewpoint.

Concepts of the human relations school

Mayo and the other early workers in the human relations field studied the role of individuals, informal groups, inter-group relationships and the formal relationships within the organisation. They developed a number of concepts of which the following are the most important.

(a) People are not only motivated by financial factors but by a variety of social and psychological factors as well.

(b) An organisation is a social system as well as a technical/economic system.

(c) Informal work groups have important roles in determining the attitudes and performances of individuals.

(d) Management requires social skills as well as technical ones.

(e) Traditional 'authoritarian' leadership patterns should be modified substantially to consider psychological and social factors and should become more 'democratic' in nature.

(f) Participation in work organisation, planning and policy formulation is an important element in organisations. This meant establishing effective communications between the various levels in the hierarchy to ensure a free flow of information.

Following Mayo's pioneering work, the study of people and their motivations continued to dominate the minds of researchers and practising managers alike. It was soon apparent that motivation was influenced by many more factors than assumed by the classical theorists.

Motivation in organisations

From our view motivation can be explained as the driving force or commitment people have for doing things. A motive is a need or desire within a person to achieve some goal or objective and understanding human motivations is a complex matter with no precise answers. Although the causes of motivation are imperfectly understood, the results of having motivated people in an organisation are obvious and highly beneficial.

As a consequence managers have to try to understand the conditions and influences that motivate people so that they can manage, organise activities and create an organisational atmosphere that encourages positive motivational effects. Early management theory took a somewhat mechanistic view of human motivation assuming that:

(a) individual goals were consistent with, or sublimated to, organisational goals,

(b) individuals responded positively to authority, and

(c) that people were motivated solely by monetary reward.

Experience and behavioural research has shown that these early views are incomplete and simplistic and that people are much more complex than suggested by the early management theorists. A useful classification of the assumptions about motivation has been developed by Professor Schein and is given in the next paragraph.

Schein's classification of motivational assumptions

Professor Schein reviewed the assumptions about people that were implicit in the then current ideas about what factors and conditions motivate people at work. His four-way classification, which follows a rough historical sequence, is summarised below:

(a) *Rational-Economic man*
Assumptions: Man is primarily motivated by economics needs. He has to be manipulated, controlled and financially motivated by the organisation.
These views stemmed from the industrial revolution and were important assumptions behind the 'Scientific Management' movement of Taylor and others. Schein says that these assumptions ultimately categorise people into two groups; the untrustworthy, money-motivated majority (McGregor's Theory X people – described later) and the self-motivated, more trustworthy elite who must assume responsibility for the management of others.

(b) *Social man*
Assumptions: Man is essentially a social animal and gains his basic sense of identity through relationships with others.
This categorisation is based on Mayo's conclusions from the Hawthorne Experiment described earlier. The effect of these assumptions is that management is only effective to the extent it can mobilise and rely on these social relationships. Issues of leadership and group behaviour are therefore paramount.

(c) *Self-actualising man*
Assumptions: Man is primarily self-motivated and self-controlled. Man needs self-fulfilment, challenge, responsibility and a sense of pride in his work.
This concept is based on Maslow's hierarchy of human needs and is closely allied to McGregor's Theory Y view – both explained later. The concept of self-actualising man means that managers should seek to provide demanding, challenging work and to provide for genuine delegation of responsibility and greater autonomy. Research studies have supported the concept of self-actualising man especially for professional and managerial grades, although it is less clear whether it applies to lower grade or less skilled workers.

(d) *Complex man*

Assumptions: Man is variable. He has many motives which are arranged any one time in a hierarchy but the hierarchy may change from time to time and from situation to situation.

The result of this view is that managers need to adapt and vary their behaviour in accordance with the motivational needs of particular individuals and groups and the task in hand. Schein sees the relationship between the individual and the organisation as 'interactive and interdependence'.

It is apparent from the above that there are numerous views about how to explain human behaviour at work. The following paragraphs expand some of the categories given above and outline the more important findings of the major contributors to the theory of motivation.

Maslow's hierarchy of needs

Abraham Maslow was an American psychologist who developed the theory that people are motivated by a desire to satisfy specific groups of needs and that they tend to satisfy their needs progressively, starting with basic physiological needs and moving up to hierarchy.

Maslow's hierarchy of needs is shown in Figure 5.1.

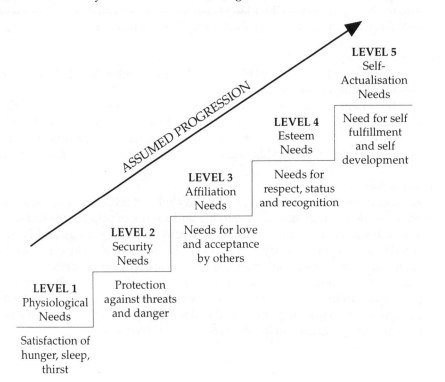

Figure 5.1: Maslow's hierarchy of needs

According to Maslow when one need is more or less satisfied another, higher level need becomes dominant. The consequence is that when a need is satisfied it ceases to be a motivator.

In a general sense Maslow's theories have intuitive appeal. A starving man is obviously dominated by the need for food, to him esteem and status are unimportant. However, above this primitive level, difficulties appear. There is doubt whether people do in fact move progressively up the hierarchy and whether higher levels can ever be considered as truly satisfied. For example, it is likely that the need for esteem and status requires continual reinforcement. Although the research evidence in support of Maslow's hierarchy is inconclusive his theories have been influential in the study of motivation.

McGregor's Theory X and Theory Y

McGregor evolved two sets of propositions and assumptions about the nature and behaviour of people in organisations. He termed these two sets 'Theory X and Theory Y', the key elements of which are shown below.

Summary of Theory X and Theory Y

Theory X

1.   The average man is inherently lazy.
2.   He lacks ambition, dislikes responsibility and must be led.
3.   He is resistant to change and is indifferent to organisational needs.
4.   Coercion and close control are required.

Theory Y

1.   To the average man, work is as natural as rest or play.
2.   Motivation, potential for development, imagination and ingenuity are present in all people given proper conditions.
3.   Coercion and close control are not required.
4.   Given proper conditions people will accept and seek out responsibility.

The characteristics of Theory X are similar to Schein's classification of Rational-Economic man and there are clear implications for management if the Theory X view is adopted. Management must direct, persuade, punish and control the activities of people and management must seek to coerce and modify people's behaviour to fit the needs of the organisation.

The assumptions of Theory Y are close to Maslow's 'Self-Actualising Man' (Schein's third category) and, if adopted, considerably alter management's priorities and tasks. Management's essential task becomes to harness the inherent qualities of people by arranging conditions and methods of operations so that people can achieve their own goals best by directing their own efforts towards organisational objectives. Co-operation rather than coercion is required.

Herzberg's motivation-hygiene theories

A further influential insight into motivation was provided by the researches of Frederick Herzberg. He concluded that certain factors led to job satisfaction, which he termed motivators and certain factors could lead to dissatisfaction termed hygiene factors. The major factors found in the two groups are summarised below.

Hygiene factors (leading to dissatisfaction)	Motivators (leading to satisfaction)
Policies and administration	Achievement
Supervision	Recognition
Working conditions	Responsibility
Money	Growth and development
Job Security	Growth
Status	
Relationships with peers and subordinates	

Herzberg's hygiene factors and motivators

It will be seen that the motivators are related to the content of the job whilst the hygiene factors are more related to the environment of the work and not intrinsic to the job itself.

Hygiene factors and motivators are not opposites. Hygiene factors, even if provided for, do not themselves induce job satisfaction; they merely prevent dissatisfaction. Motivators must be present to promote positive satisfaction. A production analogy is that hygiene factors are necessary to maintain production but motivators are needed to increase output.

Although there are some differences between Maslow's and Herzberg's approaches they both tend to assert that the individual's performance in a job is influenced by basic needs (necessary for maintaining performance) and higher order-needs (needed to improve performance). Herzberg's work has led to much of the modern interest in the design of the job and to what is called job enrichment, i.e. where the task is enriched with motivators such as responsibility and recognition.

Other investigations into motivation

There have been numerous other contributions towards the understanding of motivation and of course investigations still continue. Another American, Rensis Likert, found from his researches that successful managers built their success on tightly knit groups of staff whose co-operation had been obtained by close attention to a range of lower and higher order motivational factors. Participation was encouraged and supportive relationships within and between groups were fostered. These features led to full commitment to the organisation's goals and high performance levels.

Researchers who attempted to study the process of motivation were Vroom and Lawler who developed a set of ideas which has been named Expectancy Theory. The main part of the theory relates to how a person perceives the relationship between three factors – effort, performance and reward. The theory emphasises the importance of individual perceptions of reality in the motivational process and indicates that individuals will only act when they have a reasonable expectancy that their behaviour will lead to the desired outcomes.

Human relations and motivation – a conclusion

The preceding paragraphs have outlined (very briefly) some of the ideas developed by researchers into motivation and human relationships in the workplace. All have contributed to the understanding of the human factor at work yet none provides a complete answer and probably no research ever will. Consideration of the various theories and assumptions on which a manager subscribes will colour his views about the way to manage and the ways to deal with people.

Assumptions that man is rational-economic will lead to a bargaining approach and to a preoccupation with the intrinsic conditions of work. Believers in self-actualising or psychological man, will be more concerned with providing the right type of work in the right climate in order to create opportunities for the individual to develop and realise his talents.

Systems/contingency approach

Historically, organisational theory developed from two main sources. The Classical School with its somewhat mechanistic emphasis on structures which could be imposed on people and the Human Relations School whose laudable concentration on the needs of the individual to an extent obscured study of the organisation as a whole.

Modern workers have built upon earlier ideas in an attempt to provide a more comprehensive view of behaviour in organisations. One influential approach has been that using Systems Theory. Systems Theorists see organisations as complex social systems that interact with their environment and which must respond to numerous interdependent variables of which the following are the most important:

- ❏ People
- ❏ Tasks
- ❏ Technology
- ❏ Organisation structure
- ❏ Environment

Whilst earlier approaches considered variables in isolation, system theorists study the relationships between several of them. Their researches have suggested that there is no one best way of designing organisations, and, because of volatility and change, the 'best' way is dependent (or contingent) upon prevailing conditions. Thus the contingency approach has developed out of system's thinking. Both recognise that an organisation is a complex structure with many interacting elements and that it must continually adapt to an uncertain and changing environment.

The American researchers, Lawrence and Lorsch, first used the term contingency approach. They examined the operations of a number of firms to assess the effects on the tasks and attitudes of managers in various functions operating within different structures and environments.

The firms chosen for study ranged from plastics companies, where the environment was uncertain and volatile, through firms in the packaged food industry with a moderate degree of uncertainty, to firms in the container industry, where the environment was considered stable and predictable.

Task differentiation

The main emphasis of the Lawrence and Lorsch study was on task differentiation which covered the differences and attitudes of the managers concerned as well as the division of specialisation or functions. The functional area differences are summarised in Figure 5.2 which should be studied with the explanatory notes.

	Functions		
	Production	Sales	Research
Function structure 1	High	Medium	Low
Managerial time orientation 2	Short term	Medium term	Long term
Managerial objective orientation 3	Techno/economic	Market	Scientific and techno/economic
Interpersonal orientation 4	High task motivation	Socially oriented	Low task motivation
Sub unit environment 5	High degree of certainty	Moderately uncertain	Considerable uncertainty

Figure 5.2: Summary of functional differences

Notes

1. The function structure refers to the relative formality of the unit in terms of hierarchy, rules and procedures. For example, the production functions had clear, formalised procedures, narrow spans of control, numerous levels as compared with the more informally structured and organised research area.

2. This is the managerial expectation about the time required to produce results from their efforts.

3. This relates to the main concern of the functional area. For example, deadlines, cost reduction, efficiency are major objectives of production functions.

4. This relates to the manager's motivation towards establishing personal relationships as compared with task performance.

5. The environment of each function – or sub-unit of the organisation – differs because each one is engaged in different types of activity, interacts with different part of the environment and has greater or lesser contacts with the environment external to the organisation as a whole.

The study also examined the extent of integration and amount of internal conflict within the organisation. Integration was considered to be the quality of the collaboration that existed between the departments and function and was discovered to be an important factor in controlling the conflicts which inevitably arise between functions with the widely differing characteristics outlined in Figure 5.2.

Task differentiation study – conclusions

In spite of some criticism of their methodology the Lawrence and Lorsch study was an important landmark in the development of a theory of organisation which took account of change, uncertainty and the interaction of key variables. The main conclusions were as follows:

(a) The more volatile and diverse the environment the more task differentiation, and consequent integration, is required to achieve successful organisation.

(b) More stable environments do not require as much differentiation but still need substantial integration between the functions that exist.

(c) It is more difficult to resolve conflict in organisations with a high degree of differentiation.

(d) Better methods of conflict resolution result in higher performance and lead to types of differentiation and integration that suit the organisation's environment.

(e) In a predictable environment integration is achieved through the management hierarchy, particularly at higher levels, and through rules, procedures, budgets etc. In an uncertain environment, integration is achieved at lower levels mainly through personal inter-relationships with only a moderate use of administrative methods.

Adaptation and environmental variability

Another important study using the contingency approach was that conducted in Britain by Burns and Stalker. A number of electronics firms were studied to see how they adapted to changes in their environment particularly with regard to changes in market and technical conditions. The studies resulted in a classification of organisations into what were termed mechanistic and organic systems; the properties of which are summarised in Figure 5.3.

Mechanistic systems	Organic systems
Stable environment with high certainty & predictability	Uncertain environment, low predictability
High functional specialisation	Low functional specialisation
Detailed differentiation of duties and responsibilities	Less structured management with more adjustment and Re-definition of roles
Hierarchical control, authority and communication with largely vertical interactions	Lateral communications with a network of control and authority
Authoritarian style with clear superior/subordinate relationships and emphasis on loyalty and obedience	More consultation with information and advice being communicated rather than decisions and instructions
Low rate of innovation	High rate of innovation

Figure 5.3: Properties of mechanistic and organic systems

Mechanistic and organic organisations in practice

The two systems were seen as extremes with many intermediate forms possible. Traditional industries, for example, steel, textiles and shipbuilding are mechanistic in nature where management controls and methods are based on well defined rules and procedures which experience little change.

Industries facing rapidly changing environments, for example, computers, pharmaceuticals and so on have to adapt their systems of management in order to survive so that, according to the Burns and Stalker findings, organic systems are more appropriate. This latter point has met with some criticism as it is far from proven that full organic systems are necessary in order to cope with change.

Some large organisations have coped with change quite successfully even though having a substantial degree of structure and formality by ensuring that they are sensitive to changes in the organisation's environment and by a process of step-by-step or incremental adjustment. Indeed the avoidance of unexpected and traumatic large scale abrupt change by making continual incremental adjustments appears to be a feature of many successful companies. A classic British example of this process is Marks and Spencer who avoid the need for unsettling, large scale change by a continual process of incremental adjustments which are in tune with the needs of the market place.

Technology and the organisation

The studies of manufacturing firms conducted by Joan Woodward observed that many organisational characteristics were directly related to the technology used by the firm. The organisations were categorised on the basis of the technology used as follows:

(a) Small batch or individual item production.

(b) Large batch or mass production including assembly line production.

(c) Continuous process production including refineries, chemical and gas production and so on.

Based on this categorisation Woodward found that there were clear patterns relating to things like the span of control, chain of command and systems of management. The various features found are summarised in Figure 5.4.

	Categories of technology		
	Small batch/ individual item	Large batch/ mass production	Continuous production
Number of levels in chain of command	Few	Medium	Numerous
Span of control Top management	Small	Medium	Large
Span of control Middle management	Large	Medium	Small
Span of control Supervisors	Small	Medium	Small
Ratio of management/ operatives	Low	Medium	High
Type of management system	Mainly organic with fewer rules and close personal relationships	Mainly mechanistic with clear cut procedures and more rules and impersonal relationships	Mainly organic with fewer rules and close personal relationships
Communication	Mainly verbal with little paperwork	Mainly written with considerable paperwork	Mainly verbal with little paperwork

Figure 5.4: Organisational characteristics and technology

Woodward's findings

Woodward found that the more successful firms in each group were those whose various organisational characteristics, as summarised above, tended to bunch around the average of their particular category. This means for example, that a mass production firm would tend to be more successful if operated in a formal, mechanistic way with a flatter and broader organisation structure than a process production company.

The importance of the Woodward studies was the conclusion that the method of production was an important factor affecting organisation structure and that there was a particular type of structure and management style suitable for each of the type of production. It was found that the ideas of the classical theorists seemed only to be appropriate for firms engaged in large batch and mass production, not for the other categories studied.

The work of Woodward was continued and extended by other studies into structure, technology and the environment, an example being the work done at Aston University by Pugh and others. The Aston group's study examined more variables than Woodward and the findings to some extent contradicted Woodward's, partly due to the inclusion of larger companies in the sample studied.

The Aston group found that size was an important factor in determining structure as well as the technology used. As firms grow they become more formally structured and the study found that larger size tends to lead to:

- more standardisation
- more formalisation of structures, procedures and decision rules
- more specialisation of tasks and functions but
- less centralisation, i.e. the concentration authority.

Centralisation, and its converse, decentralisation, are important influences on organisations and are dealt with in more detail later in the book.

Systems/contingency approach – conclusion

Although there is a natural yearning for the certainties and simplicities of the classical approach it is now generally accepted that there are no universal solutions to organisational problems. It is recognised that what is right for one organisation is not necessarily right for another and what is right for a given organisation at one time may not suit the organisation at a different stage of development or when the environment changes.

Organisations are always faced by the two opposing forces of uniformity and diversity. By nature, they prefer the predictability and efficiency of uniformity but the need for adaptability and the uncertainty of the environment require diversity.

Key point summary

- Motivation is the driving force or commitment people have for doing things.

- Schein's classification of assumptions about motivation is: Rational-economic man, Social Man, Self-Actualising man, Complex man.

- Maslow's hierarchy of needs range from physiological needs to self-actualisation needs and Maslow suggests these are satisfied in sequence.

- McGregor's Theory X person is lazy and needs close control. The Theory Y person will accept and seek out responsibility.

- Herzberg considered that factors called motivators led to satisfaction whereas other factors known as hygiene factors could lead to dissatisfaction.

❏ There is no complete understanding about what motivates people but the assumptions a manager uses strongly influences the way he carries out his task.

❏ Modern approaches emphasise the need to take individual circumstances into account when designing organisations.

❏ The contingency approach to organisations was pioneered by Lawrence and Lorsch.

❏ Their studies studied the differences between the tasks carried out by managers in different functions.

❏ The main conclusion from their studies was that the more volatile the environment the more diversity is required but that integration becomes more difficult.

❏ Burns and Stalker categorised organisations into mechanistic and organic.

❏ The type of technology used by the firm was found to influence the organisational structure.

❏ Woodward's studies of technology and organisation concluded that there was a particular type of structure and management style suitable for each type of production and that formality increased with size.

Self review questions

1. *What view did the early management theorists take of motivation?*

2. *Define and explain Schein's classification of motivational assumptions.*

3. *What is Maslow's hierarchy of needs and why is it important in the study of motivation?*

4. *What are the characteristics of Theory X and Theory Y people?*

5. *Distinguish between motivators and hygiene factors and give examples.*

6. *Why is it necessary to study motivation?*

7. *What is the key thrust of the modern approach to the study of organisations?*

8. *What is the task differentiation and why was this studied by Lawrence and Lorsch?*

9. *What are mechanistic and organic systems?*

10. *Summarise the main findings of Woodward's studies of technology and the organisation.*

6 Organisations: structure

Objectives

After you have studied this chapter you will:

☐ *Understand the relationship between the formal and informal organisation.*

☐ *Know the advantages and disadvantages of both types of organisation.*

☐ *Be able to describe the ways that departmentation may be achieved.*

☐ *Understand functional, geographical, product or service specialisation.*

☐ *Know what is meant by matrix structures.*

☐ *Know the characteristics of flat and tall organisation structures.*

☐ *Understand centralisation and decentralisation.*

☐ *Understand the main types of legal structures.*

Elements of organisation

From previous chapters we are aware that organisations are more than just groups of people.

Organisations:

☐ have purpose i.e. their objectives.

☐ have formal patterns of relationships i.e. their structure.

☐ practise division of labour i.e. who does what?

☐ specify formal sources of authority i.e. who makes decisions?

These are the key elements of organisation and the way that they are dealt with largely determines the nature of the organisation, what departments and functions it contains the forms of relationships and communication practised, the levels of management, the amount of centralisation/decentralisation, and so on.

That an organisation exists, by definition means that there is some form of structure or formality. However, within the *formal organisation* also exists an *informal organisation*.

Formal and informal organisations

The formal organisation is the pattern of relationships and tasks defined by official rules, policies and systems. The formal organisation is designed to achieve the objectives of the organisation in a rational, efficient manner. It is usually depicted on organisation charts. These are diagrams which show the official relationships, departments, levels of management and so on which make up the formal organisation. Organisation Charts are described in detail later in the book.

The way that the organisation works is affected not only by official procedures and relationships but also by the behaviour of the people who work in it. People form small groups and social relationships and develop non-standard, informal ways of getting things done.

This is known as the informal or unofficial organisation and exists, to a greater or lesser extent, within every organisation. The social groups develop behavioural patterns, beliefs and objectives which are different from, and sometimes opposed to, the requirements of the formal organisation.

The informal organisation exists because:-

☐ formal relationships are considered too impersonal.

☐ it fulfils human needs for friendship and belonging.

☐ the security of the group provides psychological support for the individual.

☐ it provides a power base for those dissatisfied with their official influence.

☐ the formal organisation is not considered efficient or flexible enough.

This latter point is particularly important regarding communication and information flows. As everyone knows, news travels far quicker through the 'grapevine' than through official channels!

The possible advantages and disadvantages of formal and information organisations are summarised in Figure 6.1.

The two types of organisation are not alternatives, they exist side by side in every organisation. Accordingly, it is vital that management try to harness the beneficial aspects of informal organisations and to ensure that the formal organisation, as far as possible, meets the needs of their employees. If not, people will give more attention and loyalty to the informal organisation with a consequent reduction in organisational efficiency.

	Possible advantages	Possible disadvantages
Formal organisation	Unity of objectives and effort	Less innovative and adaptive
	Clear hierarchy of command and control	More 'red tape', formality and inflexibility
	Well defined relationships, duties and responsibilities	Slower, more cumbersome decision making
	Stability and predictability	Inefficient information flows
	Assists control and co-ordination	Lack of individual fulfilment
Informal organisation	May improve communication	Managerial authority may be undermined
	May use unofficial but efficient methods	Group objectives may run counter to organisational objectives
	May provide more personal satisfaction	Rumours and distortions rather than facts may be communicated
	Activities may be co-ordinated better	More loyalty and effort may be given to group than organisation
	More flexible and adaptive	Bad decisions may result from protecting group interests

Figure 6.1: Formal and informal organisations

Specialisation and departmentation

Specialisation is concerned with the division of labour. This means that the various tasks and activities needed to meet the objectives of the organisations should be suitably grouped and divided up. In virtually all organisations the tasks and activities are grouped into departments, hence the term departmentation. By specialising, people are able to concentrate on one task or group of related tasks and develop proficiency, knowledge and expertise, thus raising organisational efficiency. As organisations grow in size and complexity there seems an inevitable tendency for there to be more specialisation and departmentation.

For example, a small business is likely to have one person responsible for all aspects of sales and marketing. By the time the organisation reaches the size of say, ICI there will be numerous departments dealing with specialised aspects e.g. Market Research, Advertising, Brand Management, Retail Sales, Trade Sales, Export Sales etc. etc.

Depending on the nature and objectives of the organisation departmentation can be achieved in various ways. For example, by function, by product or service, by geography or by some mixture of these. The various forms are explained below.

Functional specialisation

This means that tasks are linked on the basis of common functions; for example, Production, Finance, Personnel and so on. This basis is the most widely used and seems to be logical.

Figure 6.2 shows how a manufacturing company might be departmentalised on a functional basis.

Figure 6.2: Functional organisation structure for a manufacturing company

Advantages of functional specialisation:

(a) Professional expertise is enhanced.

(b) Usually effective in practice.

(c) Because it is the traditional form and widely encountered it is readily accepted by employees.

Disadvantages:

(a) May encourage narrow departmental interest to the detriment of overall objectives (known as sub-optimality).

(b May be difficulties in adapting to change e.g. geographical dispersal, product diversification.

(c) Narrow functional experience is less suitable as training for management.

Geographical specialisation

The activities of many organisations are dispersed across the country rather than being concentrated in one place. Examples include; banks, insurance companies, multiple retail outlets and so on. In such circumstances the organisation is often divided up on a regional basis and local management given responsibility for the activities of the branch, area or region as the case may be.

Advantages of geographical specialisation:

(a) On the spot decision making using local knowledge.

(b) Speedier reactions and better service creates customer goodwill.

(c) Some operating costs are lower e.g. transport, storage and so on.

(d) The all round experience is good training for managers.

Disadvantages:

(a) Loss of control by head office.

(b) Problems of co-ordinating local activities.

(c) Duplication of some jobs (note that local units rarely have responsibility for all activities. Some activities usually remain centralised; one typical example being Finance).

Product or service specialisation

Another commonly encountered form of organisational specialisation is by category of product or service. This is frequently encountered in large organisations – in both the public and private sectors – which have a wide range of services or products.

For example a local authority organises its employees into service related areas typically; Education, Social Services, Highways, Rating and Valuation and so on. The National Health Service groups its employees (nursing, paramedical and others) according to the nature of the service i.e. psychiatric, orthopaedic, gynaecology, surgery and so on.

In the private sector, a tyre and rubber manufacturer might be organised on a product basis as shown in Figure 6.3.

Advantages of product or service specialisation:

(a) Develops expertise in dealing with a particular product or service.

(b) Enables responsibilities to be clearly identified which may increase motivation. For example, a manager is given responsibility for all aspects of Product X, including profitability. In effect it becomes his own business.

(c) Diversification and technological change is easier to handle.

Disadvantages:

(a) Managers may promote their product or service to the detriment of the organisation as a whole.

(b) Possible co-ordination problems and loss of top-management control.

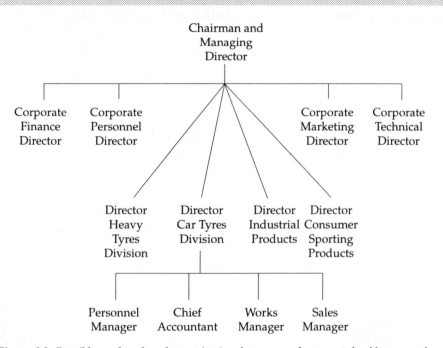

Figure 6.3: Possible product-based organisational structure for tyre and rubber manufacturer

Mixed forms of structure

Organisations choose structures which are thought to be the most efficient for their particular circumstances and operating conditions. This means that they often use a mixture of types in an attempt to combine the best features of functional, product, and geographical specialisation. For example within an organisation grouped into Product Departments, functional areas such as marketing, production, personnel still operate. Mixed forms of structure are commonly encountered reinforcing the contingency view of organisations that the best way depends on individual circumstances and that there are no universal answers.

One unusual form of mixed structure developed to meet particular needs, the *matrix structure*, is described below.

Matrix structures

Organisation structures are constantly evolving in order to overcome the deficiencies of earlier forms in coping with new activities, relationships and technological change.

One particular concept that has developed from the aerospace and other high technology industries is the *matrix form.*

In matrix structures, project teams, each with a designated manager, are combined with a conventional functional structure. The project teams are multi-disciplinary and are formed to achieve specific goals such as; the launch of a new product, the development of a new automatic gearbox, the development of a new system of collecting taxes and so on. The project leaders liaise with the functional heads for services and the functional heads provide technical expertise and facilities and give structure to the organisation. In addition to the functional relationships mentioned, the project manager has a direct or line relationship with his superior, usually the Chief Executive or General Manager.

An illustration of a matrix organisation applied to a manufacturing company is shown in Figure 6.4.

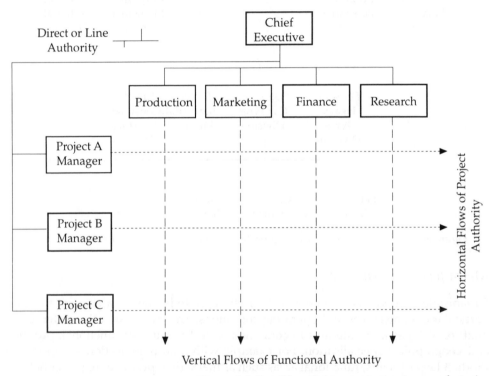

Figure 6.4: Possible matrix organisation in manufacturing

The matrix form attempts to combine the efficiency and stability of the more conventional departmental and functional form with the flexibility and directness of a project based approach. It is a compromise between a traditional functional organisation and a full scale programme based approach such as that used for the American space developments, such as Apollo, Skylab and the Space Shuttle.

The matrix form of organisation can increase motivation and is a help in directing productive effort. However, it does suffer from the disadvantage that conflicts may arise over divisions of responsibility between project groups and functional heads and the consequent way resources are allocated. Also, particularly if newly introduced, functional management may resent the apparent down-grading of their responsibilities.

The various forms of specialisation or departmentation described in the paragraphs above show typical ways in which organisations arrange the tasks to be done. However, it is not sufficient merely to consider the reasoning behind the departments by the numbers of department and the consequent levels of management. A major influence on this is the span of control.

Span of control

It will be recalled that the span of control is the number of subordinates over which a supervisor has direct control.

The classical theorists tended to favour a narrow span of control; Urwick for example recommended a maximum of 6, but practice varies greatly with organisations successfully using spans ranging from one to fifty or more. Smaller forms of control are common in technical, professional and managerial groups where the work is diverse and complex. Larger spans are usually found where the work is routine.

In general, where the span is too wide for the particular conditions the supervisor may spend too much time supervising and co-ordinating and will thus have insufficient time for decision making, training and support. Where the span is too narrow the tendency will be for the manager to become too involved in routine tasks and to interfere in the tasks he has delegated to others causing frustration and the breakdown of trust.

The number of subordinates cannot be determined in advance but will always depend on a variety of factors; the main ones of which are:

☐ the complexity of the work. The more complex, the narrower the span.

☐ degree of environmental change. Fast rates of change require narrow spans to increase adaptability.

☐ ability of subordinates. More able and better trained people require less supervision and support.

☐ riskiness or danger associated with the work. If mistakes could be costly or there are physical hazards, narrower spans are required, and finally,

☐ the ability of the manager. Good organisers and communicators will be able to deal with larger numbers.

Within a given organisation the spans of control will vary. They are likely to be narrower at higher levels and broader at the lower operational levels. The number of levels of management or authority varies from organisation to organisation and is dependent on a variety of factors. The number of levels determines the configuration or shape of the organisation.

Configuration and levels

An organisation may contain many levels of authority or management such as for example, in the Civil Service, or it may have just one or two as in many small businesses. It is the number of levels between the workers and top management which determines the configuration or shape of the organisation.

In general, organisations can be *flat* or *tall* in relation to their size as shown in Figure 6.5.

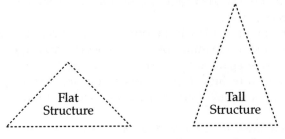

Figure 6.5: Flat and tall organisational structures

Numerous factors influence the number of levels in an organisation, the main ones of which are:

- Size of organisation
- Complexity and nature of operations
- Production methods
- Technology
- Management style and attitude to authority
- Amount of delegation practised
- Spans of control
- Ability of management and personnel

The characteristics of flat and tall structures are summarised below.

Flat organisation structures

The key features of flat structures are:

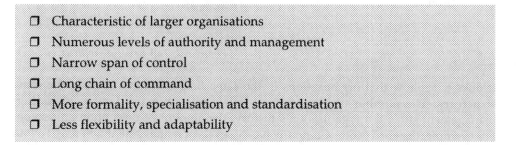

- Relatively small size (but not always)
- Few levels of authority and management
- Short chain of command
- Tendency to suit mass production operations (Woodward studies)
- Broad span of control

As an example Figure 6.6 shows an organisation with 4 levels, typical of many small and medium sized organisations.

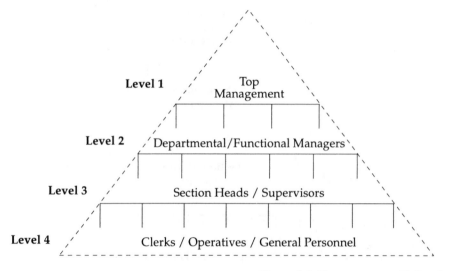

Figure 6.6: Flat structure with four levels

Tall organisation structures

Although there is a tendency for the number of levels to increase with the size of organisation this relationship does not continue indefinitely. It would be rare to find more than 8 or 10 levels of authority even in very large organisations.

The key features of tall structures are:

- Characteristic of larger organisations
- Numerous levels of authority and management
- Narrow span of control
- Long chain of command
- More formality, specialisation and standardisation
- Less flexibility and adaptability

Figure 6.7 shows a possible structure for a medium/large organisation.

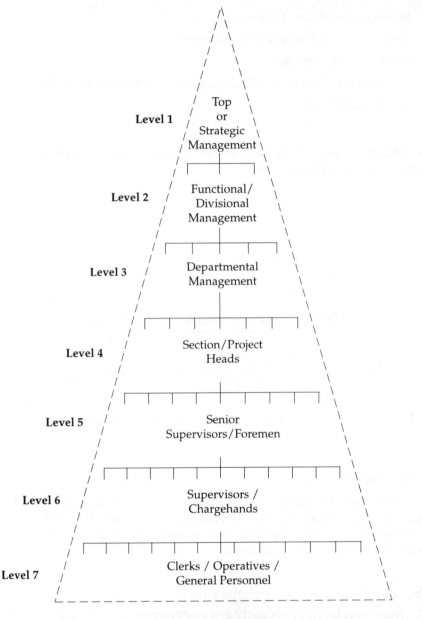

Figure 6.7: Tall structure with seven levels

It does not follow that organisations in the same field will have broadly the same structures. The number of management levels reflects many factors including; management style; the organisation's history, the amount of delegation and so on. For example, the Ford Motor Company has 13 levels of management whereas Toyota has 6.

Shorter and flatter organisations increase discretionary power in the lower and middle levels. Organisations where risk is unacceptable, where there is a reluctance to delegate, will keep the spans of control small and the number of levels high.

Possibly the most serious consequence of tall structures is their lack of flexibility and slower responsiveness to operational needs. As a consequence the 1990's have seen many organisations attempting to flatten their structures, cut out middle levels of management and to become leaner and fitter. This trend is apparent in both private and public sector organisations. To take two examples from two widely different areas the Sheehy Report proposes that management levels are scrapped in the hierarchy of the UK Police force and the multi-national computer firm IBM are giving more responsibility to lower level employees and cutting out layers of middle management.

Studies conducted by Aston University researchers found that as organisations grow they tend to become taller with an inherent loss of flexibility but that they are able to support a greater degree of specialisation.

Two other key influences on organisation structures are centralisation and decentralisation.

Centralisation and decentralisation

Drucker states that 'decentralisation is the best principle of organisation *where it fits*' but warns that the requirements for its application are stringent. Decentralisation, in the organisational sense, refers to the *dispersal of authority* to the parts of the organisation and does not describe physical locations.

Accordingly, a decentralised organisation is one where authority to commit resources (e.g. personnel, materials, money) and to take real decisions, is spread throughout the various levels of the organisation, as compared with a centralised organisation where authority is exercised only by top management.

As organisations grow and there is more specialisation, the organisation has to decide how much authority, and of what type, it can delegate from the centre. A. P. Sloan in the 1920's, then President of General Motors, was a pioneer of decentralisation in organisations and expressed his philosophy as: 'decentralised operations with centralised policy control'. This remains a good description of how successfully to decentralise.

What functions can be decentralised?

Because of their nature certain functions are more easily decentralised than others. Production and Marketing would be in this category whilst Finance and Research are examples of functions which often remain centralised even in a largely decentralised organisation. To avoid fragmentation of the business, Drucker argues that three main areas of decision must always be reserved for top management alone i.e.

□ decisions about what technologies, markets and products to go into and what businesses to start or to abandon.

□ decisions on corporate finance.

□ decisions on corporate personnel policy and on key appointments.

If these types of decision are not centrally controlled the organisation will become fragmented with no real cohesion.

There are no absolute standards to judge the extent to which an organisation is decentralised. An organisation may have numerous operating divisions but with all decisions of any significance taken at the centre whilst another may have few or no identifiable divisions yet has genuine, decentralised decision making.

The natural consequence of a policy of decentralisation is the creation of semi-autonomous operating divisions where the local management has considerable, but not absolute, discretion and has responsibility for divisional profitability. It is in such circumstances that formal performance appraisal and monitoring systems become necessary and good information flows vital.

Factors for decentralisation

Properly organised and controlled, decentralisation should:

(a) Improve local decision making. Divisional management are in close touch with day-to-day operations and are in a position to make more informed and speedier decisions.

(b) Improve strategic decision making. Central management are relieved of much lower level and routine decision making and thus able to concentrate on strategic considerations.

(c) Increase flexibility and reduce communication problems. The ability to take decisions near the point of action reduces response time and means that adjustments can be made more swiftly to cope with changes in market or supply conditions. The shorter communication lines mean quicker decisions and fewer chances of errors caused by communication channels.

(d) Increase motivation of divisional management. This is a key feature of decentralisation and arguably is the most important factor contributing to increased efficiency. Research shows that people value greater independence and respond in a positive manner to increased responsibility particularly when this is linked to the reward system of the organisation.

(e) Better Training. The spread of genuine decision making and the increased responsibility this entails provides better training for junior management. In many organisations there are movements within divisional management and between divisional and central management thus enhancing career opportunities for able and ambitious managers. The existence of these opportunities helps to attract people of the right calibre and increases morale and motivation.

Problems with decentralisation

Inevitably there are potential problems with decentralisation and these include:

(a) Possible sub-optimal decision making. This is potentially the greatest problem and occurs when local management take decisions which benefit their department or division but where the local gains are more than offset by increased costs or losses of benefit in other parts of the organisation. Where there is any conflict between local and organisational objectives those of the organisation should be paramount. This is not easy to achieve and well designed reporting and information systems are essential.

(b) More problems of co-ordination. With a decentralised organisation, top management must ensure that the parts of the organisation work together. They must ensure that local, parochial attitudes do not develop to the detriment of the organisation as a whole. Without overall co-ordination it becomes difficult for the various functions to integrate their activities. For example, production, selling, distribution and stocking activities must be meticulously co-ordinated to avoid losses in efficiency, increased costs and customer dissatisfaction.

(c) Problems of control, monitoring and communication. Although one of the advantages of decentralisation is that certain aspects of communication are improved, for example, that relating to operational decisions which, being taken locally, do not have to travel up and down several levels of the organisation, top management must have sufficient information to maintain overall control. There must be the correct type of information so that top management can monitor the performance of junior management with regard to the tasks delegated to them.

(d) The supply of the right type of manager. Decentralisation places extra demands upon junior management so that there is a continuing need to recruit, train and develop well motivated and intelligent personnel. Although most people react positively to increased responsibility, some do not and top management need to monitor personal performance closely and must ensure that the organisation's personnel policies and practices attract and retain the right people. Whilst decentralisation puts extra responsibility on to junior managers it also requires top management to reconsider and redefine their own tasks and responsibilities.

As well as commercial companies, organisations in the Public Sector are also encountering the need to be more flexible and efficient:

In 1991 the Audit Commission, which reports on the effectiveness of public spending, said that it had found wide variations in organisation between the 43 police forces in England and Wales.

Some had 10% of staff working on administrative jobs at headquarters; others had 20%. The commission said that moving police officers out of the central offices would lead to more flexible groups of officer's fully accountable for the quality of day-to-day policing in their areas.

If decentralised forces were to be created the police's divisional officers, effectively the middle management level, could become redundant. The commission reported that 'those forces which have reviewed their divisional structures have tended to reduce or remove them'.

Centralisation combined with decentralisation

Recent research by Peters and Waterman suggest that more successful companies practice both centralisation and decentralisation. Centrally, clear performance guidelines are established with core values relating to the quality of product and service and then decentralisation by the operating units is encouraged.

For example, within organisations such as Courtaulds, Lucas and BTR the operating units – which may be subsidiary companies or designated business units – are encouraged to be more entrepreneurial and to act as largely independent entities in order to achieve the designated targets in their own individual ways. With this style of operation, the organisation as a whole becomes more flexible and responsible whilst adhering to centrally imposed values and targets.

The need for flexibility is affecting even the giants of industry.

IBM was once the world's most profitable company and operates on a world-wide basis. IBM's earnings peaked in 1985 but increasing competition, mainly from more flexible small companies, caused earnings to decline in the late 1980's and early 1990's. IBM have identified that there are management and structural problems as well as the more obvious problems of maintaining technical leadership in the fast moving electronics field. As a consequence, operating companies throughout the world are being given much more freedom to take decisions and to react quickly to local competition. IBM is changing from a highly centralised organisation to a more decentralised one. It is becoming leaner and more flexible.

Overall, whilst there are undeniably more advantages than disadvantages of decentralisation, it is well to recall Drucker's remark quoted earlier that decentralisation is excellent, 'when it fits'.

Legal structures

An all pervasive influence on organisations, their structures, rights and obligations is their legal status. There is an enormous range of legal possibilities from a *sole trader* to a *public limited company*, from a *partnership* to a *local authority* or *nationalised industry* and so on.

A brief summary of the more common legal structures follows.

Sole trader: This is a simple and common form of business organisation. The owner has total control and has unlimited liability for the debts of the business. The business does not have a legal identity separate from the owner.

Partnership: This is where two or more people own and carry on a business together. Normally the number of partners is limited to 20 although accountants, solicitors or members of a recognised Stock Exchange may be in partnerships with more than 20 partners. The activities, rights and obligations of partnerships are covered by the Partnership Act of 1890. Normally all partners have unlimited liability. However, limited partnerships are possible where all the partners, bar one, may enjoy limited liability. There must always be one partner with unlimited liability and those with limited liability are not allowed to take part in the management of the business. These types of partnerships are covered by the Limited Partnership Act of 1907.
Note: sole traders and partnerships are known as *unincorporated associations*.

Limited liability companies: These forms of organisation account for the overwhelming proportion of business activity. Their key features are that they are legal entities in their own right i.e. separate from the individuals who own them and their owners, known as shareholders, enjoy limited liability. Limited liability means that the liability of the shareholders is limited to the amount paid, or to be paid, on the shares taken up by them. This means that shareholders know their total potential liability in the case of failure. The legal framework of companies is governed by the Companies Act. Originally passed in 1948 this is progressively amended every few years; the latest version being 1989. Companies are of two types; private or public.

In general, private limited companies are smaller than public companies, and have the following main features. The numbers of shareholders is limited to 50 and the private company cannot offer shares and debentures to the public. On the other hand, public limited companies may offer their shares and debentures to the public and there is no limitation on the number of shareholders. Some public companies are very large enterprises indeed; for example Hansons, Glaxo, British Telecom and so on. By law private companies must have the words, 'limited' or 'Ltd.' in their name and public companies 'public limited companies' or 'PLC'.

The concept of limited liability is universal in all industrialised economies and developed because the sole trader and partnership forms are less appropriate for larger enterprises with substantial capital requirements. Limited liability has the significant advantage that shareholders may invest money in an enterprise without taking part in the management of the business or having unlimited liability for the debts of the business. This is not an abstract, theoretical idea; it has real practical consequences as investors in Lloyds have found.

> Lloyds of London is the long established insurance market famous throughout the world. Its investors, known as names, provide the funds to back up the insurances undertaken and their individual liability is unlimited. From the late 1980's to the early 1990's Lloyds had disastrous results with total losses of over £5 billion. This has meant that Lloyds have called upon the names to find more funds to settle claims. On a personal level this has proved disastrous as many names have had to sell all their possessions to meet their liabilities and have been ruined. A natural consequence of these problems is that investors are reluctant to invest funds where their liability for debts is unlimited and Lloyds are having to introduce limited liability for investors for the first time in their 300 year history.

Special forms of companies

The limited liability companies mentioned above are by far the most common and important. However other forms exist including *chartered companies* and *statutory companies*.

Chartered companies are companies incorporated by Royal Charter. Statutory companies are rare and are those formed by a specific Act of Parliament.

Public sector organisations

In spite of extensive de-nationalisation or privatisation during the 1980's e.g. Telephones, Water, Gas, Electricity and so on, public sector organisations and nationalised industries still represent a major part of the economy.

There is an enormous range of public sector organisations. Some are akin to commercial companies, trading or supplying services which have to be paid for. Examples include, British Coal and British Rail. Others have a commercial element but supply many free services e.g. the National Health Service, the British Broadcasting Corporation, others have a purely administrative rôle e.g. the Department of Social Security and so on.

The following list, although not exhaustive, shows the main types of public sector organisations:

- Central Government including the various government departments such as Environment, Transport, Social Security
- Defence including the armed forces, ordnance factories and depots.
- Security including police, jails.
- Nationalised industries including British Rail, British Coal.
- Local government including District and County Councils.
- Education including Schools, Colleges and Universities.
- National Service organisations including the National Health Service, the BBC, and so on.

Many hitherto conventional Civil Service departments have been turned into quasi-commercial agencies operating to targets and expected to earn profits by selling goods and services to the public and to industry.

This process is being carried out under what is known as the Next Steps Programme. By 1991, 75 agencies had been launched with another 64 units operating on Agency lines. Each Agency has a contract with central government, known as the Framework Document which covers such things as; Aims and Objectives, Reporting and Accountability, the Financial Regime. Some examples of Agencies currently operating are; Central Office of Information, the Benefits Agency, Passport Office, Ordnance Survey, Patent Office, Driver and Vehicle Licensing.

Key point summary

- Within every formal organisation exists an informal one.

- Departmentation is the result of grouping people by specialisation.

- Different forms of specialisation exist including; functional, geographical, product or service.

- Mixed forms of specialisation frequently occur.

- Flat structures have a short chain of command with a broad span of control and tend to occur where decentralisation is practised.

- Taller structures tend to occur with increase in size and produce more specialised and formal organisations.

- Decentralisation occurs when authority is dispersed from the centre.

- Decentralised organisation can be more responsible and flexible but overall control and co-ordination are more difficult.

❐   The legal status of organisations has a profound influence on structure.

❐   Business organisations normally range from sole traders through partnerships to limited liability companies, private and public.

❐   Public sector organisations are a major part of the economy.

Self review questions

1.   What are the possible advantages and disadvantages of formal and informal organisations?

2.   What is specialisation and how can it be achieved?

3.   What is a matrix organisation and what are its advantages and disadvantages?

4.   What are the factors which affect the number of levels in an organisation?

5.   What are the features of flat organisations?

6.   What are the features of tall organisations?

7.   Why are organisations reducing the number of management levels?

8.   What is decentralisation and what are its possible benefits and problems?

9.   What are the features of organisations which affect lateral and vertical information flows?

10. Distinguish between partnerships and limited liability companies.

Assessment and revision section

Assignments

1. Investigate several organisations (or different parts of a large organisation) and try to find out what spans of control different managers have to deal with. If they vary greatly, find out the reasons. Can you find any general guidelines which determine the span of control?

2. By observation or interviews or discussions try to find out what factors motivate a person of your choice. Do the things that motivate them also motivate you? Does anything you discover relate to the theories of motivation covered in the book?

3. Imagine you are starting a 20 person Design Consultancy employing 12 professional designers, 4 computer specialists and 4 clerical staff.
   Explain, with reasons, how you would deal with the following:
   (a) Hierarchy of Authority;
   (b) Degree of Centralisation;
   (c) Specialisation.

4. Major changes are taking place within the UK Civil Service. An important part of these changes is the 'Next Step' programme. Find out what this is. What changes in management and organisation will be necessary for this to succeed? What are the problems?

5. Try to find in the literature or by investigation examples of structural changes made by organisation to cope with change or the introduction of new technology or in an attempt to become more efficient.

6. Try to find examples where real decision making has become more decentralised. Find out, if you can, what have been the effects of this change.

Mini-Case 1 – BKM plc

BKM plc is a group consisting of numerous manufacturing plants; some in the North West, some in the Midlands and some on the outskirts of London. The Group's activities include automotive products and components and assemblies for the aerospace and defence industries. Some factories sell direct to outside customers, others both sell direct and manufacture parts which are assembled in other factories in the Group.

The Group is administered by a holding company with a substantial head office staff dealing with the following functions:

☐   Purchasing for the Group.

☐   Personnel; including recruitment, selection and training. The department also administers salaries and runs a detailed staff appraisal scheme.

☐   Industrial engineering; including designing production layouts, management services etc.

☐   Data Processing with Group wide responsibility for systems analysis, design and implementation.

☐   Central Accounting with small accounting departments at each factory reporting to head office.

Task 1 *Describe the Group's organisation structure.*

Task 2 *Give the advantages of such a structure.*

Task 3 *Give the disadvantages.*

Mini-Case 2 – Westonshire District Council

Westonshire is a largely rural D.C. with three large towns within its boundaries. Like most councils it is under pressure to reduce expenditure. There is also political pressure to use outside contractors wherever possible but the Council would like to keep as many services as possible under its own control. A preliminary investigation has shown that the performance of the Council's own domestic refuse collection and disposal service compares unfavourably with that of a neighbouring Council who use private contractors.

Task 1 *Explain how the Council may improve the performance of its own service.*

Task 2 *Investigate what has been the experience of Councils who have sub-contracted out this service.*

Task 3 *Explain what are the organisational consequences of sub-contracting out such services.*

Examination questions with answers

A1 What is organisational centralisation? Describe some of the advantages and disadvantages of organisational centralisation and decentralisation.
        ACCA – Effective Management

A2 Norman is a recently qualified management accountant. He chose this profession because he understood that high salaries could be earned by successful accountants in senior positions.

After training in various departments of a large firm he was offered a position in the consultancy division in a department concerned with advising companies in the London area on management accounting systems. The department is growing, partly because its expertise in management accounting systems is widely known. The department is therefore well provided with technical support and other resources. He enjoyed the analytical work involved and received high merit ratings in each of his two annual reviews. These resulted in substantial pay increases.

Norman is married, has a two-year old son and another baby due shortly. He loves playing with his son, and is a keen member of a choir which practises twice a week. He has purchased a house with a mortgage which is just within his financial means and he enjoys making do-it-yourself improvements to the house.

A large organisation which has over 100 establishments throughout the country has asked Norman's employers to advise them on the management accountancy systems in each of these establishments. Each of the establishments differs in its structure, due to varying local environments. Because Norman's performance has been so good, it has been suggested that he should take charge of a small new department which will be specially set up for this business.

You are required, on the basis of any relevant motivation theory (such as Vroom's Expectancy Theory or Porter and Lawler's), to analyse Norman's personal motivation and how it may be affected by the suggested change of job.

CIMA – Management

A3 Motivation of subordinates is an important aspect of a manager's job.
   (a) What do you think motivates a person to work well?
   (b) What steps can a manager take to motivate his subordinates?

ICSA – Management, Principles and Policy

A4 The use of the sole tradership and the partnership as forms of business enterprise is common in small business proprietorship. In what ways may the use of these forms of organisation assist or impede the development of innovation and entrepreneurship?

ACCA – Effective Management

A5 Compare the approaches taken by the classical/traditional theorists with the human relations/resources theorists, in understanding the nature of organisations.

CIMA – Management

A6 Classical writers on organisation structure focused on the search for a common set of principles applicable to all circumstances.
   (a) State and briefly explain any FOUR such principles.
   (b) Discuss why the Classical Approach based on principles has been criticised by later writers and whether it has anything of lasting worth to contribute to our understanding of organisational design.

IAM – Organisational Analysis

Examination questions without answers

B1 What is divisionalisation? Why do organisations make use of divisionalised structures?

ACCA – Effective Management

B2 (a) What are the main features of a bureaucratic organisation?
    (b) How effectively do bureaucratic organisations respond to changing circumstances in the environment?

ICSA – Management, Principles and Policy

B3 M Ltd employs between 200 and 300 people. It was formerly part of a large group of companies with a centralised personnel function.
    The responsibilities of this function were
    (a) recruitment services, including preparing personal specifications, and interviewing;
    (b) appraisal procedures, including the design of forms and maintenance of records;
    (c) determining salary scales, including job evaluation;
    (d) employment services, including maintaining personnel records and dealing with legal issues.
    M Ltd has now become independent, through a management buy-out. The new managing director is considering whether to establish a central personnel department to take responsibility for the above matters or whether to devolve the responsibilities to the managers of the operating departments.
    You are required to explain the implications of decentralisation versus centralisation for each of the functions (a) to (d) above.

CIMA – Management

B4 You are required to describe five features of an 'organic' organisation, explaining how these affect the operations of the organisation.

CIMA – Management

Additional reading

Organisation, J. Child, Harper & Row.

Administrative Behaviour, Simon, Harper & Row.

Management – Theory and Practice, G. A. Cole, DP Publications.

Practice of Management, P. Drucker, Heinemann.

Company Law, K. R. Abbott, DP Publications.

7 Management: introduction, roles, levels and tasks

Objectives

After you have studied this chapter you will:

❐ *Have had an introduction to the chapters on management.*

❐ *Understand the problems of managing change.*

❐ *Be able to describe Theory Z.*

❐ *Know what roles a manager must perform.*

❐ *Be able to define the basic three levels of management.*

❐ *Know, in outline, what are the key tasks of management including; Planning, Organising, Motivating and Control.*

What is management?

Fayol's classic definition of management was derived from his own experience and is repeated below.

> 'To manage is to forecast and plan, to organise, to command, to co-ordinate and to control.'

More modern definitions are largely variants of Fayol's but with more emphasis on the need to guide, lead and motivate people rather than merely command. Management is a down to earth process which has practical consequences. As Drucker says:

> 'Management is a practice not a science. It is not knowledge but performance.'

Management have to make decisions about work, people, structures and systems and some typical examples are shown.

Work of the organisation

What should it be? How should it be divided and organised? How will tasks be co-ordinated?

People in the organisation

Who should they be? How should they be treated and motivated? How will they be managed and led? Who does what?

Structure of the organisation

What will be the groups/departments? What will be their relationships? How will authority and responsibility be arranged? Where will decisions be taken? (centralisation/decentralisation).

Systems of the organisation

What systems will there be? How will the operating systems (i.e. sales, production, finance etc.) work? What type of information/communication system will there be?

Change management

The single most pressing problem that faces any organisation is how to cope with change. Change occurs in many ways including; competitive pressures (e.g. a competitor introduces a new model or reduces prices), legislation (e.g the change from the Poll Tax to the Council Tax), the operating environment (e.g. the European Single market in 1992), changing client/consumer preferences (e.g. the desire for more leisure or environmentally friendly products), the introduction of new technology (e.g. computer networks, robotics) and many more.

Organisations do not automatically adjust to change. Adaptation only occurs as a result of management actions. These may cause changes in the way the organisation takes decisions, in the processes used, in the services or products, or in the structure of the organisation itself. Only one thing is certain; the organisation that clings to rigid, traditional methods in the midst of rapid change will be an unsuccessful organisation.

Ways to manage change

Many valuable pointers to the way more successful organisations manage change and innovation have come from studies by Moss Kanter, Peters and Waterman and others. Moss Kanter found that organisations who adopt an integrated approach to innovation did it more successfully than those who adopted a more piecemeal approach, which she termed 'segmentalist'. To overcome resistance to change and inertia she suggested the following actions:

Top management must support innovation in a personal way and must think integratively.

The organisation must be made 'flatter' i.e. unnecessary layers of hierarchy should be removed and staff 'empowered' by authority being pushed downwards.

Communication should be improved especially across the organisation and staff mobility encouraged.

Achievements should be highlighted and a culture of pride cultivated.

Company plans should be made known earlier and more widely to enable staff to make suggestions and contribute before decisions are made.

Peters and Waterman also investigated how companies handled change. They defined success in handling change in terms of a mixture of above average growth and financial return, and a reputation for continuous innovation. Those that achieved success they deemed excellent companies and found that they had certain attributes in common. These can be summarised thus:

They have simplified structures with autonomous divisions without large headquarters' staff.

Entrepreneurship and initiative is encouraged with acceptance that there will be occasional failures.

Customer service is paramount and they genuinely listen and respond to customers.

They get things done; once a problem is identified and analysed, solutions are sought.

The organisation's basic values are emphasised and employees are held in high esteem but expectations are high.

Control is a loose/tight mixture. Core values such as quality and service are insisted upon but decision making is pushed downwards and not continually monitored as long as objectives are achieved and core values maintained.

It will be seen that the attributes above are the hallmarks of the modern approach to organisations and management. The distinction between the traditional and more modern approaches is summarised in the following two quotations.

> Big is better . . . make sure everything is carefully and formally coordinated . . . the manager's job is decision making . . . analyse everything . . . produce fat planning volumes . . . get rid of the disturbers of the peace . . . control everything . . . keep things tidy . . . specify the organisation structure in great detail . . . write long job descriptions.
>
> *Peters and Waterman*
>
> Companies are discarding their organisational charts and simplifying their chains of command. This gives chief executives more flexibility, keener and quicker assessment of performance, clearer and faster lines of action, and a quick grasp of the information needed to run their companies . . . they are frantically trying to push (decisions:) down to those who are closest to the marketplace, giving more autonomy to plant managers, sales people, and engineers . . . creating environments in which compensation depends on performance and freedom to improve performance provides the psychic reward.
>
> *Business Week*

Pointers to the way that organisations may adapt to change are provided by the ideas behind Theory Z organisations.

Theory Z

Theory Z is a term coined by William Ouchi to describe an ideal cultural system based mainly on the successful methods and approach used by large Japanese companies. The culture of an organisation includes the philosophies, tradition, experience and corporate values of the organisation.

> The Z culture is one characterised by:
>
> (a) a commitment to people
>
> (b) trust and effective personal relationships
>
> (c) long-term employment
>
> (d) a desire to humanise working conditions
>
> (e) consensus decision making

Theory Z claims that high levels of performance and job satisfaction go together. Although hierarchies and formal structures do exist in Type Z organisations, self direction and mutual trust to a large extent replace traditional hierarchical direction and co-ordination. Type Z organisations are more informal and egalitarian and are characterised by many semi-autonomous work groups. Ouchi reports that in Japan each employee, from top to bottom, is simultaneously a member of as many as 10 or 12 work groups, each with a different task. This flexibility should be contrasted with the rigid compartmentalisation which is a feature of many UK organisations.

Theory Z argues that although individual managers might have to accept responsibility for decisions there should be a consensus in decision-making, reached by agreement with subordinates and peer colleagues. This participative approach encourages information flows and *goal congruence* i.e. the alignment of personal and corporate objectives.

The reasoning behind Theory Z is the belief that differences between Japanese and Western management practices in part account for the better record of Japanese companies in matters such as; productivity, quality and motivation. If this is true, it means that Japan's industrial dominance is not just because they use more robots but also because they practise more effective management.

What is a manager?

Management is a process which takes place at all levels in an organisation. It is not carried out only by people with 'manager' in their job title. Section leaders, supervisors, chief clerks, foremen etc. all carry out managerial functions although obviously not all of the same type or of equal importance. It is the task which a person performs which is of importance not the job title.

The examination of what managers actually do in practice has led to a more detailed analysis of managerial roles. For example, Mintzberg has developed a list of key roles which his researches showed appeared consistently in managerial jobs.

His key roles were:

(a) Entrepreneur (planner and risk taker)

(b) Resource Allocator (organiser and co-ordinator)

(c) Figurehead/Leader (motivator and co-ordinator)

(d) Liaison/Disseminator (co-ordinator and communicator)

(e) Monitor (controller)

(f) Spokesman/Negotiator (Motivator and communicator)

(g) Disturbance-handler (motivator and co-ordinator)

This list, based on actual jobs in real organisations, illustrates the all-pervasive involvement with people and the importance of behavioural factors. A manager is concerned not only with physical processes, organisation structures and tasks, he has to deal with people and must take account of their attitudes, beliefs, values and reactions.

Although the roles above are shown clearly separated from each other this is for instructional purposes only. The reality is that the manager must blend together his roles and activities in order to be effective.

There are no artificial dividing lines between the manager as 'entrepreneur' or 'leader' or 'disturbance-handler' nor are there between the activities of planning, controlling, co-ordinating and so on.

Professor Handy has characterised the managerial role as akin to the role of the medical General Practitioner in that he must:

- Identify the symptoms
- Diagnose the cause of the trouble
- Decide how it might be dealt with
- Start the treatment

Levels of management

Although the proliferation of job titles can suggest otherwise, it is possible to differentiate three levels of management in most organisations.

Strategic management e.g. Chief Executive, Board of Directors

Tactical management e.g. all types of middle management, departmental managers, functional managers such as the personnel manager, accountant, sales manager.

Operational management e.g. foremen, supervisor, chief clerk, charge hand.

A major factor in deciding the category of management is the planning horizon. This ranges from long term at the highest level to short-term, almost day-to-day, at the lowest level. Figure 7.1 summarises the typical responsibilities, decision types and information needs of the three levels.

Although in many organisations the three levels of management discussed above are still readily discernible there is evidence of the erosion of the middle management level. This is caused by various factors, including;

- the creation, within large organisations, of semi-autonomous business units with considerable discretion over operations. Examples include; Rank Xerox, IBM, Hanson Industries. This has been well described as 'small within big is beautiful'.

- the developments in information technology and communication networks enabling information to be received by Strategic Management direct from the operational level.

☐ the growing ability of computer based systems to take decisions which traditionally were taken by middle managers. Examples include; stock replenishment decisions in supermarkets, credit scoring in banks and so on.

Level of Management	Typical Responsibilities	Planning Horizon	Decision Types	Information Characteristics			
				Orientation	Source	Aggregation	Accuracy Required
Strategic	☐ Definition of Objectives, Policies for whole Organisation ☐ Long Term Planning ☐ Large Scale Investment Decisions ☐ Middle Management Appointments ... and so on	Wide ↑	Unstructured ↑	External & Future ↑	External ↑	Aggregated ↑	Low ↑
Tactical	☐ Establishment and Monitoring of Budgets ☐ Acquisition of Resources ☐ Developing Operational Policies and Objectives ☐ Appointing Staff ... and so on			Internal Achievement Future/ Historical			
Operational	☐ Effective Use of Existing Facilities & Resources within Budget Constraints & Prescribed Objectives ☐ Making Routine Day-to-Day Decisions ... and so on	Narrow	Structured	Internal Transactions & Historical	Internal	Detailed	High

Figure 7.1: Levels of management and characteristics of information

The tasks of management

A useful way of grouping the tasks of management is into the following categories:

Planning

All activities leading to the formulation of objectives or goals and deciding upon the means of meeting them.

Motivation and leadership

Behavioural processes where a manager influences others to contribute to the achievement of objectives by gaining their commitment.

Organising and co-ordinating

Determining the necessary activities, structures and responsibilities and combining these factors to achieve the required objectives.

Control

A monitoring process where actual results are compared with planned results in order to bring activities in line with plans or to amend the plans.

In addition the all-pervasive task of decision making takes place within each of the above categories

Each of these tasks is covered in detail in the chapters which follow.

Key point summary

☐ There are numerous definitions of management but Fayol's original one remains relevant.

☐ Change occurs in many ways and adapting to change is a primary management responsibility.

☐ Factors which have been identified as important in successfully managing change include; flexibility, delegation, regard for customers and core values, tight/loose control.

☐ Theory Z organisations are characterised by trust, good personal relationships and consensus decision making.

☐ Management takes place at all levels.

☐ Various roles have been identified as appearing in a manager's job including: Entrepreneur, Spokesman, Figurehead, Monitor and so on.

☐ Decision making, which is choosing between alternatives, is an integral part of all management tasks.

☐ The main three levels of management are: Strategic, Tactical, Operational.

❐   There is a constant interchange of information, advice, decisions, results and so on between the levels.

❐   Management tasks can be grouped into: Planning, Motivating, Organising, Control with Decision Making taking place within each.

Self review questions

1. *How has Fayol's original definition of management been modified by modern writers?*

2. *Give examples of change which affects organisations.*

3. *How do organisations adapt to change?*

4. *Describe a Theory Z organisation.*

5. *What are the seven roles identified by Mintzberg?*

6. *Define the three basic levels of management and give the typical responsibilities of each level.*

7. *What are the reasons for the decline in importance of middle management?*

8. *Give the functions of management and explain what each means.*

8 _Planning and decision making_

Objectives

After you have studied this chapter you will:

☐ _Understand the relationship between planning, decision making and control._

☐ _Be able to define key terms used in planning._

☐ _Know how planning is carried out at the three management levels._

☐ _Understand the elements of corporate or strategic planning._

☐ _Understand the key elements of decision making and the distinction between pro-grammed and non-programmed decisions._

☐ _Know how decision making varies between the levels of management._

☐ _Be able to distinguish between rational, descriptive and consensus decision making._

Planning, decision making and control

Planning, decision making and control are intimately related managerial tasks. Although these activities are often separated for instructional purposes, as they are in this book, in practice they are effectively inseparable and this point should be kept in mind whilst studying the chapters which follow.

A complete cycle containing these tasks would include the following phases:

(a) Objective setting

(b) Planning

(c) Decision making and action

(d) Accomplishment

(e) Feedback

(f) Control

What is planning?

Planning is the managerial process of deciding in advance *what* is to be done and *how* it is to be done. Planning is not an end in itself, its primary purpose is to provide the guidelines necessary for decision making and resulting action, throughout the organisation. Planning is done on both a formal and informal basis and the planning process uses information from internal and external sources. The process gathers, translates, understands and communicates information that will help to improve the quality of current decisions which are based on future expectations.

In summary, planning means decisions by management about

☐ *what* is to be done in the future

☐ *how* to do it

☐ *when* to do it

☐ *who* is to do it

Because planning deals with the future uncertainty is always present. This means that flexibility must be incorporated into plans. Even where there is considerable uncertainty, plans give direction and purpose to an organisation.

Without plans, the organisation is rudderless. The essence of planning is well captured by the Vice Chancellor of Aston University in the foreword to the University's Academic Plan.

'Whether as individuals or as members of departments and professions; whether at the level of the Faculties or of the entire University, we all make plans for the future. To be realistic, they must take account of our personal strengths and weaknesses, and of externally-imposed constraints on our actions. If they are well formulated, they will anticipate threats and opportunities that might arise, and be capable of dealing with them as contingencies.

Of course, they will not be able to foresee all threats and opportunities, but that only strengthens the argument for planning thoughtfully, and retaining as much flexibility as possible. Counsels of inaction deriving from the fact that the future can never be perfectly known must be rejected if progress is to be made.'

Planning terms

In the literature on planning a bewildering variety of terms are used, not always consistently. For clarity the terms used in this book are defined below.

Objectives: general statement of aims or goals to be achieved.

Plans: statements of specific actions and activities to achieve objectives.(Plans are sometimes described as strategies).

Policies: limits to acceptable behaviour expressed in terms of priorities, ethical and moral values, standards, social responsibilities and so on.

Thus objectives are *ends*, plans are *means* and policies are *statements of conduct*. Policies are not actions in themselves but they cause management to take actions in certain ways. For example it is the policy of Marks and Spencer only to sell goods under their own brand name of St Michaels.

Figure 8.1 shows the relationship of the planning elements described above.

RELATIONSHIP OF PLANNING ELEMENTS

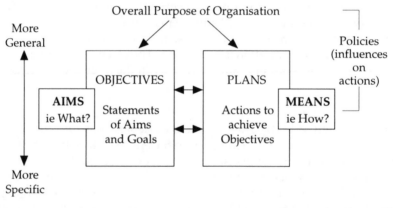

Figure 8.1

Because of their importance in providing direction to the whole organisation objectives and policies are further described below.

Objectives

The objectives of the organisation are usually of two levels of detail. At the highest level there are those that state the purpose or overall objective of the organisation. Naturally these are in broad general terms intended to be relatively permanent. In addition somewhat more detailed objectives would be set stating the organisation's long-term aims. These should be specific enough so that it is possible to assess, say over a 5 year period, whether or not they have been achieved. If the objectives are highly specific and quantifiable they are likely to be tactical or operational level objectives rather than true strategic ones.

The nature of overall or strategic objectives is influenced by many factors including; the attitudes of the owners, political pressures which reflect different views of society, the history of the organisation, the type of business or service and so on. Traditionally in profit seeking organisations there was a heavy emphasis on financial objectives such as; return on capital employed, earnings per share, profit levels. This was a relatively narrow view which has been termed the *shareholder theory of the firm*.

A more modern tendency is what is called the *stakeholder theory*. When this view is adopted objectives are set not only for the good of the organisation but also for the other groups which are beneficiaries of the organisation, known as the stakeholders. These may include; employees, customers, suppliers, the public at large.

As an example of organisation which takes the stakeholder view consider the objectives of Sainsburys plc.

Sainsbury's p.l.c. objectives

☐ To discharge the responsibility as leaders in our trade by acting with complete integrity, by carrying out our work to the highest standards and by contributing to the public good and to the quality of life in the community.

☐ To provide unrivalled value to our customers in the quality of goods we sell, in the competitiveness of our prices and in the range of choice we offer.

☐ In our stores, to achieve the highest standards of cleanliness and hygiene, efficiency of operation, convenience and customer service, and thereby create as attractive and friendly a shopping environment as possible.

☐ To offer our staff outstanding opportunities in terms of personal career development and in remuneration relative to other companies in the same market, practising always a concern for the welfare of every individual.

☐ To generate sufficient profit to finance continual improvement and growth of the business whilst providing our shareholders with an excellent return on their investment.

Note the balancing of the needs of the various stakeholders; the customers, staff and shareholders, with the needs of the community as a whole. Note also the part of the first objective relating to the public good and quality of life in the community. This is the area of *social responsibility* which is taken seriously by many leading organisations which initiate or contribute to activities in the Arts, Education, Welfare and so on. For example:

In education: support for universities e.g. Nottingham (Boots), Liverpool (Littlewoods), funding of Chairs e.g. by Lloyds, Arthur Andersen and others.

Community projects: Sainsbury, Tescos and other firms support numerous local and National projects. Boots are sponsoring a scheme to beautify towns and cities.

Arts: donations to the National Gallery, Royal Philharmonic by the Getty Foundation, Bankers Trust Company and others. Financing of a major extension at the National Gallery by Sainsburys, sponsorship of the Royal Shakespeare Company by Allied-Lyons.

Business assistance: funding of the London Business Agency to help small business jointly by Marks and Spencers, Barclays Bank, BP, United Biscuits and others.

Activities such as those above are predominantly charitable in nature and should be distinguished from promotional activities such as sports sponsorship which are usually funded from the advertising and public relations budgets of the large organisations concerned.

Because of the increasing world-wide attention to environmental matters a number of organisations have, in addition to more normal objectives, also established specific environmental objectives. For example:

Environmental Objectives - ICI plc.

☐   Compliance with regulatory legislation and standards wherever ICI operates is the minimum basis of the Group's four environmental objectives.

☐   To require all its new plants to be built to standards that will meet the regulations it can reasonably anticipate in the most environmentally demanding country in which it operates that process. This will normally require the use of the best environmental practice within the industry.

☐   To reduce wastes by 50 per cent by 1995, using 1990 as the baseline year. It will pay special attention to those which are hazardous. In addition, ICI will try to eliminate all off-site disposal of environmentally harmful wastes.

☐   To establish a revitalised and more ambitious energy and resource conservation programme, with special emphasis on reducing environmental effects so as to make further substantial progress by 1995.

☐   To establish a clear policy and practice on waste recycling.

The importance of environmental issues was underscored by the first ever listing in 1993 of corporate environmental performance by 'Fortune', the international business magazine.

Policies

Policies are a guide to managers causing them to take actions in certain ways. They express the organisation's official attitude to various forms of behaviour. When the organisation's objectives have been established, policies provide guidance on the way they will be achieved.

Policies are formal expressions of the organisation's culture and belief systems. Some are so fundamental that they form the rationâle for the whole organisation. For example, the Fairtrade Foundation has a policy of ensuring that Third World growers of coffee receive a higher price than the normal world market price for their coffee beans. At present Café Direct is their only product and is being sold in an increasing number of supermarkets. There are plans to apply these same policies to the cocoa and chocolate trade.

Examples of policies published by other organisations include

Marks and Spencers has policies of selling goods only under their own brand name and of concentrating their buying in the UK.

The Body Shop has strong environmental policies which include the avoidance of animal testing, recyclable containers, natural ingredients.

Levels of planning

All levels of management make plans but naturally the type of planning done at each level varies in scope and time scale. Planning has a natural hierarchy and must commence at the strategic or top level of the organisation. Planning at tactical and operational levels takes place within the guidelines of strategic plans which is obviously essential otherwise the organisation will not have a direction or overall purpose.

Figure 8.2 shows an outline of the three levels of planning with indicative time horizons.

Planning problems

Planning is a vital process in all organisations yet it is often shirked and management sometimes seek ways to avoid planning if at all possible. There are numerous reasons for this of which the following are the most important.

(a) Planning is an intensive, time consuming task and there often seems to be more important jobs to be done.

(b) Planning is hard mental work so it may be neglected.

(c) Planning makes evident the uncertainty of future events so that paradoxically, the future may seem more uncertain after planning than before.

(d) Lack of confidence by managers about their ability to meet targets.

(e) Planning reduces the apparent freedom of action. When plans are made managers are committed to a narrower range of actions than when no formal plans are made.

(f) Lack of knowledge about the purpose and objectives of the organisation and of other departments. Good planning encourages co-ordination.

(g) Lack of appropriate information.

(h) Plans are often made and then ignored. This tends to happen with imposed plans which do not represent real agreement.

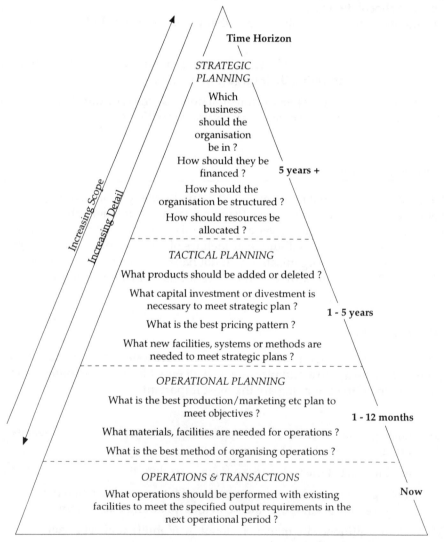

Figure 8.2: Levels of planning

Strategic or corporate planning

As previously pointed out, planning within an organisation must start from the top or strategic level. Strategic planning, or as it is sometimes known, *corporate planning*, seeks to obtain a consensus among the top people of the organisation about the overall direction of the organisation over the medium or long term. It is more than 'business planning' (which produces plans for parts of the business), it is more than 'budgets' (which are tactical plans expressed in money terms), it is more than finance, marketing or manpower panning.

Corporate planning is about issues which affect the *whole organisation at the highest level*; it is a top-down process whereby the organisation as a whole is given planning guidelines which spell out the direction which the organisation will take and how the parts of the organisation fit into the plan.

In summary, corporate planning can be defined as the systematic planning of the direction and total resources of an organisation so as to achieve specified objectives over the medium to long term.

Excessive detail should be avoided because this has a tendency to reduce flexibility and the scope for opportunism and initiative; vital factors in dealing with future problems and opportunities. Argenti recommends that the corporate plan should provide 'a coarse grained strategic structure for the long term future'.

In the early days of corporate planning it was thought that corporate planning should be a very detailed, numeric exercise carried out by specialist planners using sophisticated planning techniques. Nowadays it has been realised that true corporate planning must be done by top management themselves, that the plan should address only the topmost issues facing the organisation and that few advanced techniques are relevant. Although the overall process has become more informal and less numerate, a methodical approach is still necessary.

Figure 8.3 summarises the corporate planning process and shows its relationship to shorter-term tactical and operational planning. The following paragraphs expand some of the stages shown in the diagram.

The planning team

The task facing the planning team is to tackle the top issues facing the organisation. This is not something that can be delegated away or given to a specialist corporate planning department. Accordingly the planning team must consist of the Chief Executive, however designated, and other members of top management. The planning team would normally be served by a planning assistant (or several) whose task is to write reports, make calculations, undertake investigations and generally provide what assistance the top management require.

The assessment stage

The primary task is for the planning team to establish the overall purpose of the organisation, i.e. the corporate objective. To do this some assessment of the numerous factors that influence the organisation is required. These range from the expectations of what can be termed the 'stakeholders' i.e. shareholders, employees, customers, ratepayers etc., to the planning team's judgement of the future. Assessment may be on an informal basis or it may take the form of special investigations and reports by the planning assistant.

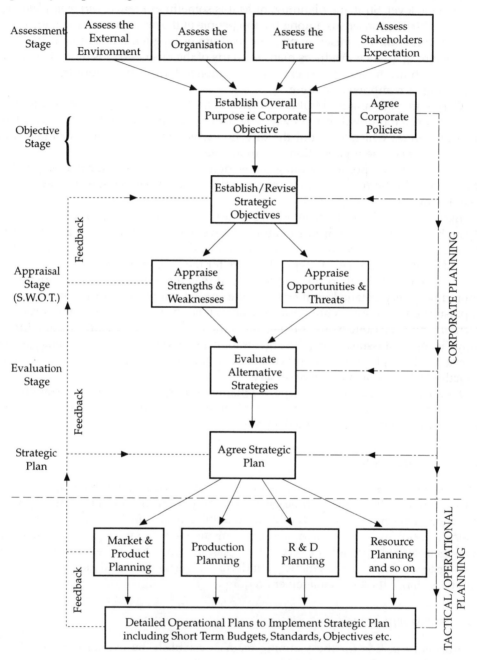

Figure 8.3: Overview of corporate planning

The objective stage

This is in two stages; firstly the statement of the overall objective or purpose of the organisation followed by the establishment of the strategic objectives or aims of the organisation over the medium to long term.

The statement of purpose for the organisation is intended to be relatively permanent and would be framed in broad, general terms, for example:

'to achieve a return on shareholders' capital at least 2% better than the average in industry', or

'to provide a service to ratepayers, visitors and the business community'.

Although the overall purpose of, say, a public limited company manufacturing consumer products, would seem to be self-evident, this is not so for many types of organisations. For example, consider the problems involved in arriving at a corporate objective for a charity, a mutual insurance company, a building society and so on.

Strategic objectives

Within the framework of the overall purpose, the strategic objectives are also written in general terms and relate to different parts of the organisation. For example, within a Local Authority, strategic objectives could be set for Housing, Education, Social Services, Planning and so on whilst in a manufacturing company they could relate to marketing, finance, personnel etc.

Top management will also establish corporate policies which provide guidelines on the manner in which the organisation expects its objectives to be achieved. Policy statements reflect the organisation's culture and belief system and can be powerful influences on the ways activities are carried out and decisions taken. Consider the difference in policies between two local authorities; one a Conservative controlled rural area and the other a Labour controlled inner-city authority.

It is during this stage that gaps will become apparent between what the planning team want to achieve and what forecasts, based on current strategies, show is expected to be achieved. The *gap analysis* often shows the size of the strategic task facing the organisation.

The appraisal stage

This is colloquially known as SWOT analysis (i.e. Strengths, Weaknesses, Opportunities, Threats). By a process of discussion, analysis and comparison of internal factors, the planning team should attempt to rank what are considered to be the main strengths and weakness of the organisation. These could be found in any area of the organisation. They could, for example, relate to the price, range, reliability (or otherwise) of the products; the training, age structure, morale of the workforce; size, age, capability of equipment and so on.

Although all the details are not known it seems clear that a detailed analysis of this type was undertaken by John Egan (now Sir John) when he first took over Jaguar Cars. This identified product reliability and quality as the major weakness which was remedied in a highly professional manner, resulting in the turn-round of the whole company.

Next the planning team should consider the environment within which the organisation operates to try to identify the trends and factors which will have a material effect on the organisation in the medium to long term. This process will involve considerable discussion with outside experts and analysts, perhaps special investigations, examination of national and international statistics and so on. Depending on the size and scope of the organisation the appraisal could include local, national or international factors. Threats and opportunities may be identified in various aspects of the environment, for example:

(a) Political factors such as privatisation, changes of government at home and abroad, legislation, wars and so on.

(b) Market factors such as new and current competitors, market share, change in distribution (e.g. city centre to out of town shopping) and so on.

(c) Economic and social factors such as unemployment, inflation, social mobility and so on.

(d) Technology factors such as automation and robotics, new materials, process and so on.

It has to be recognised that all these appraisals mean trying to peer into a misty and uncertain future. When change is in a continuous pattern it is possible to project existing trends and thus make reasonable assumptions as to the actions and reactions required. The problem is that much change is discontinuous and unexpected.

With truth it has been said that the only thing we know for certain about the future is that the unexpected will happen. This unpredictability means that judgement and intuition always play a part in long-term forecastings. Statistical forecasting, of whatever level of sophistication, is based on the implicit assumption that existing trends, patterns and cycles will continue in the future. Of course, they may but on the other hand they may not.

Evaluating alternatives

By this stage the planning team will be aware of:

(a) the scale of the strategic task ahead; i.e. the gap between what it is hoped to achieve and what is likely to be achieved using current plans, methods and facilities.

(b) the major forecasted trends and factors which are expected to influence the organisation either as threats or opportunities;

(c) the aspects of the organisation which are strong and those which are weak.

The team are now able to consider alternative corporate strategies which will form the basis of the agreed corporate plan. The strategies should be sufficiently clear so that they can be evaluated as to whether they have been achieved or not, but not so specific that they constrain the organisation. Specific targets can only be set at tactical and operational levels for shorter periods of, say, up to one year.

The information system of the organisation can be of considerable assistance to the planning team when considering alternative strategies. The team will continually require answers to a series of questions beginning, 'What would happen if ... ?' The exploration of alternatives and the working through of the effects of differing assumptions can be assisted by appropriate computer facilities. However it must be stressed that the computer only provides rapid retrieval, calculating and comparison facilities; it does not carry out corporate planning.

The strategic plan

By this time there will be a consensus on the strategies for the organisation so that the remaining stages add increasing amounts of practical detail. The task is to prepare action plans for the various departments and functions of the organisation. These plans should contain targets and should be in sufficient detail so that tactical level management know the task they have to perform. The plan should show not only the new tasks, but how existing operations will dovetail into the new targets over, say, the next five years. The strategic plan will be used by tactical management to prepare operational plans, budgets, set short term targets and so on. An example is shown below of a 5 year Strategic Plan for Wolverhampton Council.

The Corporate Strategy embodies the principles upon which the Council works and provides the context for service strategies and organisational change. Between 1993 and 1996, Wolverhampton Council will:

☐ efficiently implement the Council Tax and any other national changes in the financial structure of local government.

☐ thoroughly reassess its own functions services and assets base in the light of changing needs, financial constraints and the priorities of its elected Councillors.

☐ continue to meet the requirement for clearer definition of purchasing and contracting roles, a controlled 'internal market' for professional services and the devolution of decision-making authority within a strong corporate framework.

❏   demonstrate that services to be provided in-house are at least as effective and efficient as those provided by private sector competitors.

❏   strengthen the working relationship with and influence the activities of public agencies delivering services and setting policies for Wolverhampton.

❏   strengthen the processes of formal and informal consultation with the business community, residents and tenants, voluntary and community groups.

❏   develop a positive and consistent presentation of Wolverhampton Council and its work through a new strategy for public relations and communications.

Monitoring and controls

There is little point in any planning exercise if progress is not monitored after the plans have been implemented. This is to see whether activities need to be adjusted to bring them into line with the original strategies or to see whether, because of unforeseen circumstances, it is time to review the strategies themselves.

Monitoring and control at all levels works by the feedback of information which is a major function of the information system of the organisation and is dealt with in detail later in the book.

Formal and informal planning

In the 1960's and 70's the vogue was for highly formal planning systems and for formal information systems to support them. Informal planning and information systems were thought of as imprecise and somehow amateurish. Experience and major unforeseen disturbances such as the oil price explosion of the mid 1970's,the stock market crash of 1987, the collapse of the property market in 1990 and others showed that highly structured systems are slow to respond to change, perpetuate static organisational assumptions and offer little or no protection from unpredictability. Indeed a survey by Grinyer and Norburn found no correlation between formal planning procedures and financial performance; instead informality and diversity of information, especially from external sources, seemed to be the critical factor.

Informal systems are more flexible and adaptable. They deal with information which is more current and significant and, because of the social contact involved, they can convey nuances which formal systems cannot handle. They do, however, suffer from bias, and do not always provide a complete picture. What is required is a blend of formal and informal so that the completeness, accuracy and detail of the formal systems complement the flexibility and adaptability of the informal.

Various reviews of formal planning procedures suggest that they can encourage inflexibility whereas the real requirements, especially at the strategic level, are responsiveness and adaptability. The greatest care must be taken to ensure that the environment is continually scanned and monitored so that the organisation can adapt in a progressive, controlled fashion. This is always more efficient than enforced traumatic changes made after a period of stagnation.

By now it should be apparent that planning requires a great deal of information. The types of information and their sources will naturally vary from organisation to organisation but there is one general principle. For long term planning, environmental information is of critical importance. At lower levels, and in the short term, internal information is important but for planning the long term direction of the organisation and ensuring survival and success, external information is all important.

What is decision making?

Decision making can be defined as making choices between future, uncertain alternatives. It should be noted that *all decision making* relates to the *future* and that a decision is a *choice* between *alternatives*.

Decision making is an integral part of management and occurs in every function and at all levels. Naturally the type of decisions taken vary enormously but all decision makers have to go through a similar process. All of them must decide by some means to choose the outcome or outcomes which are considered necessary or desirable to them and to do so after some form of appraisal of the situation.

H.A. Simon, a leading authority on management decision making, considers that decision making comprises four principal phases: finding occasions for making decisions, finding possible courses of action (i.e. alternatives), choosing among courses of action, and evaluating past choices.

Figure 8.4 shows a summary of these phases using Simon's terminology.

Phase 1	INTELLIGENCE	– Searching the environment for conditions calling for decisions.
Phase 2	DESIGN	– Inventing, developing and analysing possible courses of action. This involves processes to understand the problem, to generate solutions and the testing of solutions for feasibility.
Phase 3	CHOICE	– Selecting an alternative or course of action from those available. A choice is made and implemented.
Phase 4	REVIEW	– Assessing past choices.

Figure 8.4: Simon's phases of decision making

Decision making is an iterative process and although it is useful to separate out the various phases in order to discuss them, very few decisions are taken in this neat, logical sequence. There is feedback, inter-relationships between decisions, there is flair, intuition, judgement and creativity.

Decision making is based on information. Information is the trigger to knowing there is a problem, information is needed to define and structure the problem, information is needed to explore and choose between the alternative solutions and information is needed to review the effects of the implemented choice.

Programmed and non- programmed decisions

Simon classified decisions into two categories according to the extent that the process of decision making can be pre-planned. The categories are *programmed* and *non-programmed*, as follows:-

Programmed decisions

Characteristics: repetitive, routine, known decision rules or procedures, often automated, usually involve 'things' rather than people, can be delegated to low levels in the organisation.

Examples: inventory control decisions, machine loading decisions, scheduling.

Non-programmed decisions

Characteristics:- novel, non-routine, decision rules not known, high degree of uncertainty, cannot be delegated to low levels, may involve 'things' but always involve people.

Examples: acquisitions, mergers, launching new products, personnel appointments.

Note: Alternative terms for these two categories are structured and unstructured.

The two categories should be thought of as the extreme ends of a range of decision types with many decisions containing elements of both categories. The terms programmed and non-programmed are not related to computer processing. They refer to the nature of the decision process and to the extent that the process can be pre-planned.

There is some relationship between the level of management and the decision type; broadly more programmed decisions at lower levels and more unstructured decisions at higher levels, but this is not an absolute rule. Some high level decisions contain structured elements, an example being a costly plant replacement decision which is likely to be taken at the highest level and for which decision rules are available using replacement analysis and investment appraisal techniques.

Levels of decision making

Decision Making takes place at each level of management in organisation although there are markedly different characteristics at each level. Each level has substantially different information requirements and Figure 8.5 summarises the main characteristics and information requirements of the various levels.

The tactical level of management occupies an intermediate position between the two extremes with some of the characteristics of both. Much of the development of formal aids to decision making, such as, for example, optimising models, has been directed at the operational and tactical levels of management.

Management Level	Decision Characteristics	Information Characteristics
Strategic	Long time horizons, large scale resources, much creativity and judgement, usually unstructured, problems difficult to define, infrequent, much uncertainty	Largely external, informal sources important, forward looking, qualitative information important, precision unimportant, instant access not vital, wide ranging, incomplete
Tactical	↑↓	↑↓
Operational	Repetitive, short time scale, small scale resources, usually structured, clear objectives and decision rules, little or no discretion	Largely internal, mainly historical, detailed, often quantitative, high precision, instant availability often critical, narrow in scope, comprehensive

Figure 8.5: Levels of decision making

At the strategic level, decision making is much more dependent on human factors and judgement. Such decision making is based on guided trial and error and because of uncertainty and ambiguities, all possibilities cannot be explored. This type of decision making is known as *heuristic* and is based on rules of thumb rather than explicit decision rules.

Figure 8.6 shows some examples of typical decisions at the three levels with their information requirements.

The preceding paragraphs and diagrams are not absolutes and indicate tendencies only. In practice, decisions should be taken at the level where they are most effective.

Peter Drucker says decisions should be made at the *lowest possible level* which accords with their nature, and as close to the scene of action as possible. They should always be taken at the level which ensures none of the activities and objectives affected are forgotten.

Management level	Decision examples	Information requirements
Strategic	Mergers and acquisitions, new product planning, capital investments, financial structuring	Market and economic forecasts, political and social trends, legislative, environmental and technological constraints and opportunities
Tactical	Pricing, capacity planning, budget preparation, purchasing contracts	Cost and sales analyses, performance measures, summaries of operations/ production, budget/actual comparisons etc
Operational	Production scheduling, maintenance, re-ordering, credit approval	Sales orders, production require- ments, performance measures, customer credit status, deliveries, despatches etc

Figure 8.6: Decision and information examples

How are decisions taken?

There are, in effect, two approaches to this problem. One is termed the *rational* or *prescriptive* approach which can be used for structured problems where all the factors are defined and known. It is this type of problem for which numerous decision techniques exist mostly drawn from accounting economics, statistics and operational research.

On the other hand, descriptive models have been developed by behavioural scientists and seek to explain actual behaviour in decision making. Actual decision making is less structured and is not completely rational. In practice, decision makers simplify the factors involved and, because of practical difficulties are prepared to accept a satisfactory solution rather than attempt to find the theoretical optimum.

These two categories are expanded below.

'Rational' decision making

This model of decision making, developed from classical economic theory, is summarised in Figure 8.7.

This model assumes perfect knowledge of all factors surrounding the decision and adopts a rational, mechanistic approach to decision making. It will be realised that all the criteria of the model: single, known objective, perfect information and so on – are rarely met in practice, yet many decision making techniques make these assumptions and are widely used. Examples include, linear programming, invest-ment appraisal, statistical decision analysis, cost/volume/profit analysis.

The use of the pure rational decision making is more suited to operating and tac-tical levels of management where the factors are more clear cut and there is less uncertainty. The decisions are more structured so that formal decision rules and the organisation's information system are likely to be of value. However, care is always necessary to ensure that the particular 'rational' decision making technique being used actually does suit the individual circumstances. Various studies have shown that things are not always as clear cut as they seem; for example.

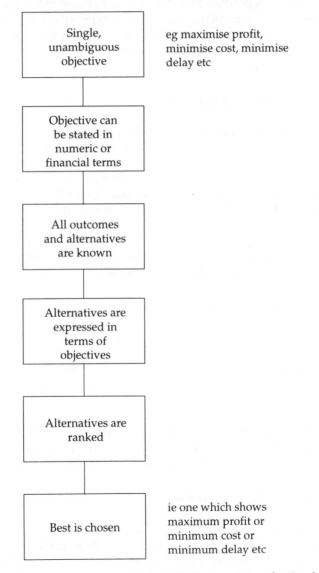

Figure 8.7: Characteristics of rational decision making

> 'Users tend to explain their actions in terms of rational behaviour, whereas their actual performance may be governed by intuition rather than by rational analysis. Studies of managers at work have shown that there is a discrepancy between how managers claim to take decisions and their actual observed decision-making behaviour'.
>
> *Argyris and Schon*

In many cases the results produced from a rational decision making technique are not used uncritically. They are treated as one of many types of information and management may well adjust to the apparent 'optimal' decision because of other factors. These could include; conflicting objectives, uncertainty, social, psychological, political considerations and so on.

Rational decision making objectives

The starting point of the rational decision making process is a statement of the single objective. This may be to: maximise profit, or maximise return on capital employed, or minimise cost per unit, or maximise utility (used in the economic sense of satisfying wants or desires), or, where risk exists, maximise expected value.

Expected value is a widely used decision making criterion and can be defined as the total of the probability or likelihood of each outcome times the value of each outcome.

As an example, assume that this is required to choose between three alternatives A,B and C each of which has three possible outcomes. The objective is to maximise profit and all outcomes and probabilities are known, as follows:

	Alternative A		*Alternative B*		*Alternative C*	
	Prob'y	*Profit*	*Prob'y*	*Profit*	*Prob'y*	*Profit*
Optimistic Outcome	0.2	5000	0.3	4000	0.1	3000
Most Likely Outcome	0.6	7500	0.5	7000	0.7	6500
Pessimistic Outcome	0.2	9000	0.2	9500	0.2	10000

Solution

Expected values:

Alternative A   (0.2 x 5000) + (0.6 x 7500) + (0.2 x 9000)   = 7300
Alternative B   (0.3 x 4000) + (0.5 x 7000) + (0.2 x 9500)   = 6600
Alternative C   (0.1 x 3000) + (0.7 x 6500) + (0.2 x 10000) = 6850

Thus, in terms of the objective, Alternative A is preferred.

Expected value is commonly used and has the advantages of arithmetically taking account of all the variabilities and being easy to understand. It suffers from the fact that by representing the various outcomes by a single summary figure, it ignores other characteristics of the distribution, such as the range and skewness.

Furthermore, expected value can strictly only be interpreted as the value that would be obtained if a large number of similar decisions were taken with the same range of outcomes and associated probabilities. Hardly a typical decision making situation!

Decision trees

Often decisions are not taken in isolation but as part of a sequence. In such circumstances the analysis can usefully be presented in the form of a decision tree. Decision trees are a pictorial way of showing a sequence of inter-related decisions and outcomes. They invariably include probabilities and are evaluated using expected values. By convention, decision points are represented by square nodes and outcomes (which vary according to circumstances) by circles. Figure 8.8 shows the general form of a decision tree.

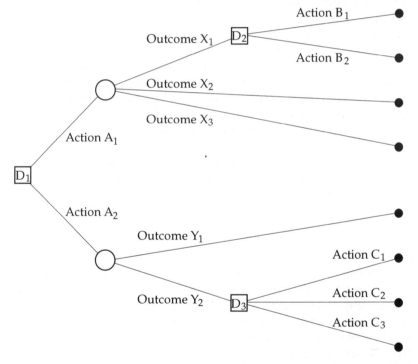

Figure 8.8: Decision tree

Notes on Figure 8.8

(a) The decision nodes are points where a choice exists between alternatives and a managerial decision is made based on estimates and calculations of the returns expected.

(b) The outcome nodes are points where the events depend on probabilities, e.g. assume that Action A1 was – Build branch factory – then outcomes X1, X2, and

X3 could represent various possible sales; high, medium and low, each with an estimated probability.

Decision trees are evaluated from right to left, working back from the later decisions to the first.

Satisficing or bounded rationality

This view of decision making is a descriptive, behavioural model which takes account of imperfections of knowledge and behaviour.

The term *satisficing* was coined by Simon to describe the behaviour of decision makers operating in a complex and partially unknown environment. Decision makers are not fully aware of all the alternatives available nor is there always a single, clear cut objective. They make only a limited search to discover a few satisfactory alternatives and finally make a decision which satisfies their aspirations, hence the term satisficing.

There is not complete rationality but bounded rationality which means that decision making is rational but within the imperfections of information and the decision maker's ability to perceive alternatives and outcomes. The choice of an alternative which is good enough, from a limited range of possible alternatives, is a practical approach to day-to-day managerial pressures and problems. Observation and personal experience show clearly that satisficing behaviour is commonplace.

An important consequence of this type of decision behaviour is that subjectivity, judgement and rules of thumb are used to make decisions rather than the use of explicit decision rules. This means that wide ranging background information and ways of exploring alternatives become much more important than mechanical decision rules and procedures.

Consensus decision making

Where the agreement of people and groups in positions of power is necessary for the effective implementation of a decision then consensus decision making is practised, i.e. a decision is reached which is acceptable to all. This is a common strategy in government and many large organisations. The conventional wisdom, at least in the West, is that this form of decision making is most appropriate where there are only small changes to existing policy and it is not suited to radical changes.

This viewpoint can be questioned by examination of the Japanese method of decision making. Their method is decision making by consensus with discussion and argument throughout the organisation until there is agreement. The Japanese focus is on determining what the decision is all about i.e. what is the question first, not what is the answer. They then bring out dissenting opinions which helps to explore the alternatives available.

This helps to clarify at what level a decision should be taken and, importantly, it eliminates the 'selling' of a decision in order to get effective action and support. This method has been used for the most radical decision making and although it has been criticised in the West as being long-winded, once a decision has been reached, implementation and action follow with great speed and effectiveness.

By its nature consensus decision making involves more people so that there is more chance of the real problem being identified. This is a vital, if not the most vital, part of the process. The recognition of what is the real problem requires much questioning and thought.

For example, a firm is experiencing a drop in sales. What is the real problem? Is it the price of the product, the quality, appearance, style, capability? Is it poor sales and marketing? Is it the lack of advertising or of the right type of advertising? Is it the lack of an appropriate incentive scheme for the sales force? Is it the appearance on the market of a superior competing product? Have the consumers' tastes changed? etc.

Only when the real problem has been identified can alternatives be developed to deal with it and a decision made.

Key point summary

☐ Planning is deciding in advance what is to be done and how it is to be done.

☐ Common terms used in planning include; objective, plans, policy.

☐ Planning is long term at strategic levels and virtually immediate at operational levels.

☐ Corporate or strategic planning is about issues which affect the whole organisation.

☐ Corporate planning is the key task of strategic management.

☐ Strategic objectives are set within the overall purpose of the organisation.

☐ The appraisal stage is known as SWOT analysis.

☐ The output of the corporate planning process is the strategic plan.

☐ It is important to use a blend of informal and formal planning.

☐ There are numerous sources of planning information, external and internal, formal and informal.

☐ Simon considers that decision making has four phases – Intelligence, Design, Choice and Review.

☐ Decisions can be categorised into programmed or structured, and non-programmed or unstructured.

☐ The characteristics and information requirements of the levels of decision making vary greatly.

❒ All decision making has problems of risk, unquantifiable factors and how to recognise the real problem.

❒ Prescriptive decision models tell the manager how to make decisions whereas descriptive models explain how decision making takes place.

❒ Rational decision making assumes perfect knowledge of all factors and is a mechanistic approach.

❒ Expected value is a well known decision making criterion.

❒ Decision Trees are a useful way of presenting a sequence of decisions.

❒ Satisficing or bounded rationality acknowledges that imperfections exist and that to seek a satisfactory outcome is a practical approach.

❒ Consensus decision making, although protracted, saves time in implementation.

Self review questions

1. *Define planning.*

2. *Define the following terms: objectives, strategy, plans, policy.*

3. *What is the relationship between aims and means in planning?*

4. *What are examples of the areas covered by the three levels of planning?*

5. *Define corporate strategy.*

6. *Who should carry out corporate planning?*

7. *What takes place during the objective stage of corporate planning?*

8. *What is 'gap analysis'?*

9. *What is SWOT analysis?*

10. *What is the strategic plan?*

11. *What is decision making and what are Simon's four phases?*

12. *Distinguish between programmed and non-programmed decisions.*

13. *What are the decision and information characteristics at the three management levels?*

14. *What are some of the practical problems in decision making?*

15. *What are the stages of 'rational' decision making?*

16. *What is expected value?*

17. *What is consensus decision making?*

9   *Leadership, organising and co-ordinating*

Objectives

After you have studied this chapter you will:

❑ *Be able to classify the main theories of motivation.*

❑ *Be able to define leadership and explain its importance.*

❑ *Understand the trait, style and contingency theories of leadership.*

❑ *Know the importance of organising work.*

❑ *Be able to describe job enlargement and job enrichment.*

❑ *Understand what is meant by participation and delegation.*

❑ *Know the principles of MBO.*

❑ *Be able to draw the various types of organisation charts.*

❑ *Understand the importance of co-ordination and some of the ways it can be improved.*

Management and motivation

The objectives of any organisation will be achieved more efficiently when the people who work in it have drive and commitment, in other words, when they are *motivated*.

Management try to increase motivation by using motivators (e.g. pay, status, recognition etc.), by their style of management, and the way they practise leadership.

There are numerous theories about motivation and the kind of theory a manager believes in, even at a sub-conscious level, influences his approach to management. Some of the earlier motivation theories have already been covered (Maslow's Hierarchy of needs, Herzberg's hygiene factors and motivators and so on) and these theories can be grouped under three headings.

Satisfaction theories: these theories suggest a satisfied employee will work harder although there is little evidence to support this view.

Incentive theories: these suggest that a person will work harder to obtain a reward. There is some evidence that positive reinforcement can work if the individual performance can be recognised and rewarded.

Intrinsic theories: these theories suggest that people will work hard to realise higher-order needs contained in the job itself; self fulfilment, responsibility, participation and so on.

Motivation in practice

The manager trying to increase motivation is faced with a complex problem with no universal solutions. Managers in practice may adopt the carrot or stick approach. The stick approach could include; reprimands, demotions, or threats of dismissal. On the other hand, the more positive carrot approach may be achieved by either external motivators such as pay or promotion or by offering 'internal' satisfaction for the individual through a sense of achievement or responsibility.

Management use a variety of methods to make jobs more fulfiling and more motivating including; job enrichment, job enlargement and job rotation, delegating authority to subordinates, and encouraging participating in decision making, all of which are dealt with later in this chapter. Before this it is necessary to consider leadership for there seems general agreement that behaviour in organisations is affected by leadership styles and leadership behaviour. Accordingly, the following paragraphs analyse individual leadership characteristics in organisations and the influence of leadership on motivation.

Leadership defined

In general terms, leadership can be defined as the ability to influence the behaviour of others. The definition can be expanded when considering leadership in organisations to include the fact that the leader exerts influence within a working group in order that the group may achieve group tasks or objectives.

Although there is no doubt that leadership is a vital factor and greatly influences the whole organisation, (consider, for example, Ricardo Semler at Semco, Alan Sugar at Amstrad and other similar leaders) it is very difficult to lay down general rules for effective leadership to fit all situations. According to Bennis and Nanns, many organisations are over-managed and under-led. The difference is crucial; managers are people who do things right, but leaders are people who do the right things.

Some of the more important leadership studies and theories are briefly described below, the more modern ones of which indicate that leadership is always related to the situation. There is a growing awareness that there is a continuous interaction between the factors present in any given situation, including for example, the personal characteristics of the leader, the tasks, the environment, the technology, the attitudes, motivation and behaviour of the followers and so on.

The approaches to the problem of trying to explain leadership are described under the following three headings:

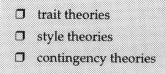

Trait theories

The earliest studies of leadership attempted to discover the distinguishing personal characteristics, or traits, of successful leaders. The assumption was that the individual was more important than the situation and that there were innate qualities of leadership in certain people. The various studies identified numerous characteristics including:

- Intelligence
- Initiative
- Self Assurance
- Imagination
- Courage
- Decisiveness
- Energy
  and so on

Unfortunately the different studies produced highly variable results. Professor Handy has pointed out that in over 100 studies of these kind only 5% of the traits discovered were common throughout. Accordingly, trait theory in its original form has been heavily criticised and largely discredited as a basis for a workable theory of leadership, although more modern studies are beginning to highlight once again the importance of the individual amongst many other factors.

Style theories

These theories concentrate on the behaviour or style of the leader rather than his personal attributes, i.e. they concentrate on the way he manages. The assumption is that employees will work harder for managers who employ particular styles than they will for managers who use other styles. The two extremes of style usually compared are the authoritarian or structured style and the democratic or participative style; the main features of which are summarised below.

Authoritarian management style:

☐ All power resides in the leader.

☐ Decision making is carried out by the leader alone.

☐ Only the leader can exercise control, reward, punishment etc.

Democratic management style:

☐ Group participation and discussion.

☐ Shared power.

☐ Group decision making, control etc.

☐ Delegation.

Clearly the above two positions represent extremes and management style in practice is likely to be somewhere between the two. The fact that there is a continuum between the polar positions is aptly demonstrated by Figure 9.1 which was developed by Tannenbaum and Schmidt who wished to demonstrate that managers have choice in selecting a leadership style. They considered that the choice is influenced by three factors; the manager himself, his subordinates, and the requirements of the situation.

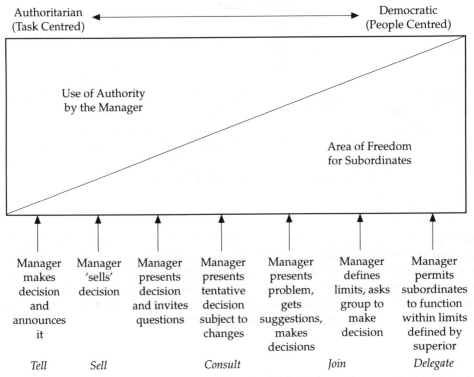

Figure 9.1: Tannenbaum and Schmidt's continuum of leadership styles

There is some evidence, by no means conclusive, that participative styles are associated with higher-producing work groups. It seems that such styles bring increased subordinate satisfaction and reduce inter-group conflict and tend to satisfy higher order/personal needs such as esteem and self-actualisation. There is also evidence that some people prefer to be directed and that in repetitive work a structured style of leadership leads to higher productivity, at least in the short term. It does seem however that leadership effectiveness is dependent on more than style alone. Hence what are called *contingency theories of leadership.*

Contingency theories

The contingency theories, pioneered by Fiedler, consider that leadership effectiveness depends on (is contingent on) a range of factors; in particular, the task, the work group and the position of the leader within the work group.

Fiedler's view was that group performance depends on the manager adopting a style appropriate to what he termed the 'relative favourableness' of the situation. He found that a more authoritarian style was most effective when the situation was very favourable or very unfavourable to the leader. When the situation was only moderately favourable then the participative style worked best. Fiedler thought that situations favourable to the leader were characterised as follows:

(a) the leader was liked and trusted by the group

(b) the task was clearly defined;

(c) the power of the leader in respect of the group was high and where he had organisational backing.

Fiedler's findings seem to be supported by practical experience. A strong, well respected leader with a clearly defined task would get best results by being fairly directive. Where the task is ill-defined and he is in a weak position, best results are still likely to be achieved by a more authoritarian style. Alternatively, a respected leader confronted by an ambiguous task (i.e. only a moderately favourable position) would probably obtain best results by drawing out from the group all the contributions they can make.

Fiedler's researches have received some criticism but his approach is useful in that it emphasises that there are occasions where the best results are achieved by a more formal, task-centred approach rather than the apparently more appealing democratic style. He considered that organisations could do much to help the individual leader by either:

(a) defining and structuring the task more clearly; or

(b) improving the leader's formal power vis-a-vis his group; or

(c) changing the composition of the group.

Fiedler's original contingency approach has been, and continues to be, refined and modified as further research is undertaken. In general terms this seems to indicate that even more factors need to be analysed before leadership can be even partially understood. An example of a modified contingency approach is that developed by Professor Adair, called *Action centred leadership*.

Action centred leadership

This theory, developed in the UK by Professor Adair, is based on what the leader *does* to meet the needs of the *task, group and individual*. The theory recognises that there will not be a perfect match between the three elements of task, group and individual so that the leader's job is to be aware of the three key variables and to manage each situation by giving suitable priorities to the inter-acting elements.

Figure 9.2 summarises the functions of leadership applied to the three inter-acting variables.

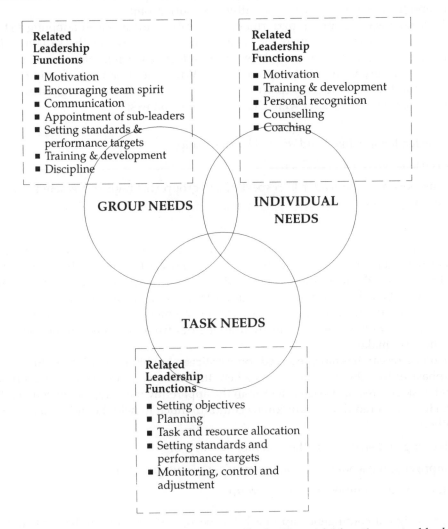

Figure 9.2: Functions of leadership – Adair's action centred leadership

Changing social attitudes to authority and the need for adaptability are causing major changes in management styles. Maccoby's study of leadership styles showed that

modern managers exhibit more 'flexibility about people and organisational structure, and a willingness to share power'. Thus, rather than acting as a traditional 'boss' or 'decision maker', leaders are becoming more like a coach, teacher and catalyst.

Leaders have to cope with a rapidly changing world and the most successful organisations are those that continually adapt and re-organise. Managers must accept that change is normal and vitally necessary for long-run success and survival.

In addition to being leaders, managers are also responsible for *organising* and *co-ordinating* activities.

Organising and co-ordinating

This is a key task of management and has been included in just about every definition of management from Fayol onwards. There are numerous facets to this aspect of management which can be summarised as follows:

(a) deciding what activities and tasks are necessary to achieve the plans;

(b) deciding how the tasks are to be arranged and responsibilities allocated;

(c) deciding upon an appropriate structure so that tasks, activities and responsibilities can be effectively co-ordinated.

An important part of organising, concerned with the organisation structure itself, has already been dealt with in earlier chapters. It will be recalled that these chapters dealt with the influences of factors such as technology and the environment, the degree of functionalism, the extent of centralisation and decentralisation, the contributions of managerial theorists over the years and so on.

Although the design of the total organisation is outside the scope of most managers, every manager has some responsibility for the design of jobs under his control. The scope of the jobs, the amount of responsibility accorded to individuals, the type of control and supervision exercised, the amount of participation and other similar problems must be faced by every manager. Accordingly, the following paragraphs deal with these issues.

Design of the job

Designing or redesigning jobs is not easy. It causes change in the tasks to be done, in job relationships, in supervisor/supervised relationships, in the pattern of working groups, in training and skill requirements and so on. When work is designed effectively the individual can benefit from more challenging and satisfying tasks and the organisation may benefit from improved productivity. Poor design and organisation may result in stress and tension, low motivation and reduced productivity.

The Department of Employment has suggested that the following factors are important if a job is to satisfy human needs:

(a) Every job should have some goal to aim for and the job-holder's role should be made clear.

(b) There should be a degree of autonomy over the way tasks are to be achieved and people should be responsible for their own work and the resources used.

(c) There should be an element of variety in the job with a minimum of repetition and where possible the job should enable the completion of a complete item or cycle.

(d) There should be some arrangements for providing job-holders with feed-back on their performance.

(e) The job should be arranged to provide some social contact.

(f) There should be opportunities to learn and to extend the job-holder's knowledge and skills.

There are several ways of designing jobs to increase employee satisfaction and the following are covered in this book:

❑ Job enlargement
❑ Job enrichment
❑ Autonomous working groups
❑ Participation
❑ Delegation

Job enlargement

This can be termed 'more of the same' or the horizontal enlargement of jobs. It is done by adding tasks of the same type and level but without adding more responsibility or needing more skill. Rotating jobs within the same grade, which is commonly practised, is a form of job enlargement. This approach does increase variety and there is some evidence that the process may increase morale and productivity. However, there are limits to the extent that job enlargement will increase motivation. As Child points out:

> '. . . adding one Mickey Mouse job to another does not make any more than two Mickey Mouse jobs.'

Job enrichment

This is the process of increasing the scope, challenge and breadth of a task. It is a vertical extension of job responsibilities so that the job-holder has a more rounded job. It is a reaction to the industrial engineering approach to work with its emphasis on the micro-division of labour. The process is a conscious effort to implement some assumptions about the motivation to work by including in a job factors which Hertzberg has termed motivators.

The approach gives an individual more scope, more autonomy, more responsibility, more variety, and seeks to satisfy an individual's higher order needs. Numerous organisations such as Shell, Philips, IBM, Volvo etc. have reported success with job enrichment schemes.

Care is needed with job enrichment and some schemes have ended after a period because their usefulness came to an end. Not everyone is capable of doing a bigger job so that selection, placement and training become much more important. Job enrichment is not a once-off process, it needs constant self-renewal. Properly done it does appear to offer genuine advantages to both the individual and the organisation.

Autonomous work groups

These are self-organised work groups which are held responsible for the rate and quality of their output. These groups have been used successfully in Scandinavia, especially at Volvo, where quality improved, overheads were reduced and job satisfaction increased. Within the group the employees are multi-skilled and accept full responsibility for the deployment of group members and for the designated task in terms of quality and output. Although there have been dramatic success stories with this type of work organisation, there appears to be some doubt as to how long the effects will last.

Participation in decision making by employees is a form of both job enlargement and job enrichment.

Participation

This is a word with a wide range of meanings; from mere consultation at one extreme to full worker control at the other. The most relevant meaning from our point of view however is that participation means *the sharing of decision making between managers and managed*. Although there is an intuitive feeling in us all that participation is always good, it may not always produce beneficial results in practice unless certain criteria are met. These can be summarised as follows:

(a) The manager must genuinely want participation and not indulge in it because he feels he ought to.

(b) The invitation to employees to participate must be genuine. If the decision is already taken or if the group decision is not accepted, then there is not genuine participation.

(c) The decision must be worth the time and effort of all concerned. Trivial matters, matters outside the individual's or group's concern, situations where there is no effective control over the factors concerned and so on will cause participation to become meaningless.

Where these conditions are met, participation will tend to result in increased commitment from the individual although studies of participation in practice have been inconclusive. Job enrichment and autonomous work groups are examples of participation at the job level and clearly are limited in their scope. The existence of job enrichment does not, for example, mean that there is participation in strategic decision making which is likely to affect the individual far more than decision making at the task level.

An important consequence of participation is the need for more information at lower levels. Effective decision making requires good information so that pushing decision making down the hierarchy requires radical changes in the organisation's information system as well as a change in management style.

Delegation

This is the process where a manager transfers part of his own authority to a subordinate so that the subordinate can carry out some task. The responsibility for the task remains with the manager and is not delegated. True delegation is delegation with trust and the minimum of necessary controls. The art of effective delegation is about getting the trust/control ratio right and there are two main guidelines:

(a) The area of trust for each individual must be clearly defined and the individual must be allowed full control within the defined limits.

(b) There should be control of results not means. The monitoring of results after the event is not a violation of trust but control of the ways of achieving the result will generally be seen as a violation of trust.

Reasons for delegation

In effect a manager who delegates is sharing his workload with a subordinate in whom he has confidence. The main reasons why delegation is practised are:

(a) A manager is relieved of some less important or less immediate tasks and thus has time for higher-level work.

(b) Delegation can be more efficient because decisions are taken lower down the hierarchy and communication delays are reduced or eliminated.

(c) Delegation is good training for junior personnel. They learn to make decisions and to live with the consequences. It is more challenging for them.

(d) Delegation makes the organisation more flexible and adaptable.

(e) Delegation satisfies 'higher-order' needs and is a necessary part of job enrichment programmes and is consciously practised by many organisations as part of staff development programmes.

Delegation guidelines

There is always risk involved with delegation because the manager may not be sure that the subordinate can be trusted to carry out the delegated task, yet knows he still carries ultimate responsibility for its successful completion. Such risks can never be eliminated entirely but the following guidelines will help to reduce them as much as possible.

To ensure effective delegation the manager should:

(a) set clear objectives and indicate the standards of performance expected;

(b) clearly define the level and limits of authority delegated and ensure that sufficient resources are allocated;

(c) give what briefing, advice, training and guidance is necessary;

(d) establish a control system to monitor results;

(e) ensure that the task is completed and review the performance with the subordinate.

Some managers find it difficult to delegate and when they do, they continually interfere during the execution of the task. Others do not delegate because they think they may lose touch with day-to-day operations or because they feel threatened by the thought that a subordinate is doing part of their job.

It is generally recognised that in any organisation above the very smallest management must delegate some authority. However by delegating authority to subordinates the manager takes on two extra tasks:

(1) The need to monitor the results of decisions and the performance of subordinates.

(2) The need to co-ordinate the efforts of different subordinates.

Management by objectives (MBO)

MBO is a structured form of delegation which seeks to harmonise the goals of the individual with those of the organisation. MBO concentrates on results achieved (in relation to objectives) rather than on the process of achieving results. A key element of the system is that there must be participation by the managers concerned in the goal setting process. This helps to achieve a sense of common purpose and direction throughout the organisation.

A system of MBO develops logically from the overall planning system of the organisation whereby corporate and department objectives are broken down into individual manager-objectives. At its best MBO is an all-embracing approach to management both from the point of the organisation's need to achieve objectives and the needs of the individual.

The distinctive features of MBO are given below:

(a) clear definition of individual responsibilities;

(b) clear definition of key tasks and targets expressed in terms of results;

(c) participative goal setting;

(d) development of agreed measurements for both qualitative and quantitative factors;

(e) joint review and appraisal with recognition of achievement in current post;

(f) joint review of a manager's potential ability in his next job.

Although much broader in scope, there are clear similarities between the above features of MBO and the guidelines for effective delegation given earlier.

The MBO process is summarised in Figure 9.3.

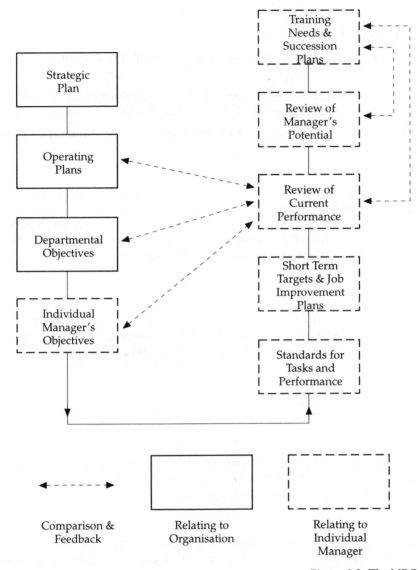

Figure 9.3: The MBO process

The advantages and disadvantages of MBO are:

Advantages of MBO

☐ A scheme for converting strategic plans into management action plans.

☐ Helps planning, control, co-ordination and communication.

☐ Each manager knows what is required of him and the agreement of targets ensures commitment to them.

Disadvantages of MBO

☐ It can be a time consuming process with the possibility of creating inflexibility.

☐ It requires a major change in the attitudes of senior management and in the style of leadership, which is not easy to achieve.

☐ It can overstress the need for individual achievement at the expense of teamwork.

Numerous aspects of the management task of organising have been dealt with in the preceding paragraphs. When management are considering the structure of the organisation, the responsibilities of managers, the relationships between departments, tasks and jobs it is often useful to show the structures and relationships in a diagrammatic form. These diagrams are known as organisation charts.

Organisation charts

Organisation charts can be drawn to show various aspects of the organisation including the different types of authority and relationships, the levels of hierarchy, job and departmental duties and so on. Before considering the various forms of chart it is useful to define three key terms used to describe relationships and authority namely; *line, functional* and *staff.*

Line

Line authority is the authority each manager exercises over his subordinates. Line authority is the essence of the chain of command. Thus a manager has a line relationship with his subordinates and his superior.

Functional

Functional authority is the authority of a specialist manager (e.g. Personnel, Finance etc.) to be able to direct others including other managers, in relation to agreed aspects of their specialist area. For example, the Personnel manager has line authority over the staff in the Personnel Department and also functional authority for personnel matters throughout the organisation. Thus line managers have functional relationships with specialist managers.

Staff

Staff activities are those which primarily exist to provide advice and service. The line manager may call upon a staff advisor, for example, a data processing specialist, but he may accept or reject the advice.

In today's complex and rapidly changing environment line managers need specialist advice and guidance. This means that there has to be an integrated effort so that pure line authority is invariably qualified by functional authority.

What do organisation charts show?

An organisation chart is a visual representation of the formal structure of an organisation at a particular date. Appropriately drawn an organisation chart may show all or some of the following:

- ❏ the line relationships in the organisation
- ❏ the functional relationships between managers and functional specialists
- ❏ the levels of responsibility and authority of individuals and posts
- ❏ the hierarchy of the organisation
- ❏ the span of control of managers and supervisors
- ❏ the main formal lines of communication
- ❏ the main duties of different functions, managers or departments

Naturally no single chart could be expected to show all the above. To attempt to show everything on a single chart would be complicated and would make the chart difficult to understand. This would defeat a key objective of organisation charts which is to show structures and relationships in a simple, visually appealing manner.

Types of organisation charts

Charts may be drawn in a variety of ways; vertically, horizontally or in a circular format. Provided they show the required information simply and clearly the exact format is not important. Although not universal it is common for line relationships (i.e. superior - subordinate) to be shown as solid lines. Dotted lines are often used to indicate functional relationships but again this is not universal so care must be taken in interpreting any chart.

Various examples of organisation charts are shown below together with notes explaining their key features.

Figure 9.4 is a traditional vertical organisation chart showing line relationships only. If it was required to show functional relationships these could be shown as dotted lines from one function to another but naturally these would clutter up the chart. This organisation could equally have been depicted in a horizontal format. Note that the organisation is organised on functional lines i.e. Personnel, Finance etc. The chart automatically shows the hierarchy of the organisation and shows staff of equal grade level with one another. Note that the relationships between staff of the same level are known as lateral relationships.

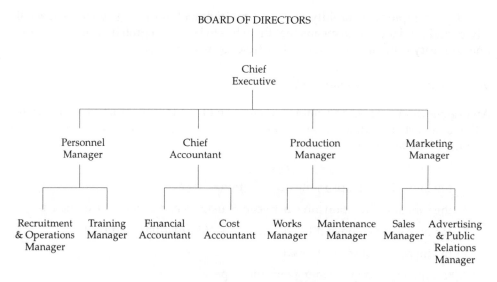

Figure 9.4: Vertical organisation chart

This type of vertical chart is commonly used and frequently includes the names of the various post-holders at the time of drawing up the chart. The chart could, of course, be extended to show lower levels in the organisation.

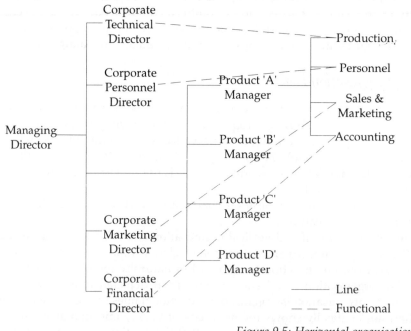

Figure 9.5: Horizontal organisation chart

Figure 9.5 is drawn in a horizontal format. The firm is organised on a product basis. This means that there are Production, Personnel, Sales and Accounting tasks carried out separately for each of the products. Note that, for clarity, only those for Product 'A' have been shown but these tasks are also carried out for the other three products. The chart also shows the main functional relationships between the corporate or group functions and the tasks carried out for Product 'A'. Although not shown, there are similar functional relationships for Products B, C and D. Organisations structured on a product or service basis are commonly encountered both in the private sector and in the public sector for organisations which provide a range of services e.g. the National Health Service.

Figure 9.6: Circular organisation chart

Figure 9.6 illustrates a circular format. It shows the relationships and line responsibilities of an Office Services Manager in a large organisation. Charts do not have to illustrate the whole structure of an organisation hence this example for a particular service department. The chart shows the establishment and grade of each position. For example, the establishment for Audio Typists is 6 posts with a B6 grade. This type of information commonly appears in detailed charts used internally in organisations such as the Civil Service, Local Government and large private sector companies. This type of information could, of course, be shown equally well on vertical or horizontal charts. It is claimed that circular charts are more democratic because they denote the senior person as the hub rather than the top of a status pyramid.

Advantages and disadvantages of organisational charts

The main advantages are:

☐ they show the main formal lines of authority and responsibility thus providing an overall view of the balance of the organisation.

☐ they may help in suggesting improved structures or ways to re-organise.

☐ they communicate a clear over-view of the organisation which is useful for outsiders and new employees.

Disadvantages:

☐ if badly drawn or out of date they may cause confusion.

☐ they may cause a status conscious attitude to develop.

☐ they may cause organisational inflexibility and stifle initiative.

☐ they can only show some of the formal relationships and none of the vital informal ones thus are always incomplete.

Co-ordination

Co-ordinating is a primary management function and can be defined as:

the process of integrating the work of individuals, sections and departments towards the effective achievement of the organisation's goals.

A co-ordinated organisation meshes together as a team, with obvious benefits. However a lack of integration brings problems of which the following are examples:

☐ Complaints by clients, customers about poor service, late deliveries and of receiving conflicting messages from different parts of the organisation.

☐ Conflicts and 'buck passing' between individuals and departments.

☐ The presence of excessive rules, committees and 'red tape' in an attempt to enforce integration.

☐ Repeated short term 'panic' decision making to cope with today's crisis.

Reasons for poor co-ordination

Any one, or combination of the following reasons could contribute to poor co-ordination in an organisation and to loss of morale.

Possible reasons for poor co-ordination.

☐ Poor communications between departments and between individuals.

☐ Poor organisation structure and inappropriate departmental groupings.

☐ Inadequate planning and objective setting. Does each department know, in detail, what it has to do?

☐ Differences in leadership style.

☐ Inter-departmental and inter-personal dislikes and rivalries.

☐ Difficulties of combining different disciplines. Can the accountants work with the marketing people?

Improving co-ordination

As with many management problems there is not a single, universally applicable, solution.

Management have to examine the particular circumstances and difficulties and try to deal with them in a progressive fashion. Some of the approaches found useful in practice are as follows:

Administrative procedures

Standardising rules, procedures and specifications. These will have been derived from clearly defined operational plans and policies. A well developed information system is essential to disseminate the required information.

Committees and meetings

Formal and informal committees and meetings provide a simple but effective structure by which co-ordination may be improved. Membership should be drawn from the pool of interested people/departments. The greatest care must be taken to ensure that committees have specific tasks to perform and do not become just talking shops. Committees should not consist of the unwilling, drawn from the unfit, doing the unnecessary.

Establishing co-ordinating roles and departments

These would act as intermediaries between existing departments or functions. For example, between Social Services and the local Health Authority, between Research and Marketing and so on.

Project teams

These are used to combine and integrate different functions and departments to achieve a project objective. In effect they are a stage in the development of a full matrix structure.

Making structural changes

Depending on circumstances co-ordination may be improved by combining specialisations in different ways, or by creating more coherent service or product groups or some other structural change.

Apart from these formal changes management should try to cultivate an attitude for co-operation between departments and should actively foster teamwork.

Key point summary

❐   A manager's beliefs about motivation affects his style of management and how he leads.

❐   The theories on motivation include those based on satisfaction, incentives and intrinsic or personal fulfilment.

❐   Leadership is the ability to influence others.

❐   The more modern views on leadership consider that successful leadership must always relate to the specific factors in the situation.

❐   Trait theories attempted to identify the personal characteristics of successful leaders.

❐   Style theories concentrated on the way a manager manages, the two extremes being Authoritarian and Democratic.

❐   Contingency theorists consider that leadership effectiveness is dependent on such factors as the task, the work group and the position of the leader.

❐   Organising includes: deciding what tasks are necessary, how tasks are to be arranged and designing an appropriate structure or the organisation.

❐   There are numerous factors influencing job design including; provision of goals, some autonomy and feedback, variety, social contact and the opportunity to learn.

❐   Job enlargement is essentially more of the same.

❐   Job enrichment involves more scope, more autonomy and seeks to satisfy higher order needs.

❐   The conditions for genuine participation must be met otherwise there will be pseudo-participation.

❐   Delegation is where a manager transfers part of his authority (but not responsibility) to a subordinate.

❏ When delegating the manager should set clear objectives, provide what training etc. is needed, monitor results and review performance.

❏ Management by Objectives (MBO) is a formal, structured form of delegation where the emphasis is on results achieved, not on the ways that the results were obtained.

❏ Organisation charts are a visual representation of the authority and relationships in an organisation.

❏ Organisation charts can be drawn in vertical, horizontal and circular formats.

❏ Co-ordination is the process of integrating work to achieve the organisations objectives.

Self review questions

1. *Why is it necessary to study motivation?*

2. *What are the three main theories of leadership?*

3. *What is the problem discovered by investigations of the traits of successful leaders?*

4. *What are the characteristics of an authoritarian? a democratic style?*

5. *What are the key features of the contingency approach?*

6. *What elements are included in the organising function?*

7. *What factors do the Department of Employment suggest are needed in the design of jobs?*

8. *What is Job Enlargement?*

9. *What is Job Enrichment and what are its advantages and disadvantages?*

10. *What is an autonomous work group?*

11. *What guidelines should be followed to ensure successful participation?*

12. *What is delegation?*

13. *Why do managers delegate?*

14. *How should you delegate?*

15. *What is MBO?*

16. *Distinguish between Line and Functional Authority.*

17. *What do Organisation Charts show?*

18. *What types of Charts are there?*

19. *What is co-ordination?*

20. *How can co-ordination be improved?*

10 Control

Objectives

After you have studied this chapter you will:

❏ *Understand the importance of the control function.*

❏ *Be able to describe the basic elements of the control cycle.*

❏ *Know the importance of feedback loops.*

❏ *Be able to distinguish between single loop feedback and double loop or higher order feed-back.*

❏ *Be able to describe Pareto analysis.*

❏ *Be able to explain feedforward and describe its importance.*

❏ *Know that multiple control factors are necessary in complex organisations.*

❏ *Understand that more flexible, decentralised organisations need changed forms of control.*

Control in management

Control is a primary management task and is the process of ensuring the operations proceed according to plan. A comprehensive definition of management control given by Mockler is reproduced below:

> 'Management control can be defined as a systematic effort by business management to compare performance to predetermined standards, plans, or objectives, in order to determine whether performance is in line with these standards and presumably in order to take any remedial action required to see that human and other corporate resources are being used in the most effective and efficient way possible in achieving corporate objectives.'

The type of control activity varies according to the level of management, and the amount of time spent controlling also varies according to level. As an example, control activities will occupy most of the time of a supervisor or foreman at the operational level and most operational control systems use formal, systematic rules with clear, unambiguous targets expressed in quantitative or financial terms. At higher levels, planning and control are more interlinked, with management being concerned both to monitor progress against the original plans and to review the suitability of the plans themselves for current and anticipated future conditions.

Control is necessary because unpredictable disturbances occur and cause actual results to deviate from the expected or planned results. Control activities seek to keep the system outputs in line with the original plan, what is known as 'steady state', or to enable the system to change safely to meet the new conditions.

Disturbances can range from minor matters such as a short delay in the delivery of raw materials, to disturbances which threaten the organisation itself, for example, the unexpected entry of a large, new competitor into the market.

Control of systems

To be successful, any organisation, whether a factory, local authority, school or whatever, must produce outputs in the form of goods, services, or facilities that meets its objectives. To do this planning must take place and, when the plans have been implemented, control must be exercised to ensure conformity to the plans and that the plans remain relevant.

It is meaningless to consider any form of control activity without a clear idea of what is to be achieved i.e. a plan. Correspondingly, a vital element in any planning process is consideration of the controls and control systems necessary to ensure adherence to the plan. In physical systems, control is an integral part of the design and is based on direct and immediate measurement and sensing of voltages, pressures, temperatures, flows, weights and so on. Well known examples being engine governors, heating thermostats and overload switches.

In organisational and management systems the need to monitor activities is not always so apparent and there must be a conscious effort to include appropriate control systems throughout the organisation. A crucial difference between organisational and mechanical systems is that in organisational systems, control is exercised by the use of information. Most managers do not see the actual operations and rely on information about the activities that have taken place in order to be able to exercise control. It is this fact which makes formalised information systems so essential, particularly for operational and tactical level management.

Basic elements of control cycles

Control is the activity which measures deviations from planned performance and provides information upon which corrective action can be taken (if required) either to alter future performance so as to conform to the original plan, or to modify the original plans. The elements of the complete control cycle are:

(a) A standard specifying the expected performance. This can be in the form of a budget, a procedure, a stock level, an output rate or some other target.

(b) A measurement of actual performance. This should be made in an accurate, speedy, unbiased manner and using relevant units it measures. For example, time taken, £'s spent, units produced, efficiency ratings and so on.

(c) Comparison of (a) and (b). Frequently the comparison is accompanied by an analysis which attempts to isolate the reasons for any variations. A well known example of this is the accounting process of variance analysis.

(d) Feedback of deviations or variations to a control unit. In an organisational context the 'control unit' would be a manager. This type of feedback is *single-loop feedback* which is described more fully below.

(e) Actions by the control unit to alter performance in accordance with the plan.

(f) Feedback to a higher level control unit regarding large variations between performance and plan and upon the results of the lower level control units actions. This is *double-loop feedback* which is described more fully below.

Feedback loops

Control is exercised in organisations by *feedback loops* which gather information on past performance from the output side of a system, department or process, which is used to govern future performance by adjusting the input side of the system by, for example, altering the amount of finance available, the number of staff, the amount of equipment etc.

Figure 10.1 shows the outline of single-loop and double-loop feedback.

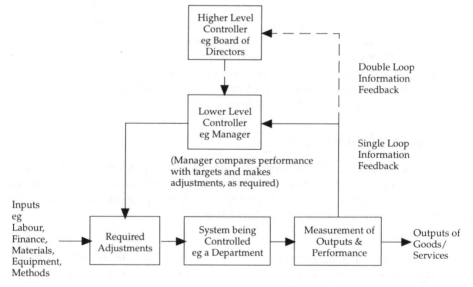

Figure 10.1: Control and feedback cycle

Single-loop feedback

Single-loop feedback, usually expressed simply as 'feedback', is the conventional feedback of relatively small variations between actual and plan in order that corrective action can be taken to bring performance in line with the plan. The implication of this is that existing performance standards and plans remain unchanged.

This type of feedback is that associated with the normal control systems at operational and tactical levels. Examples include; stock control, production control, budgetary control and standard costing. At lower levels these systems are closed in that they do not interact with their environment, and relatively mechanistic in that the performance standards do not change.

Double-loop or higher order feedback

This is a higher order of feedback designed to ensure that plans, budgets, organisational structures and the control systems themselves are revised to meet changes in conditions. Ross Ashby maintains that double-loop feedback is essential if a system is to adapt to a changing environment and, as already pointed out, adaptability is the primary characteristic of organisations that survive.

The business environment abounds with uncertainties – competitors' actions, inflation, industrial disputes, changes in tastes and technology, new legislation – and the monitoring of trends and performance so that appropriate adjustments can be made to plans is likely to be more productive than the rigid adherence to historical plans and budgets which were prepared in earlier and different circumstances.

The timing of information flows and of control decisions differs from level to level. In general at the lowest level there is the need for more or less immediate information and decision making whereas at higher levels, weekly, monthly and longer review periods are more effective. As an example, reviewing quality on an automatic production line needs to be done minute by minute whereas reviewing the performance of the factory as a whole is likely to be done on a monthly or quarterly basis.

Timing of control action

Control action is likely to be most effective when the time lag between the output and corrective action – via the information loop – is as short as possible. Not only will the control action be able to commence earlier but it will be more appropriate. Too great a time lag may cause the resulting control action to be the opposite of what it should be.

Two factors which influence the speed of control are the *organisational structure* and the *reporting period.*

If an item of information has to pass through several levels of the organisation's hierarchy before effective action can be taken then there will inevitably be delays. Peter Drucker has said that decisions should always be made at the lowest possible level, consistent with the nature of the decision and as close to the scene of action as possible. Effective control and organisational protocol may thus be in conflict.

There is a tendency for some types of control information, for example budgetary control and standard costing reports, to be produced in accordance with conventional accounting periods – monthly or four weekly – for all levels in the organisation. Because of the procedures involved, such reports are frequently not available until halfway through the next period and consequently much of the information is out-of-date and is misleading as a guide to action.

There is no complete answer to this problem but there should be recognition that the most effective control period is not necessarily the same as an accounting or calendar period such as a week, or month or year. At lower levels in the organisation rapid feedback of a relatively restricted range of matters is likely to be more effective, whilst at higher levels there is less immediacy. Organisations where decentralisation is practised have shorter communication lines and control information, and hence control action, is more immediate and hence is likely to be more effective.

Research into formal managerial control systems, such as budgetary control indicates that they are by no means as effective as top management would like to believe. Many managers considered the control systems to be ineffective and virtually ignored the reports and statements produced by the systems. The studies showed that there were five main reasons for management's failure to use the information provided:

- ❏ Subjects covered were outside the manager's control.
- ❏ The information arrived too late for effective action to be taken.
- ❏ Insufficient detail was provided.
- ❏ The information supplied was thought by the manager to be inaccurate.
- ❏ The information was provided in a form which could not be understood.

The first two factors were by far the most important so repay close attention by everyone concerned.

Concentration of control effort

The full control cycle – continual monitoring of results, comparisons with plans, analysis of variations and reporting – is an expensive and time consuming process. Accordingly it is important that the effort is concentrated where it can be most effective such as areas of high expenditure, vital operations and processes, departments whose objectives are vital elements in the fulfilment of overall objectives and other similar areas.

A good example of this is the use of Pareto analysis (sometimes called ABC analysis or the 80/20 rule) in stock control. It is commonly found that 20% of the items account for 80% of the total inventory value and accordingly the major control effort would be concentrated on these items and correspondingly less time spent on detailed analysis and control of items which have insignificant values. The application of this simple concept is, of course, much wider than just inventory control and its use makes it more likely that control activities will be cost effective.

Feedback and control example

To bring together the ideas on feedback and control covered so far a diagram (much simplified) is shown in Figure 10.2 of a typical production system.

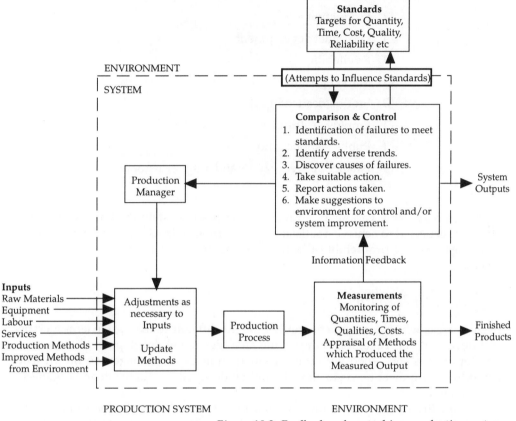

Figure 10.2: Feedback and control in a production system

Figure 10.2 depicts a relatively structured application for which a standardised feedback control system based on internal factors is suitable. In more complex and uncertain conditions where both external and internal influences need to be considered a more flexible and broader control system is required.

Multiple control factors

Complex organisations such as commercial and industrial firms contain a large number of elements and pursue a range of objectives. The consequence of this is that simple control systems which have traditionally concentrated solely on financial factors cannot be expected to control the multi-faceted activities of a complex organisation.

Whilst the profit factor is important, especially in the long-run, there is general recognition that it is only one facet of the management task. Profit is relatively objective and is easily measurable whereas some of the other factors are less so. Numerous organisations have attempted to deal with the problem and one of the pioneers was the General Electric Company of America.

General Electric identified eight key result areas which are summarised below.

- Productivity
- Personnel development
- Profitability
- Market position
- Product leadership
- Employee attitudes
- Public responsibility
- Balance between short- and long-term goals

Within each key area various performance targets were established and a manager would be expected to achieve a satisfactory performance level across all eight facets.

A high score of profitability would not compensate for poor performance elsewhere.

Non-quantifiable control factors

Even in areas which are conventionally thought difficult to assess, General Electric laid down criteria. Take, for example, the area 'Personnel development'. Personnel development is concerned with the systematic training of managers to fill present and future manpower needs to allow for both individual development and organisational growth.

The quality of the programme offered by a General Electric department was appraised by informal interviews covering the staff's views on; selection, periodic performance reviews, training available and so on. Also a manning audit was taken annually to assess how well the department could fill its own promotional needs by examining the preparation and training of each manager and the amount of internal and external training undertaken. Finally a ratio was devised of the number of people actually promoted to the number deemed promotable in the department.

Personnel development and other parts of a manager's task are long term in nature and if no attempt is made to measure performance in such areas, a manager might be tempted to ignore them and merely concentrate on a short term factor such as profitability.

Even at operational levels there is an awareness that a single control factor cannot satisfactorily monitor the richness and diversity of any operation. J.G. Miller carried out an international survey to find out what performance measures were used to control and monitor production in Europe, the United States and Japan. The key results are summarised below.

Performance measures listed in order of importance

	Europe	United States	Japan
1	Outgoing quality	Incoming quality	Manufacturing leadtimes
2	Unit manufacturing costs	Inventory accuracy	Direct labour productivity
3	Unit material cost	Direct labour productivity	WIP turnover
4	Overhead costs	Manufacturing leadtimes	Incoming quality
5	On-time deliveries	Vendor leadtime	Vendor leadtime
6	Incoming quality	Set-up times	Indirect productivity
7	Direct labour productivity	WIP turnover	Material yield

Multiple control factors in the public sector

Public sector organisations are equally complex and face a similar range of control problems to those in a typical private sector company. As an example, when in 1988 the government accepted a report from the Civil Service Efficiency Unit that free-standing Agencies should be set up to carry out specific activities, they were faced with the problems of controlling the Agencies. The main objective of the programme, called the Next Steps initiative, was to bring about better performance in the provision of Central Government services. It was realised that to manage better and to improve reporting there was a need for more comprehensive and timely information on all aspects of performance, not just financial performance.

To date over 100 Agencies have been established employing over 350,000 people. There is an enormous range of functions and size. For example, the Social Service Benefits Agency employs approximately 65,000 people whereas the Historic Royal Palaces Agency employs approximately 330. It was decided that performance would be monitored and controlled across four broad headings.

- ❏ Financial performance
- ❏ Volume of output
- ❏ Quality
- ❏ Efficiency

Within these broad headings targets are set specifically related to the activities, services or products of the particular Agency and control exercised by comparing actual performance with the targets.

Examples of targets set by the Agencies under the four headings are shown below.

Area	Target	Agency
FINANCIAL PERFORMANCE	Full cost recovery plus unit cost targets	Civil Service College, Central Office of Information and others
	Commercial revenue to offset costs	Met Office
OUTPUT	Number of tests performed	Vehicle Inspectorate
	Number of course days provided; number of students taught	Civil Service College
	Arrange 1.3 million placings (16 per cent long-term claimants; 2.4 per cent people with disabilities; 34 per cent inner city unemployed)	Employment Service
QUALITY OF SERVICE		
(a) Timeliness	Same-day clearance for Social Fund crisis loans	Benefit Agency
	Time to handle applications	Passport Office, Vehicle Certification Agency and others
	Time to issue patent search reports	Patent Office
(b) Quality of product	Proportion of course evaluation indicators in top categories	Civil Service College
	95 per cent of work completed to time and to standards	Military Survey
	Number of print orders delivered without fault	HMSO
(c) Availability	All documents to be available within five days of receipt	Companies House
	23,000 additional basic scale maps available	Ordnance Survey
EFFICIENCY		
(a) Efficiency/economy	Percentage reduction in price paid for stationery and paper	HMSO
	20 per cent reduction in the cost of common services over five years	Patent Office
(b) Unit cost	£20.89 for a car test	Driving Standards Agency
	£472 per productive professional day	Occupational Health Service

Feedforward

Close examination of any real system such as a private or public sector organisation will show that there are two types of control loop; *feedback loops* which monitor past results to detect and correct disturbances to the plan and *feedforward loops* which react to immediate or forthcoming dangers by making adjustments to the system in advance in order to cope with the problem in good time.

In any organisation it is unlikely that pure feedforward or pure feedback control would operate in isolation. Feedback control on its own may be too slow and feedforward control too risky, so that some balance between the two is desirable.

> Feedback monitors the past. Feedforward looks ahead.

Figure 10.3 shows an outline of the two types of control.

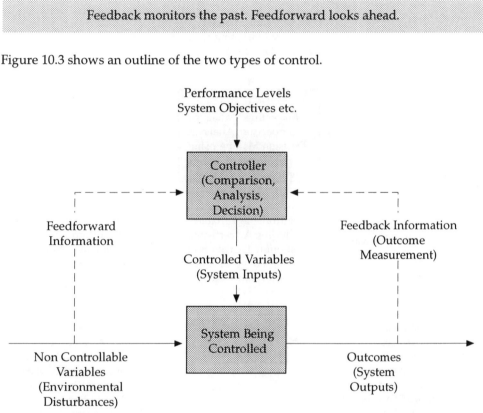

Figure 10.3: Feedforward and feedback loops

Feedforward uses flair and insight and relies heavily on information about the environment to anticipate critical changes in the non-controllable variables before they have an effect on the system. Feedforward is open-loop and does not feed back through the process as does closed-loop feedback control. The ability to sense impending problems and to take prior corrective action, which is the essence of feedforward control, are also the hallmarks of successful managers and businessmen.

Examples of feedforward

Practical examples of feedforward include the following: news of political instability in a country which was a major supplier of an important rare metal would cause astute buyers to buy before prices went up and their own stocks were depleted (in contrast a pure feedback system would not react until stocks had actually fallen), a company hearing of a possible industrial dispute would make alternative production arrangements, such as sub-contracting or engaging non-union labour, in advance of the withdrawal of labour and so on.

Figure 10.4 provides an example of feedforward and feedback in a marketing system.

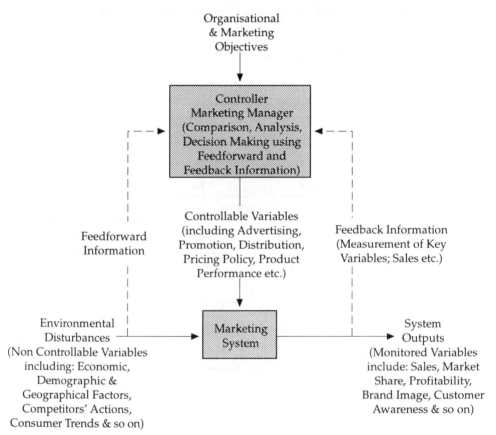

Figure 10.4: Feedforward/feedback in a marketing system

Changing styles of control

Traditionally, controls in organisations have been hierarchical moving from lower to middle to higher management in a regulated way. This pattern suits stable conditions where real decision making is concentrated at the top.

However, conditions are changing rapidly and organisations have to adapt. There is the need for more flexibility and local decision making. This has led to the growth of decentralised decision making and the establishment of smaller, autonomous units operating with considerable freedom and flexibility within a larger framework. Many business organisations already have, or are moving towards this style of operation e.g. Proctor and Gamble, IBM, Rank Xerox etc. and the same tendency can also be clearly seen in the Public Sector, for example.

❑ In education the Local Management of Schools is being introduced. This means almost total transfer of responsibility for the running of the school from the Local Authority to the Governors of each school and the Head Teacher. This includes financial management of all expenditure, including salaries.

❑ In a similar manner hospitals within the National Health Service have opted for Self-governing Trust status. Trust hospitals have virtually complete control over their operations which include bidding within the competitive market set up in the Health Service. With Trust hospitals, the 'middle management' level, represented by the District Health Authority, is bypassed and the Trust Hospital answers directly to the Department of Health. Numerous major hospitals have already opted for Trust status including, Guys in London, St James in Liverpool and many others.

As organisations and the style of operations change so must the style and method of control. Old report-based detailed controls passing up and down the hierarchy stifle initiative and inhibit flexibility. The solution to the problem of achieving both control and freedom is to combine tight control of performance with freedom of operation. This is described by Peters and Waterman as

'Simultaneous loose-tight properties'.

This means that individuals and units are held accountable for mutually agreed goals while being free to achieve the results as they see fit. Results and performance are controlled; methods are not. This places more reliance on individuals and encourages initiative.

Operating units become self managing organisations which are innovative and adaptable.

The effectiveness of another feature of traditional control systems, that of post-event monitoring, is increasingly being questioned. Take for example, labour cost control. Typically, labour costs are collected and at the end of a period an assessment is made as to whether the labour is being used effectively and costs controlled.

However, there is a growing awareness that the factors which influence labour costs are mainly determined at the planning stage i.e., the investment decisions about the machine, equipment and methods to be used. Once these earlier decisions have been made labour costs are effectively predetermined and so traditional post-event 'control' is largely illusory.

Proper planning is thus the best method of control. This philosophy has been fully accepted by the Japanese particularly in the all important area of product quality. Take an automatic pop-up toaster as an analogy for a production system. If, from time to time, the toaster pops up burnt toast the traditional Western approach, called Quality Control, is to set up an elaborate recording system to record the number of burnt slices and then a rectification system to scrape them. The Japanese approach is to fix the toaster.

Planning and control example

To bring together the chapters on planning and control an example of the inter-relationships found in one company are shown in Figure 10.5, opposite.

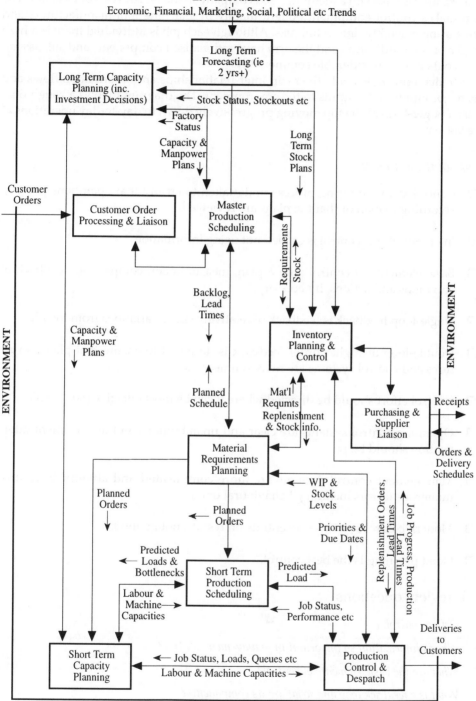

ENVIRONMENT
Economic, Financial, Marketing, Social, Political etc Trends

Figure 10.5: Manufacturing planning and control example

The example is based on a medium sized company in the North West of England. The firm makes control equipment bought mainly by machine tool manufacturers and firms using assembly line techniques. Although each job is individual there is a high degree of standardisation and the firm have rationalised components and sub assemblies so there is a considerable commonality.

The diagram shows only the main inter-relationships and information flows and the major inputs and outputs to the environment. The diagram follows a rough time scale. Longer-term at the top moving progressively down to day-to-day operations at the bottom.

Key point summary

- ❏ Control is a monitoring process undertaken to ensure that operations proceed according to plan or that the plans are reviewed.

- ❏ In organisations control is carried out using information.

- ❏ Basic elements of control are:- a plan, measurement, comparison, feedback of variations and actions, if necessary.

- ❏ Single-loop feedback is feedback of relatively small variations from the plan.

- ❏ Double-loop or higher order feedback is designed to ensure that plans, structures and control systems are revised if necessary.

- ❏ Control effort should be directed where it can be most effective (80/20 rule).

- ❏ Operating control systems are clear and unambiguous and management intervention should be rare.

- ❏ Management control systems are more complicated and attempt to control numerous factors including behavioural ones.

- ❏ Modern control systems concentrate on results, not methods.

- ❏ Good planning is the best control.

Self review questions

1.   *Define control.*

2.   *Why is information so important in management control?*

3.   *What are the basic elements of control?*

4.   *What is a feedback loop and what are its components?*

5.   *Describe single and double-loop feedback.*

6.   *What is negative feedback?*

7. *What is Pareto analysis?*

8. *Why is it necessary to consider Multiple Control Factors?*

9. *What multiple control factors did General Electric identify?*

10. *Give examples of multiple control factors used in the Public Sector.*

11. *What is feedforward and why can it be dangerous?*

12. *What is 'simultaneous loose-tight control'?*

Assessment and revision section

Assignments

1. Try to find the Organisation Charts of different organisations. If you find that an organisation does not have a chart, develop one for that organisation. Why do the charts differ between organisations? How many management levels are there?

2. Find out the policies of two organisations on matters such as race, colour, religion, the environment etc. and contrast them. What evidence can you find that the official policies are implemented in practice?

3. Carry out a SWOT analysis on yourself (try to be honest!). Get a friend to do a SWOT analysis on you independently. Compare the results.

4. Find examples of management by exception being used in practice. How are exceptions recognised? Does the procedure aid management control?

5. In an organisation known to you, find two examples each of strategic, tactical and operational level decisions. What are the key information needs for each decision?

6. Find a practical example of each of the following.
    (a) Negative feedback
    (b) Higher order feedback
    (c) Feedforward

7. An organisation is considering the purchase of a sophisticated, high-volume photocopier. List the factors which would need to be considered before a decision was taken.

8. The objectives of Sainsburys are given in the text. Find other examples for:
    (a) a not-for-profit organisation such as a college, local authority, a charity etc.
    (b) a profit seeking organisation
    How are the needs of the various stakeholders reflected in the objectives?

Mini-Case 1 - Decision tree

A company is considering whether to launch a new product. The success of the idea depends on the success of a competitor in bringing out a competing product (estimated at 60%) and the relationship of the competitor's price to the firm's price.

Table A shows the conditional profits for each set of prices by the company and its competitor.

Table A (£000's)

| Company's Price | Competitors Price | | | Profit if no Competitor |
	Low	Medium	High	
Low	30	42	45	50
Medium	21	40	45	70
High	10	30	53	90

The company must set its price first because its product will be on the market earlier so that the competitor will be able to react to the price. Estimates of the probability of a competitor's price are shown in Table B.

Table B (£000's)

| If company prices | Competitor's price expected to be | | |
	Low	Medium	High
Low	0.8	0.15	0.05
Medium	0.20	0.70	0.10
High	0.05	0.35	0.60

Task 1. *Draw a decision tree and analyse the problem.*

Task 2. *Recommend what the company should do.*

Task 3. *Consider what other information the company should try to find out.*

Mini-Case 2 - Setting a target selling price

Japanese manufacturing companies use radically different methods to set selling prices than their Western counterparts who frequently use a form of cost-plus based on existing engineering standards.

The Japanese process is market driven and starts with a specification of what features the new product should have. A target selling price is set based on market research, into which is incorporated the profit margin specified in the strategic plans of the firm. The differences between the two represents the 'allowable cost' for the product which is usually well above the currently achievable cost. As product design proceeds, value engineering and redesign takes place in a continuous cycle until the target cost is reached. The process is shown in Figure MC1.

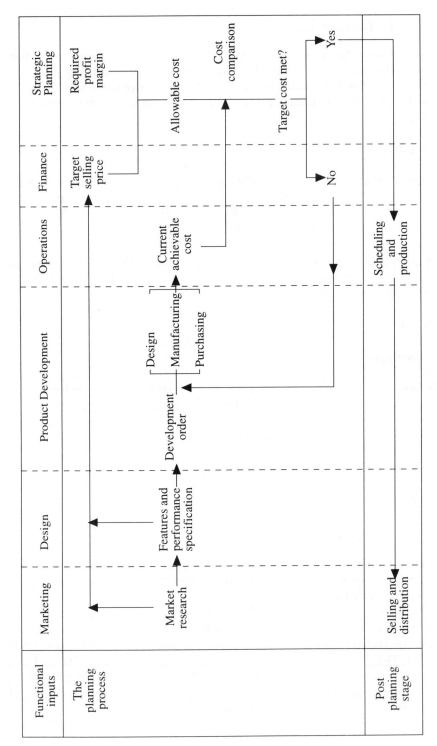

Figure MC1: Setting a target selling price

Task 1 *Classify the information used into internal and external.*

Task 2 *Explain the key differences between the Japanese approach depicted and that tradi-tionally used in the West.*

Task 3 *Describe the main decision points in the Japanese system.*

Mini-Case 3 - W.H.Jones p.l.c.

W.H.Jones p.l.c. has a nationwide chain of retail outlets specialising in the sale of magazines, books, stationery and related products. Competition is increasing and various ways of reducing costs are being examined. One possibility is to eliminate one of the in-store management levels saving three or four staff at each store.

Task 1 *Describe the main effects of eliminating the management level.*

Task 2 *Give the advantages and disadvantages of the proposal.*

Task 3 *Give examples of the changes in management and staff practices and attitudes that will be necessary to make a success of the elimination.*

Examination questions with answers

A1 Describe and compare Theories X, Y and Z as styles of management. To what contingencies may the choice of management style be subject?

ACCA – Effective Management

A2 You are required to explain the features of each of the following management styles, indicating the circumstances under which each might be appropriate:
(a) autocratic
(b) missionary;
(c) consultative;
(d) democratic.

CIMA – Management

A3 The word leadership is sometimes used as if it were an attribute of personality, sometimes as if it were a characteristic of certain positions within an organisation, and sometimes as an aspect of behaviour. Discuss.

ICSA - Management, Principles and Policy

A4 Describe what you understand by a system of management by objectives. What do you think are the advantages and disadvantages of such a system?

CIB – Nature of Management

A5 What personal competences and attributes would you look for in a potential departmental supervisor or junior manager? Give reasons for your choice.

ACCA – Effective Management

A6 'Effective delegation is often preached but rarely practised'. Describe the essential actions managers should undertake for delegation to be effective.

IAM – Manpower Administration

A7 Recent articles have focused on summary information for running a business and on a 'balanced scorecard' approach, using a number of performance measures. You are required to explain
(a) the arguments for using the profit measure as the all-encompassing measure of the performance of a business;
(b) the limitations of this profit-measurement approach and of undue dependence on the profit measure;
(c) the problems of using a broad range of non-financial measures for the short- and long-term control of a business.

CIMA – Management Accounting, Control and Audit

Examination questions without answers

B1 What are the major steps in the decision-making process? Identify and explain the key considerations in each step.

CIB – Nature of Management

B2 'The ability to deal with almost any situation is the essence of good management'. Discuss with a special reference to leadership styles and working groups.

IAM – Manpower Administration

B3 (a) In recent years, many organisations have developed mission statements. It has become increasingly common for such statements to be published within the organisation and also externally.

You are required to contrast the viewpoints that a mission statement is either an embodiment of the prevailing organisational culture or an attempt to change it. Explain other motives for publishing these statements.

(b) In discussing not-for-profit organisations, Bowman and Asch state:
'. . . even if the goals are clear but achievement of them is not measurable, then assessing the performance of the organisation becomes extremely difficult'.

Strategic Management, Bowman & Asch

You are required to explain how the performance of a not-for-profit organisation could be assessed.

CIMA - Management Accounting, Strategic Planning & Marketing

B4 Describe and compare line, staff and functional forms of managerial authority. How and why may the management of an accounting and finance department apply each of these three forms of authority within the organisation, and what problems may be associated with their application?

ACCA – Effective Management

B5 Mary has just been appointed to be in charge of Organisation and Method in Y plc. From her previous experience and knowledge of companies of a similar size and nature she is of the opinion that the ratio of first-line managers, i.e. foremen and section heads, to workers in Y plc is too high. Pressure from competition means that any potential savings in overhead must be made as rapidly as possible. She is concerned that even after early retirements and reassignment of some of these managers, some redundancies will be inevitable. The specialised nature of the work and a tight labour market mean that existing workers and managers cannot easily be replaced.

Mary proposes to reduce the number of first-line managers by increasing their span of control.

You are required to recommend actions she could take to achieve increased spans of control.

CIMA – Management

Additional reading

Planning and Control Systems, G. Davis and M. Olson, McGraw.

The New Science of Management and Decision, H. Simon, Harper & Row.

Quantitative Techniques, T. Lucey, DP Publications.

Theory Z, W. G. Ouchi, Addison-Wesley.

In Search of Excellence, T. Peters and R. Waterman, Harper & Row.

Corporate Planning, J. Argenti, Allen & Unwin.

11 *Management functions: marketing*

Objectives

After you have studied this chapter you will:

☐ *Be able to define marketing and the marketing process.*

☐ *Know the four elements of the marketing mix.*

☐ *Understand the Product Life-Cycle.*

☐ *Know the key importance of Pricing.*

☐ *Be able to describe various approaches to Pricing including; marginal analysis, cost-plus, demand-based.*

☐ *Be able to distinguish between the channels of distribution and physical distribution methods.*

☐ *Know the main activities used to promote the product including; advertising, personal selling, publicity.*

☐ *Understand the purpose of marketing research and the main methods used.*

Management tasks and functions

The last four Chapters have described the tasks which all managers have to perform. These include; planning, decision making, organising, coordinating and control. Most managers are specialists that is, they work in a particular functional area of the organisation.

Thus they plan, organise, control and so on within their area of expertise. This might be the Works Manager re-organising a production line to increase efficiency, the Chief Accountant dealing with a loan from the bank, the Personnel Manager arranging the training programme for new recruits and so on.

Accordingly we now turn to descriptions of the key functional areas of business. Marketing is dealt with in this chapter and Personnel, Production and Finance and Accounting are dealt with in following chapters.

Marketing–definition and importance

Peter Drucker has stated that marketing is the primary management function and that it is 'the whole business seen from the point of view of its final result that is from the customers' point of view'.

There are numerous definitions of marketing but a useful one is:

> the process responsible for identifying, anticipating and satisfying customer requirements profitably (for trading organisations) or effectively (for non-trading organisations).

The above definition emphasises the point that marketing is equally applicable to both trading and non-trading organisations. All have to consider the customer's point of view, which is the essence of marketing.

Organisations that adopt a market-oriented approach focus on the needs of their customers. Thus, production – or the provision of services – must respond to the demands of marketing not the other way round. With a market-oriented approach the customer forms the starting point for the development of the organisation's corporate strategy and marketing is regarded as an activity shared by all, not merely those working in the Marketing Department.

Marketing is thus a philosophy which influences the whole organisation. It is much more than just selling. Selling is trying to get the customer to want what the organisation already has: marketing tries to get the company to produce what the customer wants. Ideally, marketing should result in a customer who is ready to buy, thus making selling superfluous.

What is the marketing process?

The marketing process is a way of developing a customer based strategy that meets the organisation's objectives. Although the details will obviously vary from organisation to organisation it is a process to identify, anticipate and satisfy customer wants. Typical components of the process include:

> *Market research:* acquisition and analysis of information about; existing and potential markets, and marketing methods.
>
> *Product development and planning:* development of new products, services, features etc. to meet customer wants, and reviewing current products.
>
> *Pricing:* setting appropriate prices having regard to product status, competitive pressures, desire for market share, costs etc.
>
> *Distribution:* consideration of the channels of distribution e.g. wholesaler, retailer, mail-order, and of physical distribution.
>
> *Promotion:* identifying appropriate and cost-effective methods of advertising promoting and selling the product.

The stages shown above are used to develop the marketing stategy for the organisation i.e. the market situation is identified (customers, suppliers, competitors etc.) and decisions are taken to target the market.

It is at this stage that the *marketing mix* becomes crucial.

Marketing mix

The marketing mix is defined by Kotler as

'the set of controllable variables and their levels that the firm uses to influence the target market'

Originally expounded by Professor Borden of Harvard the marketing mix has been simplified to the four Ps; Product, Price, Place, Promotion as shown in Figure 11.1

Figure 11.1: The marketing mix (four P's)

The diagram shows some of the detailed elements under each of the four Ps. It attempts to show how the variables interact with each other and how management seeks to obtain the right mix of factors to meet conditions in the target market at a particular time.

Organisations may consider the market reasonably homogeneous and develop a single marketing mix to satisfy everyone. Alternatively there may be *market segmenta-*

tion where consumers wants vary across the whole market requiring the organisation to develop various marketing mixes to meet the needs of the various market segments. For example, car manufacturers have different marketing mixes (discounts, facilities, promotion methods etc.) to deal with fleet buyers as compared to private buyers.

Each of the four Ps are developed in the paragraphs which follow.

Product

The term 'product' includes physical objects such as a video-recorder, a packet of detergent or a cake and also service products e.g. legal and accountancy services, dental treatment, banking and insurance services and so on.

The range of products offered by an organisation is known as its *product mix*. Most organisations keep their product mix under constant review; adding, amending or deleting in response to, or anticipation of, market changes.

Especially in consumer products *branding* is of particular importance. Consumers' loyalty is encouraged by brand identification and brand advertising for everything from detergents (Persil, Bold, Daz etc.) to beers (Guinness, Bass, Heineken etc.). Some brands have become so well known that they have become synonymous with certain types of product. Examples include Hoovers for vacuum cleaners and Biros for ball-point pens.

Packaging is also vitally important not only for brand identification but also for protection and convenience in use. Examples include; ring-pull cans for soft drinks, pet foods, beers and re-fillable containers for detergents, shampoos, washing-up liquids.

The provision of technical support, after-sales service, guarantees and similar benefits is of particular importance with complex mechanical and electrical products. Examples include; cars, washing machines, televisions, computers, videos.

Consideration of the features and benefits of the product must also take account of the *product life-cycle.*

Product life cycle

Experience shows that many products pass through a series of phases from development to introduction and growth through to eventual decline and elimination. The product life-cycle is an attempt to recognise distinct stages in a product's sales history. It is important to try to identify at what stage a product is in its life-cycle because sales and profitability will vary at different stages and thus adjustments to marketing tactics (i.e. different marketing mixes) will be required. Figure 11.2 depicts a typical product life-cycle.

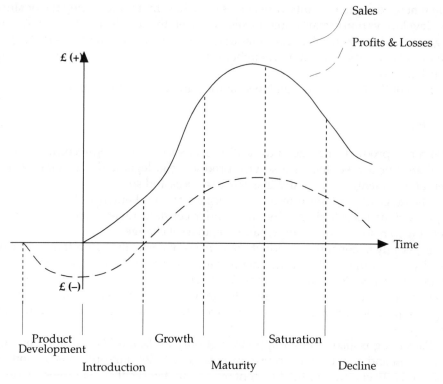

£ (+)

Sales

Profits & Losses

£ (–)

Time

Product
Development

Introduction

Growth

Maturity

Saturation

Decline

Figure 11.2: Phases of a typical product life-cycle

The key elements of the six phases shown in Figure 11.2 are as follows:

Product development

Characteristics:

- ❏ Identification of market opportunity
- ❏ Research and development of product
- ❏ Development of marketing plans and preliminary marketing mix prior to launch
- ❏ Expensive and loss making phase

Introduction

Characteristics:

- ❏ Low sales, dificult to gain acceptance
- ❏ Low output and high unit costs
- ❏ Often high prices but still likely to be loss making
- ❏ Often radical adjustments required to marketing mix
- ❏ Likely teething problems

Growth

Characteristics:

❐ Sales rise strongly
❐ Start making profits
❐ Production rises, unit costs fall
❐ Relatively static price levels
❐ Growth in sales attracts competition
❐ More expenditure on product improvement, promotion
❐ to obtain strong position

Maturity

Characteristics:

❐ Sales rise but at slower rate
❐ Branding, packaging, product identification essential
❐ to maintain position
❐ Severe competition, possible over-capacity in market
❐ Product modified and new market segments sought to prolong
❐ product life
❐ Good profits but under pressure from competition

Saturation

Characteristics:

❐ Sales level off and start to decline
❐ Profits start to fall
❐ Weaker companies leave the market

Decline

Characteristics:

❐ Rapid sales decline
❐ Obsolescence of product
❐ Profits decline and losses may occur
❐ Superior products appear
❐ Consideration given to elimination or, if possible, extension

If decline is considered irreversible then the product is likely to be eliminated although sentiment and the loyalty of the remaining customers often makes this a surprisingly difficult decision. On occasions, alterations in the marketing mix e.g. altering promotion methods, re-packaging, adding new features to the product and so on, may prolong the profit-earning life of a product.

The length of time for the whole product cycle varies enormously between products. Many leisure, fashion and 'fad' items have life cycles measured in months. Other products have long-term life cycles. For example, the Mini motor car was first produced in 1959 and is still in production.

Price

Price is a key element of the marketing mix. It is the only element of the mix which produces revenues; the others represent costs. In competitive markets pricing is constantly reviewed as it is probably the most flexible element in the market mix. Price changes, either direct or indirect through devices such as 'no-deposit', or 'interest-free credit', enable the organisation to react swiftly to changes in the market place. These may be caused by changing consumer preferences, the appearance of new competing products, price changes by competitors and many other causes. Price is important at all times but especially so at certain points. Examples include:

New product introduction.
When competitors change prices.
When entering new markets with existing products.
At times of rapid cost change.
When competitors improve/enhance products without changing their prices.
When positioning individual products in a product range.
When substantial legal or political changes occur which affects the market.
When new competitors enter the market.

Before considering pricing policies used in practice it is useful to review the theoretical economic background to pricing.

Theoretical background to pricing

Micro-economics has provided much of the theoretical background to pricing and whilst there are difficulties in applying the basic theory in practice, it serves as a useful starting point.

The theory states that firms should seek the price which maximises profit and will thereby obtain the most efficient use of the economic resources held by the firm. This price is at that level of sales where the addition to total revenue from the sale of the last unit (the marginal revenue, MR) is equal to the addition to total costs resulting from the production of that last unit (the marginal cost, MC).

This is shown in Figure 11.3 in relation to the most common type of market that of *imperfect* or *monopolistic competition* where there are differentiated products, thus enabling the firm to pursue an independent pricing policy.

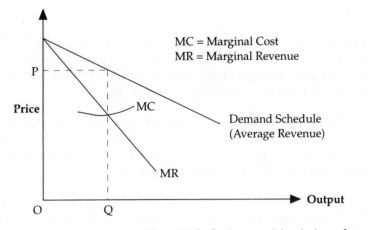

Figure 11.3: Optimum pricing in imperfect competition

At price P, output is the level of Q and profit is at a maximum. The optimal price P represents the price ceiling in any situation. The price floor could theoretically be zero if the goods are already produced, or if it is still to be produced and there is spare capacity, the price floor could be marginal cost. If there are scarce resources then the price floor will include the opportunity cost of the scarce resources.

It follows from Figure 11.3 that the firm operating in imperfect competition can determine either price or output but not both. This also applies to the monopolist. A firm operating under conditions of perfect competition, where the price is determined by the market, can only determine its output.

In an oligopolistic market (where there are few sellers) firms recognise their interdependence and are influenced by each other's decisions, particularly regarding prices. All the oligopolists will tend to charge similar prices even if there is no overt collusion and in such market structures there is likely to be a price leader who will provide the bench mark for the prices of the whole industry. Although direct price competition is rare, competitive pressure is exerted by such things as discounts, extended credit, promotional activities and other variables in the marketing mix.

Limitations to the classical theory

The classical theoretical approach, often called *marginal analysis,* has numerous limitations which makes practical application of the pure theory very difficult. The following are some of the main limitations.

a) Marginal analysis assumes perfect knowledge of all the factors involved. The practical difficulties of finding such information are great particularly relating to knowledge of the demand schedule, i.e. how much will be sold at any price. Finding the true marginal cost also poses considerable difficulties.

b) Marginal analysis assumes a single maximising objective with the firm acting with complete economic rationality. Studies of practical situations show that firms do not pursue single objectives and satisficing rather than maximising behaviour appears to be commonly encountered.

c) Marginal analysis assumes that changes in the volume of sales are solely a function of price changes where as many non-price factors, e.g. advertising and sales promotion and changes in the conditions of demand such as income changes, produce significant changes in sales volume.

d) Marginal analysis assumes rational decision guided by purely economic factors. Decision makers in practice are influenced by moral, social, political as well as economic considerations. The behavioural factors which impinge upon decision makers are reflected in such common phrases as 'a fair price' or 'a reasonable rate of return'.

Despite the limitations outlined above, economic analysis makes an important contribution to pricing theory by emphasising the interaction of demand and cost information and directs attention to the importance of marginal changes in costs and revenues.

The following paragraphs deal with three common approaches to pricing used in practice; *cost-plus pricing, demand-based pricing* and *competition-based pricing*.

Cost plus pricing

There are several methods of pricing based on costs but all involve adding a profit element to the costs of production. The methods are simple to apply and are widely used, especially in industrial goods pricing, although cost-plus pricing has a number of deficiencies.

Full cost pricing adds a mark-up, say 30%, on to the full cost of production to arrive at a selling price. The full cost of a product includes both *variable costs* i.e. those that vary with production together with an allocation of a proportion of the organisation's *fixed costs* i.e. those that do not vary with activity changes. Full cost pricing is simple to apply and is widely used, especially when the firm does not have details of demand. However, it does have several problems including:

❏ It does not take account of demand and the price elasticity of demand nor of competitor actions.

❏ It does not have the flexibility to deal with changes in the market or of demand.

❏ It ignores the inherent arbitrariness of costing procedures especially relating to fixed cost allocations in multi-product firms.

Rate of Return pricing seeks to calculate what percentage mark-up should be added on to the full cost of a product in order to obtain the firm's planned rate of return on capital employed (Return on Capital Employed – ROCE – is the ratio of profit to capital employed). The following formula can be used for rate of return pricing.

$$\text{\% mark-up on cost} = \frac{\text{Capital employed}}{\text{Total annual costs}} \times \frac{\text{Planned Rate of Return on}}{\text{Capital Employed}}$$

For example, assume that the target rate of return on capital employed is 18%, the amount of capital employed is £1.5m and the estimated annual total costs are £2..25m, what is the required mark up on cost?

$$\text{Mark up \%} = \frac{1.5}{2.25} \times 18\%$$

$$= \mathbf{12\%}$$

This method of calculating a mark-up does have the advantage of relating pricing to longer term financial objectives but it will be apparent that it is only a variant of full-cost pricing with the same potential inflexibility.

Marginal pricing, also known as *variable cost pricing* or *contribution pricing* is a cost-based pricing system using only the variable costs of a product i.e. those out of pocket costs which are incurred when an additional unit is produced. The objective with marginal pricing is to set prices so as to maximise contribution to fixed costs and profit (contribution = Sales – variable costs). For short-term decision making, marginal pricing increases pricing flexibility but needs to be used judiciously.

Marginal pricing is frequently used by hotel chains, transport services, holiday providers and electricity companies. These type of organisations suffer from wide variations in demand; compare for example the load on the railways at peak commuting times and in the middle of the day. As a consequence these firms offer much cheaper prices at off-peak times in order to even out demand if possible and to earn some contribution to fixed costs.

Another example of marginal pricing is where a firm is operating below capacity and reduces prices to fill capacity. Care is always needed with marginal pricing that the market segments are sufficiently differentiated so that full-price customers cannot demand the lower prices. Marginal pricing does consider demand so more nearly approaches the theoretical framework of classical economics. Used with care, marginal pricing can assist in short-run price setting but it must not become the long-run norm. In the long-run, prices must cover all costs plus a reasonable margin of profit.

Price discrimination example

Although their operating costs are essentially the same all the year round, Cross Channel Ferry Companies charge dramatically different fares depending on the time of the year and time of the day. The highest demand times (e.g. the Friday and Saturday at the start of the school holidays) attract the highest fares.

Differential pricing example

The product sold by Air Lines is the transport of passengers. By offering more space, better comfort, food etc. they are able to charge differential prices for First Class, Business Class and Economy even though all arrive at the same time.

Demand-based pricing

This is a system which uses the demand for a product, rather than production costs, as the starting point in setting prices. Demand is related to the customers' perception of value having regard to product quality, reputation, attractiveness and so on.

A product is not necessarily always sold at the same price in all parts of the market. For example, where the market is segmented different prices can be charged to the various segments. Where the identical product is sold to different segments at different prices this is known as *price discrimination*. Where there are slight changes in the product sold in the various segments (e.g. changes in quality or packaging or finish or brand names) and different prices charged, this is known as *differential pricing*.

Particular problems arise when setting prices for a new product which is substantially different from anything else on the market. In such circumstances there is obviously little or no information available on demand or competitive prices. Two main approaches are used to deal with this problem: *skim pricing* or *penetration pricing*.

Skim pricing sets a high price initially in order to exploit the novelty value of a product and the lack of competition. The firm earns a large profit on each unit sold which helps to recoup development costs. Skim pricing is frequently used; examples include, video recorders, colour televisions, ball-point pens etc. which were all introduced to the market at high initial prices. Although popular, Peter Drucker warns that skim pricing has a dangerous flaw in that it creates a risk-free opportunity for the competition. For example, the Americans invented and produced the world's first fax machine and charged the highest prices they could get. The Japanese entered the market and priced their machines two or three years down the learning curve and thus had the American, and World Market, virtually overnight.

Penetration pricing is where a new product is priced at a low price in order to gain market share and to make it more difficult for competitors to gain a foothold. Penetration pricing would not be suitable where the product life-cycle was short or where the market could not generate sufficient volumes for the lower prices to be profitable. Penetration pricing can be spectacularly successful, for example:

DuPont has remained the world's largest producer of synthetic fibres because, in the mid-1940s, it offered its new and patented nylon on the world market for the price at which it would have to be sold five years hence to maintain itself against competition.

This not only delayed competition, but also immediately created a market for nylon that no one at the company had even thought about (for example, in car tyres). And this soon became both bigger and more profitable than the womenswear market could ever have been.

Competition-based pricing

No organisation can ignore the price of competitive products so, to an extent, all pricing is competition-based. In the economist's theoretical perfect market there is only one price so all members of the market are price takers not price setters. In markets with only a few sellers (oligopolistic) there tends to be litle or no price competition with most firms following the market leader. Until the opening of the Channel tunnel this has tended to be the position for the few Ferry Operators although the new competition may force some form of price war where the larger companies try to gain market share at the expense of smaller firms.

A prime example of competition-based pricing is that of the price of petrol from the major oil companies (Esso, B.P, Shell, Gulf and so on). The companies charge similar prices for their products and price changes by one of the companies brings an immediate response by all the others.

Having now considered the first two elements in the marketing mix; Product and Price, we now turn to the third factor, that of Place.

Place

Place is the element in the marketing mix that deals with *distribution* which is moving the product or service to the final consumer.
There are two aspects of distribution. Firstly the *channels of distribution* and secondly the means of *physical distribution*. The channels of distribution are dealt with first.

Channels of distribution

These channels are the links or institutions in the chain between the producer and eventual customer. Some channels are short and direct; for example when the producer of a service such as a lawyer or a hairdresser deals directly with customers. Most channels however are indirect, especially in consumer markets. Typically there are one or more intermediaries, such as wholesalers and retailers, between the producer and customer. Competitive pressures and more discerning customers mean that the channels of distribution are changing and in general, becoming shorter. An example is the growth in direct mail shopping thus cutting out the traditional retailer.

Figure 11.4 shows some of the commonly encountered channels.

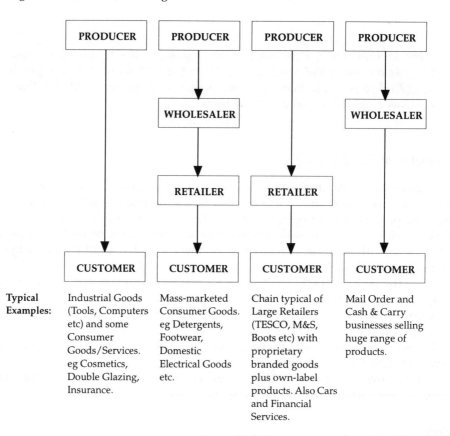

Figure 11.4: Some common channels of distribution

In addition to the distribution channels shown in Figure 11.4 various others exist to suit particular market requirements. A common variant in the import/export business is to introduce an *agent* into the chain who acts on behalf of producers to ease the flow of goods, deal with documentation and so on.

Frequently encountered links in distribution channels are wholesalers and retailers. Summaries of their key functions follow.

Main functions of wholesalers:

❑ To break bulk consignments down into quantities suitable for individual retailers.

❑ Provision of storage facilities which helps to even out flows of goods.

❑ Often provide credit facilities for retailers and may provide advice and assistance with marketing.

❑ Reduces overall distribution costs.

Main functions of retailers:

☐ Convenient service for customers with a variety of goods displayed for examination and choice.

☐ Information, technical back-up and advice available to customers.

☐ After-sales service and delivery often available.

☐ Often provide credit facilities

Dramatic changes have taken place in retailing over the past decade or so. These include; the reduction in the number of small shops and the corresponding growth of out of town shopping on 'retail parks', the use of information technology in stock control, credit cards, check-outs etc, the use of cars for shopping, week-end leisure shopping, the growth of 'high tech' shopping malls, the growing importance of the major multiples (Sainsburys, Tesco, Asda, Boots, British Home Stores and others). There is no doubt that many more changes will occur in the years ahead. Examples include; the entry into the UK market of Continental and US discount stores (Costco, Netto, Aldi etc.), the use of videos for home shopping, the impact of more liberal trading laws, especially relating to Sunday shopping.

Some producers try to ensure that as many retailers as possible stock their products. Examples include; confectionery, cigarettes, food and so on. Others pursue a more selective strategy and limit their outlets to one in each area or only to outlets considered suitable for their product. A particular example of the latter policy is that relating to high quality fragrances.

In 1993 the Office of Fair Trading asked the Monopolies and Merger Commission (MMC) to investigate complaints by Superdrug and Tescos that they were being refused supplies by leading fragrance houses (Chanel, Calvin Klein, Yves St Laurent and others) because they were not suitable outlets and sold the fragrances at a discount.

However, the MMC report said; 'Fine fragrances are marketed as luxury products and the MMC accept that the suppliers need to be able to control their distribution in order to protect their brand images which customers evidently value.' Manufacturers of luxury perfumes argued that they need to choose retail outlets where the ambience and layout as well as service and advice provided fits with the image of the product being sold. This argument was accepted by the MMC.

Selection of the channels of distribution

Numerous factors need to be considered in the choice of which channel or channels best suits a particular product. In general consumer products tend to have longer channels than industrial products or complex consumer items such as personal computers. The shorter and more direct the channel the more the producer must become involved with the marketing effort but the producer thereby obtains more control over such matters as the provision of advice, quality of service etc.

Figure 11.5 shows the tendencies and features of product which influence whether there are likely to be shorter or longer channels.

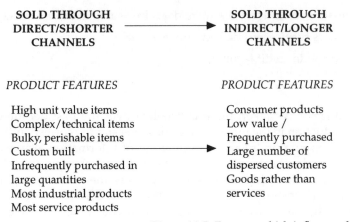

Figure 11.5: Features which influence channel length

Figure 11.5 only shows tendencies and naturally there are exceptions. For example whilst most cosmetics are sold through longer, indirect channels, Avon Cosmetics sell direct to the public via a large number of part-time agents. Conversely, whilst most services have shorter direct channels, package holidays are sold through retail outlets known as Travel Agents.

The choice of channels, and other elements of the marketing mix such as price, advertising and so on is influenced by the particular part or *segment* of the market the producer is concentrating upon. The following paragraph considers the main features of market segmentation.

Market segmentation

Virtually all markets consist of different parts, or segments, rather than a single, homogeneous whole. Each segment is characterised by different customer attributes and attitudes and consequently differences in buyer behaviour. Where the differences between the market segments is substantial, and the differences can be clearly identified, then the producer can adjust their marketing mix to suit the segment(s) targeted. Some target only one segment (for example, Sports Goods shops target the young and active) whilst others try to attract a wider range of customers (for example, Book Shops try to attract people of all ages and tastes by offering a range of titles).

The key variables used in market segmentation relate to Personal Characteristics, Geographic, and Purchasing Behaviour as shown in Figure 11.6.

Figure 11.6: Key variables in market segmentation

Although all the variables shown in Figure 11.6 contribute to market segmentation possibly the most influential relate to personal characteristics especially such things as age, sex, income and social class. Contrast for example the differences in the type of goods advertised in *The Times* from those in the *Daily Mirror*. Advertisers realise these papers reach different segments of the market and advertise accordingly. A useful summary of social grade widely used in all aspects of marketing is shown in Figure 11.7.

Social grade	Social status	Occupation of head of household
A	Upper middle class	Higher managerial, administrative or professional
B	Middle class	Intermediate managerial, administrative or professional
C1	Lower middle class	Supervisory, clerical or junior managerial etc
C2	Skilled working class	Skilled manual workers
D	Working class	Semi-skilled or unskilled manual workers
E	Subsistence levels	Pensioners or widows on basic pension; casual and lowest paid workers

Figure 11.7: Social class gradings

Physical distribution

This is the aspect of distribution which deals with moving goods from producer to eventual customer. It is a series of activities concerned with stocking, order-processing, inventory control, packaging and transport. In earlier times this aspect of operations was neglected. However it has received much more attention in recent years as it has been realised that as much as 30% of all costs can be taken up by the distribution process for a high-volume, low value product. The study and control of this aspect of marketing has come to be called *marketing logistics* or *physical distribution management (PDM)*.

Increasingly it has been realised that one part of the system affects all others and that a total or systems viewpoint must be taken to ensure the lowest overall costs consistent with meeting the customers requirements for service, availability and so on. There are numerous elements to be considered in physical distribution which can be grouped into five areas shown in Figure 11.8.

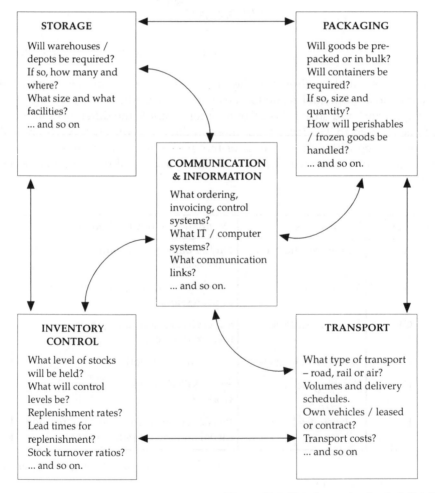

Figure 11.8: Key factors in physical distribution

Figure 11.8 attempts to show the integration required between all the elements and emphasises that one element cannot be altered without altering the others. For example, a decision to reduce stock levels to save money may cause higher costs through more frequent replenishments, more deliveries of smaller quantities, more stock-outs leading to customer dissatisfaction and so on.

We now turn to the final element in the marketing mix, that of Promotion.

Promotion

Promotion is that element of the marketing mix which draws the attention of the market to the product and emphasises its benefits, special features and advantages over the competition. Promotion is the most obvious element of the marketing mix and seeks to inform, influence and persuade customers to buy. Promotional activities can be sub-divided into five; advertising, sales promotion, personal selling, publicity, and packaging. The overall objective of promotional activities is to alter customer attitudes and behaviour from a position of Product Unawareness, through Awareness, Interest, Desire, to Adoption and Purchase.

Different promotional activities with varying emphases take place according to the product, the position on the product life-cycle and the target market. There would, for example, be a different emphasis in the Advertising for a radically new product just introduced on to the market compared with a long-established product with many competitors. The type of market also greatly influences the promotional mix. A machine tool manufacturer operating in industrial markets will spend much more on personal selling than advertising whereas the reverse would be true for a high-volume consumer product such as shampoo.

The main five promotional activities are dealt with in the following paragraphs.

Advertising

Advertising is a non-personal process directed at large numbers of potential consumers. It communicates information by one, or a combination, of the following: the spoken or written word or visual material. Advertising seeks to inform, persuade and to increase sales volume. The advertiser pays for planning, designing and inserting or displaying the advertisement in the selected medium. Naturally, advertising costs form part of total costs which must eventually be recouped from the consumer.

The main media for advertising are:

- Newspapers, magazines and journals
- Commercial television
- Direct mail
- Commercial radio
- Outdoor advertising (hoardings, buses, bill-boards)

The choice of which medium to choose is a complex decision dependent on numerous factors including

Coverage or reach i.e. what proportion of target market is covered
Cost of the medium
Selectivity
Type of product
Impact and permanence of medium

Each of the various media have advantages and disadvantages. What suits one product does not suit another. A specialist industrial product is likely to be advertised in the appropriate trade journal to ensure that it is seen by the target market. On the other hand a general consumer product (e.g. confectionery, food, detergents etc.) which does not need detailed explanations and which is aimed widely, is likely to be advertised on Television.

The main features of the various advertising media are summarised below:

Media type	Plus features	Possible drawbacks
TELEVISION	Extensive coverage Attractive, visual impact Products can be seen being used and demonstrated	Only limited information Short life High cost (but cost:1000 viewers is low) No referral possible
RADIO	Relatively low cost Regionally selective	Limited coverage Sound only No referral possible
DIRECT MAIL	Flexible Can convey detailed/voluminous information Highly selectivity possible e.g. by occupation, region, hobbies etc Can be personalised	High cost Consumer resistance to 'junk mail'
NEWSPAPERS	Good coverage at relatively low cost Some selectivity possible Flexible	Low impact (no sound/movement) Short life
MAGAZINES/JOURNALS	High selectivity Reasonable life Attractive, visual impact	Relatively inflexible No sound/movement High cost:1000 readers
OUTDOOR ADVERTISING	Long life Low cost Good coverage Colour/movement possible	Only limited information May distract Possible environmental objections Some impact lost through competing information, noise etc.

The effectiveness of advertising is difficult to assess. Its impact on sales as a whole is difficult to separate out from all the other internal and external factors which may influence sales. It is however often possible to judge the effects of specific campaigns by conducting sample interviews to assess whether people were aware of the campaign, whether they remember the name/features of the product and whether they bought the product.

Sales promotion

Sales promotion is the term given to the range of activities which aid product/brand recognition, draw attention to the product, increase usage, assist the dealer to sell the product and generally try to increase goodwill and repeat business. It includes inducements and incentives such as free samples, temporary price reductions, provision of display material, special pack offers and so on.

Sales promotion is directed both at *consumers* and the *trade* and is used most frequently for consumer products. Examples of typical sales promotion activities are shown below:

Directed at Consumers	Directed at the Trade
Coupon offers	Provision of display material
Special pack offers	Contests, with prizes, for Sales Staff
Free samples	Discounts
Point-of-sale demonstrations	Advertising schemes
Temporary price reductions	Exhibitions and functions
Competitions	
Trading stamps and tokens	
Holiday/travel/charity offers	

Those activities directed at customers seek to draw attention to the product, encourage sales, especially of slow-moving or out of season items and generally create greater customer awareness and acceptance. On the other hand those acivities directed at the trade seek to develop goodwill and try to get the dealer or retailer to push the product perhaps by giving it more or better shelf space or by encouraging the sales staff to suggest the product to customers.

Personal selling

Personal Selling is the most expensive part of the promotion mix. Although many other tasks are involved the over-riding objective of personal selling is to clinch the deal and make the sale. It is especially important in industrial markets and for more complex consumer products such as personal computers, life insurance, investment plans and so on. Where a firm follows vigorous selling policy, based on personal selling, it is following a push strategy. On the contrary where firms rely more heavily on advertising they are said to be following a pull strategy.

Some firms have a relatively restricted view of the role of their sales representatives considering sales generation and clinching sales as their prime tasks. Others take a broader, marketing view which takes account of the needs of the buyer, information flows, customer support as well as sales generation. In these situations the tasks of the sales representatives could include:

- Gathering market information including customer reactions, competitors' activities
- Advising customers on technical queries, performance, delivery, operating details
- Seeking out new prospects/customers/markets
- Building and retaining goodwill
- Product demonstrations and displays
- Advice on stock levels, merchandising etc.
- Dealing with delivery and progressing existing orders
- Closing new sales

To carry out these tasks the sales representative needs to be well motivated, well trained and suplied with a range of pertinent information including:

- Details of existing and proposed products
- The firm's structure, policies, organisation etc.
- Existing and potential customers
- Promotional material - brochures, leaflets, catalogues
- Sales territories and targets
- Details of competitors, rival products, developments
- Where appropriate relevant legislation affecting usage, disposal, environmental factors

Publicity

Publicity is information about the product or the organisation which is given in the media without charge. Good publicity is actively sought after by firms not merely because it is free but, being one stage removed from the firm, it is seen as more independent and thus more reliable and trustworthy than conventional advertising. In large firms publicity is the responsibility of the Public Relations (PR) department. It is the task of the PR department to create and maintain a positive corporate image and one of the ways this is done is to try to get as much good publicity as possible.

Ways this may be achieved include:

- ❑ Press releases about noteworthy events, personalities, achievements, products etc.
- ❑ Sponsorship of Arts and Sporting Events e.g. Concerts, Exhibitions, Tennis, Golf, Snooker etc.
- ❑ Contributions to welfare and charitable causes
- ❑ Involvement in and financial backing for local and national events
- ❑ Funding of academic posts or for research institutes

thus it will be seen that, whilst publicity is nominally free, there are often considerable costs in running publicity campaigns. Nevertheless this is considered worthwhile by most large organisations.

Packaging

The packaging of a product is a vital part of product management especially in fast moving consumer products. Apart from the basic functions of containing and protecting the product packaging seeks to:

- ❑ identify and make the product more distinctive.

- ❑ help sales promotion by making the product instantly recognisable. Consumers can instantly recognise well advertised, distinctively packaged products e.g. Terry's Chocolate Orange, red Coca-Cola cans etc.

- ❑ add to consumer convenience, e.g. easily opened/resealable packages, ring-pull cans of drinks etc.

- ❑ place the product in the required market niche e.g. the luxurious and expensive packaging used for expensive toiletries.

- ❑ re-vitalise interest in a declining or long-established product. Periodically products ranging from books to whisky are re-packaged to create more interest.

- ❑ associate the product with the manufacturer and/or other products in the range e.g. the standardised colours and logo used in Tesco's and Sainsbury's own label products.

In general, attractively packaged products create an impact with consumers and compete for attention on the shelf. Packaging is also used to promote positive images of the manufacturer. An example is the message that the package is made from recycled materials. Environmentally conscious consumers are likely to look on such products more favourably.

On occasions developments in packaging enable a new market to be developed that previously was not possible. For example:

In 1989, after much experimentation, packaging engineers at Guinness developed a new can which enabled them to market 'draught Guinness' in a can. The development responsible was a small plastic cylinder with a hole in the top secured to the bottom of the can. When the can is filled pressure forces liquid into the plastic cylinder. On opening the can this has the effect of creating a rich, creamy head in the glass, equivalent to the head on draught beer. Similar processes have now been developed by other brewers and a new market segment has been created.

Marketing research

Marketing research is the process of acquiring and analysing information to assist decision making in marketing. Marketing research is growing in importance for various reasons including:

- ❏   the growth of competition
- ❏   rapidly changing market conditions
- ❏   the move from local to national and international markets
- ❏   the increasing pace of technological change
- ❏   shorter product life cycles associated with high development costs
- ❏   the trend towards more non-price factors being used to compete.

Marketing research seeks to produce information concerning existing and potential markets and about current and proposed marketing methods. The general objective is to improve marketing decision making, reduce risks and increase the probability of success.

There are two types of data used to prepare marketing research information; *primary* and *secondary*. The characteristics, sources, methods of   collection are summarised below:

Primary Data (or Field Research Data):

- ❏   Data gathered directly from customers, dealers, general public etc.
- ❏   Methods used include; surveys using questionnaires and/or interviews, observation, discussion groups, consumer panels etc.

- ❑ Can be specific to problem being investigated
- ❑ Expensive to gather

Secondary Data (or Desk Data):

- ❑ Data gathered from existing sources both external and internal
- ❑ Typical sources: *Internal* - sales reports, accounts, stock records etc. *External* - government publications, trade publications, research and trade associations
- ❑ Unlikely to be specific, may be dated
- ❑ Relatively cheap to gather

Marketing research is such a specialised process, especially relating to the gathering of primary data, that few organisations carry out the work themselves. Most use one of the specialist agencies who have the necessary expertise and trained field staff. The agencies include; AC Nielsen, Gallup, MORI and others.

Key point summary

- ❑ Marketing is the process responsible for identifying, anticipating and satisfying customer requirements.

- ❑ The marketing mix is the set of controllable variables used to influence the market. It comprises; Product, Price, Place, Promotion.

- ❑ The full product life-cycle includes: Development, Introduction, Growth, Maturity, Saturation, Decline.

- ❑ Price is always important but especially so at certain times e.g. on introduction, when new competitors or products enter markets etc.

- ❑ Economic theory states that the key factors in pricing are marginal revenue and marginal cost.

- ❑ Cost-plus and rate of return pricing systems are widely used in practice.

- ❑ Pricing must take account of competitors' prices and demand.

- ❑ Channels of Distribution are the links or institutions in the chain between producer and consumer. Common examples include; wholesalers, retailers, agents.

- ❑ The study of physical distribution is called marketing logistics or physical distribution management.

❑ Promotional activities include; advertising, sales promotion, personal selling, publicity and packaging.

❑ The media for advertising include; newspapers, magazines, television, radio, direct mail.

❑ Sales promotion can be directed at the consumer e.g. free samples, coupon offers etc. or to the trade e.g. discounts, contests.

❑ Personal selling, although expensive, is vital in many types of market.

❑ Publicity is free of charge coverage given in the media.

❑ Packaging is to protect, attract, distinguish, to promote the product etc.

❑ Marketing research is the process of acquiring and analysing information to assist marketing decision-making.

❑ Marketing research obtains data from direct or primary, and indirect or secondary, sources.

Self review questions

1. *What is marketing?*
2. *What is the marketing mix?*
3. *What is an organisation's product mix?*
4. *What are the stages in a product's life cycle?*
5. *What is the micro-economic background to pricing?*
6. *What is cost plus pricing?*
7. *What is price discrimination?*
8. *What is penetration pricing?*
9. *What are channels of distribution?*
10. *What is market segmentation?*
11. *What is promotion?*
12. *Why does sales promotional activities differ between consumers and the trade?*
13. *What is Marketing Research?*
14. *Distinguish between primary and secondary data.*

12 *Management functions: personnel*

Objectives

After you have studied this chapter you will:

☐ *Be able to define Personnel Management.*

☐ *Understand the activities connected with Manpower Planning.*

☐ *Know what is meant by Personnel Policies.*

☐ *Be able to distinguish between Recruitment and Selection.*

☐ *Understand the main Recruitment methods and sources.*

☐ *Know the main steps in Selection.*

☐ *Be able to describe Performance Appraisal.*

☐ *Know the difference between Training and Development and the main methods used.*

☐ *Be able to describe the main duties imposed by the Health and Safety at Work Act.*

☐ *Know the main features of Stress Management and Counselling.*

☐ *Understand the principles underlying Remuneration Systems.*

☐ *Know what is meant by Job Evaluation and its purpose.*

☐ *Be able to describe the main features of Contracts of Employment.*

☐ *Understand the role and functions of Trade Unions.*

☐ *Know what is meant by Worker Participation.*

☐ *Understand Disciplinary and Grievance predecures.*

☐ *Be able to describe key developments affecting the Personnel Function.*

What is personnel management?

The Institute of Personnel Management (IPM) states that personnel management's aim is to ensure the optimum use of human resources to the mutual benefit of the organisation, the person and the community at large. A working definition of Personnel Management is:

PM is a specialist function of management dealing with all aspects of the human resources of the organisation.

It includes policy development, advising line managers on personnel matters and specific responsibilities for welfare and for recruiting, selecting, appraising, and training and developing people to carry out jobs in the organisation.

Figure 12.1 provides an overview of the various facets of Personnel Management.

Figure 12.1: An overview of personnel management

In small organisations many of the tasks and functions shown in Figure 12..1 are carried out by line managers as part of their normal duties. However, as organisations grow, there is invariably a specialist Personnel Department which liaises with line managers, give advice on personnel matters and carries out the tasks shown in the diagram. In many larger organisations the Head of Personnel is typically a Director with equal status to Directors of the other key functions of the organisation.

Subsequent paragraphs develop the elements of Personnel Management shown in Figure 12.1.

Personnel strategies

The development of personnel strategies is a high level task. The strategies developed help toward the fulfilment of the organisation's Corporate Plan and form a framework to all tactical level personnel activities including; recruitment, welfare, development and so on. Although strategic guidance on personnel matters can cover any aspect of personnel, two core items normally found are *manpower planning* and *personnel policy development*.

Manpower planning (MP)

Manpower planning seeks to make sure that the organisation will have sufficient staff of the right calibre and expertis e to achieve the organisation's corporate objectives. In essence MP consists of four inter-related activities.

Developing a forecast of future manpower requirements to meet corporate objectives.

Assessing existing manpower numbers, skills, potentials etc.

Analysing external sources, present and future.

Developing and implementing manpower plans to meet perceived shortfalls.

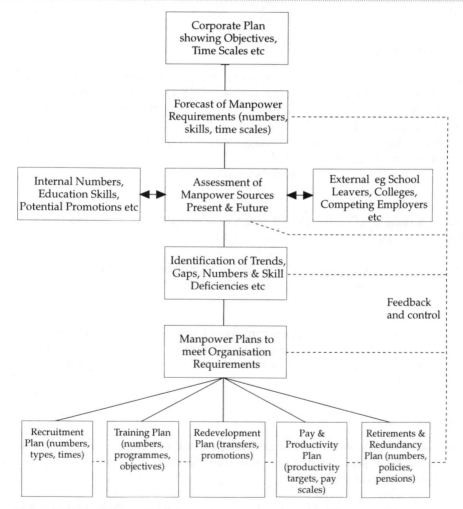

Plans to include Budgets & Targets and Allocation of Responsibilities for Implementation

Figure 12.2: The manpower planning process

MP is not merely concerned with numbers. It deals also with skills development, training and education programmes, management development and persuading people to accept and adapt to changes in methods of working technology, organisation structures, and new production and administrative systems.

The overall MP process is shown in more detail in Figure 12.2

Manpower planning affects all managers not just personnel specialists so the whole organisation must assist with the development of the plan and be concerned with its implementation. The manpower plan, like all other plans, must be reviewed frequently. Conditions change rapidly and appropriate adjustments must be made to recruitment, training, development, as the case may be, to cope with the new conditions expected. Typically the monthly budget statement provides the initial level of review with manpower numbers, pay and deployment being compared with the plan. More searching reviews would be carried out at quarterly, six-monthly and yearly intervals.

Personnel policies

It will be recalled from previous chapters that *policies* are behavioural guidelines which influence the activities of the organisation. In a similar way, personnel policies are behavioural guidelines which influence the way the organisation deals with employees and employee related activities. Personnel policies are long-term and influence all aspects of personnel management including the way that the manpower plan is developed and implemented.

Typical examples of personnel policies are

The organisation will advertise all vacancies internally before any external advertising takes place.

The organisation will conform to all relevant Employment and Health and Safety Legislation and will endeavour to follow the spirit of such legislation.

Enlightened employers publish personnel policies so that their employees, customers and the general public are aware of their attitudes and values. As an example Wolverhampton Council have published the following policies applicable to their role as an employer.

The Council will

☐ accept the challenge of changes in the organisation of work in local government in a positive manner and seek to maximise the benefits for its customers and staff.

☐ aim to provide quality jobs based upon proving quality services and a commitment to customer care.

- develop the skills of its workforce through a commitment to National Vocational Qualifications, the Management Development Programme and professional development and training.

- consult with its workforce and recognised trade unions on major changes in the way the Council's work is organised.

- be committed to wages and salaries which take account of national agreements, market conditions and organisational needs.

- be committed to provide a safe and healthy environment for its workforce and members of the public.

The Council's workforce will need to be increasingly adaptable in the turbulent 90s, meeting the challenge of the new contracting culture with energy and vision. A skilled and stable workforce is a precondition for effective service to the community.

Having briefly considered the key strategic aspects of personnel we now consider the various operational tasks of personnel management as shown in Figure 12.1, commencing with Recruitment and Selection.

Recruitment and selection

Recruitment is the process of attracting a number of suitable applicants. It is positive action concerned with generating interest, internally or externally, in the vacancy or vacancies. *Selection* means choosing the best candidate for the vacancy.

Prior to recruitment and selection there must be clarification of the *job concerned* and of the *personal characteristics* thought necessary to perform the job. In most organisations the details of the job would be contained in a *job description* which would typically contain the following items.

Typical contents of a job description:
- Title of job
- Salary/grade of job
- Purpose of job
- Principal tasks and responsibilities of job
- Organisational relationships (i.e. to whom responsible and for whom responsible)
- Number of subordinates (if any)

- ☐ Limits of responsibility
- ☐ Special equipment, facilities, resources available
- ☐ Performance targets and methods of performance assessment
- ☐ Location of job
- ☐ Special conditions relating to job e.g. hazardous working conditions, shift work, on-call requirements etc.

Job descriptions are clearly necessary for recruitment and selection but they are also useful after appointment. They provide a clear framework for the job holder and the manager and help to form a fair basis for payment and merit awards and to identify where training is required. However job descriptions become rapidly out of date and are less suitable in volatile conditions. They may also encourage a work-to-rule attitude whereby the employee is reluctant to undertake any task not specifically mentioned in the job description.

As well as a description of the job it is usual to prepare a *personnel* or *candidate specification*. This is a summary of the skills, knowledge and personal characteristics thought necessary to perform the job satisfactorily. Although many organisations develop their own schemes others use either Rodger's Seven Point Plan or Munro's Five Point Pattern of Personality. The two schemes are shown below.

Rodger's seven point plan

1. **physical attributes**
   (appearance, speech, health etc)
2. **attainments**
   (qualifications, education, experience)

3. **general intelligence**

4. **special aptitudes**
   (dexterity, speed, numeracy etc)

5. **personal interests**
   (social, artistic, sport etc)

6. **disposition or manner**
   (helpful, friendly, dependability)

7. **background circumstances**
   (family, domestic)

Munro-Fraser's five point pattern

1. **impact on others**
   (bearing, speech, appearance etc.)
2. **acquired knowledge or qualifications**
   (qualifications, education, experience)

3. **innate ability**
   (aptitude, comprehension, learning ability)

4. **motivation**
   (determination, drive, consistency)

5. **adjustment**
   (attitude to stress, emotional stability, sociability)

Either based on the organisation's own scheme or one of the Seven or Five Point systems a candidate specification would be drawn up for use in recruitment and selection. It is customary to distinguish between essential and desirable items. For example if a candidate specification was being developed for the person to fill the position of Personnel Manager in an engineering company it may be specified as *essential* that the person should be a Member of the Institute of Personnel Management and *desirable* (but not essential) that they should have an engineering background.

Recruitment sources

Depending on the type of vacancy appropriate sources of suitable candidates will be chosen. Sources include

- Advertisements in newspapers, magazines, specialist journals.
- Internal advertising using in-house magazines, noticeboards, meetings
- Recruitment agencies
- Job centres
- Career and job fairs
- Schools, colleges and universities
- Local radio and television
- Unsolicited letters and callers

Although personal experience suggests that many job advertisements are far from perfect the organisation should attempt to prepare comprehensive and informative advertisements which, ideally, should contain the following information.

Job advertisements should:
- Give brief details of the job and of the organisation.
- Outline essential and desirable personal requirements.
- Give the important conditions of employment and salary/grade.
- Give precise details how to apply and to whom.

The selection process

If done properly the recruitment process should attract a number of possible candidates. It is now necessary to select the one or ones thought most suitable for the job or jobs. Selection may involve one or more of the following:

- ❑ Assessment of written material including Application Forms, Curriculum Vitae (CV's), References, Testimonials, Certificates etc.
- ❑ Testing including Proficiency and Aptitude tests, Intelligence and Psychometric tests.
- ❑ Task performance including auditions, presentations, trade tests.
- ❑ Interviews.

Of these, the selection interview is by far the most common technique employed, typically based on a selection of applicants chosen from their Application Forms or CV's.

The aims of the interview are to find the best person for the job and to ensure that all candidates are treated fairly and understand what the job entails, their prospects, and pay and conditions. Interviewing is not easy and it is vital that the interviewer is thoroughly prepared and is able to encourage the interviewee to talk, control the interview and be able to answer any questions that the interviewee may have.

Although widely practised, interviews have several limitations as follows:

- ❑ They do not provide accurate predictions of how a person will perform in the job.
- ❑ Opinions of interviewers vary - they cannot all be right.
- ❑ Stereotyping candidates on some characteristic e.g. dress, hair, accent.
- ❑ Bias for or against candidates.
- ❑ Use of leading questions.
- ❑ Genuine difficulty of assessing abstract qualities such as; motivation, integrity.

When someone has been offered the job and accepts it they are normally provided with a contract of employment. These contain the terms and conditions of employment and specify in some detail items such as:

- ❑ Hours of work and holiday entitlement
- ❑ Salary
- ❑ Title of job
- ❑ Regulations regarding sickness
- ❑ Pension: entitlements and contributions
- ❑ Period of notice and redundancy arrangements
- ❑ Grievance and disciplinary procedures

Having briefly considered recruitment and selection procedures we now consider *employee development*.

Employee development

This is a wide area of personnel managment. In general terms employee development seeks to maintain and enhance the skill and aptitudes of all levels of emp;loyees and to develop their potential for promotion and/or more exacting jobs. This is done to increase the efficiency and flexibility of the organisation and to improve the motivation of employees.

Employee development is dealt with under three headings:

☐ Performance appraisal and needs identification

☐ Training

☐ Management development

Performance appraisal and needs identification

Appraisal of a person's performance in carrying out a job is part of the day-to-day responsibilities of the person's supervisor. This informal appraisal is done to ensure that jobs are carried out efficiently and as a help in identifying a particular training need for an individual. A training need is a shortfall between the skill, knowledge etc. required to carry out a job satisfactorily and the level of skill and knowledge currently possessed by the employee. A training need can also arise when it is known that the job will change in the future and it is necessary to upgrade the skills of the current staff. For example, if a task is at present dealt with by manual methods and is to be computerised there is a need to train the staff in keyboard skills and general computer knowledge so that they can deal with the new system in an efficient manner.

Performance appraisal is also carried out in a more formal manner, usually at annual intervals. Performance appraisal is the process of:

☐ examining the past performance of an employee to assess strengths and weaknesses and, where appropriate, to compare performance against targets.

☐ assessing the potential of an employee to carry out more demanding work and for promotion.

☐ considering how performance may be improved by training, wider experience, counselling etc.

From this process information is gathered about employees, their current performance, potential, and training needs. The appraisal frequently forms the basis of pay adjustments and merit awards. Most appraisals are conducted, in the first instance, by the persons immediate supervisor and usually include a private interview. This interview must be conducted fairly and there should be a frank exchange which may include discussion of a person's weaknesses and criticisms of their work. In rare cases the appraisal interview may be the occasion for a Formal Warning to be given.

Appraisal must be constructive and defensive attitudes, from both subordinate and supervisor, should be avoided as far as possible. Formal appraisal is often useful for assessing current performance and identifying particular training needs. However there are always difficulties in making judgements about how well a person might deal with a more senior and demanding job which requires different abilities. This particular difficulty may lead to what is known as the Peter principle. This states that by using past performance as a guide to promotion the organisation is likely to promote managers to their level of incompetence.

The appraisal of staff has many problems and difficulties and consequently may not be as efficient at evaluating staff as organisations like to think.

A paper from University College Swansea to the British Psychological Society Occupational Conference in 1994 stated that when evaluating subordinates managers favour those who are good-looking, who belong to the same ethnic group and who share their values. The research report stated that 'Managers allow personal likes and dislikes to influence their ratings - and freely admit this'. Managers used the evaluation process to 'further their own agenda, to polish their own image, to get rid of rivals and people they do not like, and to teach trouble-makers a lesson'.

Training

Although the terms are often used together *training* can be distinguished from *development* as follows

Training is a job-oriented process to provide employees with the skills and knowledge required to carry out their duties efficiently and effectively.

Development takes a broader view of knowledge and skills and is more concerned with employee potential than with the acquisition of immediately useful skills.

Training can take many forms; it may be done formally or informally, it may be on-the-job or off-the-job.

Figure 12.3 provides an outline of various training methods and their main positive and negative characteristics.

	On-the-job	Positive characteristics	Negative characteristics
In-house training	Coaching and instruction	Job specific develops immediate skills and working relations	Unstructured, bad habits may be passed on, noise and pressure problems
	Job rotation	Experience gained of various jobs, gains more insight	May be unsettling, may not suit new job
	Secondment	Experience of inter-dept. relationships and 'politics'	May be time-wasting and unproductive
	Delegation	Chance to exercise authority and discretion	May be stressful and unsettling
	Projects	Develop in-depth skills and knowledge	Difficulties in finding suitable projects and experienced leaders/mentors
	Off-the-job		
	Lectures/talks/ demonstrations	Structured, useful for factual material and basic skills	Little opportunity for participation
	Role playing exercises	Develop abilities to work with others	Need careful organisation. Feedback must be specific to be useful
	Programmed learning	Trainee can work at own pace and correct answers reinforce learning	Only really useful for basic skills and knowledge
	Group learning (T groups) and group discussions	Help to understand own behaviour, develop social skills, generate ideas	Leadership difficulties and often stressful
External training	Day release/evening and other short courses at colleges/universities	Often lead to qualifications, develop wider/deeper knowledge and skills, other viewpoints encountered	Subject matter may not directly relate to person's job. Attendance may be considered an imposition
	Longer courses at colleges/universities	Comprehensive coverage of knowledge and theory. Worthwhile qualifications gained	May be considered too theoretical and irrelevant. Lengthy
	Courses run by consultants, professional institutes etc	Professional teaching and approach. May fill gaps that organisation cannot deal with. Usually up-to-date.	Expensive. May not be specific enough
	Conferences	Often deal with up-to-the-minute topics. Opportunity to make contacts	Expensive. Possible lack of relevance

Figure 12.3: Training methods and characteristics

It will be apparent from Figure 12.3 that some of the methods shown bridge the gap between training and development. Training is vital for the organisation and, for most organisations, represents a major cost. As such it should be carried out in a systematic manner with a close control of results achieved.

Typical of the steps necessary to ensure effectiveness in training are the following.

❑ Identify training needs and gaps for individual.

❑ Establish specific learning targets in terms of skills, knowledge and performance standards in conjunction with the trainee.

❑ Take into account the strengths, limitations, experience and aptitudes of the individual.

❑ Develop a systematic learning and development programme to suit the individual.

❑ Monitor progress in collaboration with the trainee in order to adjust the programme, if necessary and to identify further needs which may emerge.

There is little doubt that targeted training which is properly carried out pays for itself many times over in terms of increased efficiency, fewer errors and increased profits.

British Telecom, the country's biggest private-sector employer, saved about £227m over two years as a result of a £7m outlay on training its junior managers, the company's own psychologists have estimated. The training programme eliminated mistakes and reduced time-wasting.

The psychologists studied mistakes by a sample of 159 junior managers before training and then scrutinised their performance afterwards. The errors, which cost £1.8m, included lost orders and the costs of remedial action. They estimate that the saving, extrapolated for all 19,000 junior managers, amounted to £227m.

Management development (MD)

MD is an extension of training and has become an important field in its own right. It is less concerned with teaching people skills required for their immediate job but more in developing individuals to be able to deal with future challenges. In Drucker's words:

'Management development should focus on tomorrow's requirements rather than those of today.'

MD in its widest sense may be seen as part of organisational renewal and succession planning. Constable and McCormick in a report for the British Institute of Management and the Confederation of British Industries entitled 'The Making of British Managers' made a number of recommendations regarding MD including:

Employees should seek to create personal development programmes for all their managers.

MD should be a major area of responsibility for Chief Executives and should be a regular item for boardroom discussions and part of long-term corporate plans.

As organisations vary in their structures and philosophies so do MD programmes. Some are informal others are highly structured. Some concentrate solely on the individual, others pay more attention to group and team development. Most MD programmes seek to enhance the knowlede and capabilities of managers in four areas:

Skills. what decision-making, problem solving, social and other skills a manager must possess.

Knowledge. what details of the job, systems, procedures and the organisation itself that the manager must know.

Personal attitudes. what is required in coping with pressure and stress, attitudes to staff, customers and the general public.

Managerial style. effects of leadership, means of motivation etc. on staff.

Although many managers do study externally for management degrees (e.g. MBAs) and for professional qualifications, if they do not already possess them, most MD programmes concentrate on in-house, experiential methods.
    Typical of the methods used are:

❏ Supported, planned experience with discovery learning.

❏ Secondments and Job Rotation.

❏ Exercising judgement/initiative and accepting real responsibilities by monitored delegation.

❏ Tackling specific tasks and projects either as an individual or member of a team.

Management development programmes and the progress of individuals are reviewed during the Appraisal process. Programmes are adjusted, speeded up or slowed down as required, after discussions with the manager concerned.

Having briefly considered the various facets of Employee Development we now turn to another facet of Personnel Management, that of *Welfare*.

Welfare

In one sense all Personnel Management is directed at the welfare of employees. However in the context of this book Welfare is taken as that part of Personnel Management which deals with

☐ Health and Safety

☐ Counselling and Stress Management

☐ Social Activities

Health and safety

There is a variety of legislation dealing with the health and safety of employees. This includes; the Common Law, the Agricultural Act 1956, The Factories Act 1961, The Offices, Shops and Railway Premises Act 1963 and the main Act applicable today, The Health and Safety at Work Act (HSWA) 1974 which codified and extended earlier acts.

The HSWA introduced a number of specific duties and legal obligations on employers with an over-riding obligation on every employer:

'to ensure so far as is reasonably practicable, the health, safety and welfare at work of his employees'

The HSWA applies to all employed persons wherever they work. It emphasises that Safety is everyone's business by making it clear that the obligations to provide safe conditions, or to work in a safe manner, apply to employees and the self-employed as well as employers.

Some of the more specific duties imposed by the HSWA are, in effect, extensions of the duties owed to employees at Common Law. Typical of the HSWA duties are the following:

☐ To maintain a safe place of work with safe entrances and exits.

☐ To provide and maintain equipment and systems of work that are safe and without risks to health.

☐ The storage, use, handling and transport of articles and substances must be carried out in a safe manner.

☐ To provide sufficient information, training, instruction and supervision to ensure the health and safety of employees.

All firms employing over 5 employees must prepare and keep up to date a written statement of safety policy. This must be drawn to all employee's attention.

Enforcement of the law on health and safety is the responsibility of the Health and Safety Executive (HSE) which have various groups of Inspectors covering Factories, Mines and Quarries, Agriculture, Nuclear Installations, Railways, and Clean Air. Although the HSE may prosecute serious or peristent offenders this is done relatively rarely. Much of the Inspector's work consists of giving advice and persuading people to take personal responsibility for health and safety.

Frequently organisatioons employ a specialist Safety Officer within the Personnel Department. The Safety Officer's main tasks are:

☐ To provide safety advice on materials, factory and office layouts, machinery, working methods.

☐ To carry out safety inspections of premises, methods, equipment to ensure that safeguards are operating, protective equipment is available, fire escapes clear etc.

☐ To provide instruction and information to all staff especially new recruits, on safety matters.

☐ To maintain and analyse accident records.

Stress management and counselling

Stress arises from a person's inability to cope with problems and pressure. Some people are able to cope adequately with domestic and work pressures; others cannot and suffer adverse reactions such as insomnia, headaches, ulcers and others which in the long-term may lead to serious illnesses, depression and possibly enforced retirement and early death.

Many of the factors causing stress arise from personal and domestic problems such as; divorce, death in the family, moving house, ageing, low self-esteem and so on. Some however are job related and to reduce stress on individuals the organisation can take various actions as appropriate. Examples include:

- ❏ Increasing a person's autonomy in their job.
- ❏ Decrease/increase personal responsibilities.
- ❏ Allow more flexible working hours, perhaps by the use of flexi-time.
- ❏ Give appropriate training.
- ❏ Where necessary provide work/job transfers.
- ❏ Eliminate any form of personal harassment.
- ❏ Provide better working conditions, including social/fitness clubs etc.
- ❏ Provide creche facilities or assistance with child care.
- ❏ Institute a counselling service.

Studies have shown that stress is more prevalent in lower grade employees than in more senior ones and is even more prevalent in the unemployed. The research indicates that an important factor seems to be the extent to which a person has control over their lives and whether they are in the position to make decisions rather than take orders from someone else. This is called job depth.

A job with high depth means that the person doing it has discretion over the job, can make decisions and can set the pace. If it is closely supervised with every detail specified then it has low job depth.

Counselling

Counselling is a joint activity in which the person seeking help shares his or her problem with a trained counsellor. Counselling is not intended to solve a person's problems or to do anything to them. It is carried out to try to get the person to put their problems into perspective and to see what they themselves can do to solve them.

Some large organisations provide an in-house counselling service, others hire external counsellors. The provision of such a service demonstrates an organisation's commitment to their employees and is a factor in improving the morale of staff.

Social activities

A normal responsibility of the personnel function, especially in large organisations, is the organisation and administration of social facilities and activities. These may include; social and leisure clubs, sports facilities and teams, parties, discos and similar events, outings, raffles, hobby clubs and so on.

This aspect of personnel work is especially well developed in public sector organisations such as the Civil Service, Local Authorities, the National Health Service etc.

Remuneration

Remuneration costs (i.e. wages, salaries, bonuses, pensions and pay administration) are a major element in the cost structure of all organisations, typically being over 50% of total costs. Accordingly, general levels of pay, the amounts paid to individuals, bonuses, increments and so on receive close attention from both the organisation itself and employees.

There are numerous influences on remuneration levels which are summarised in Figure 12.4

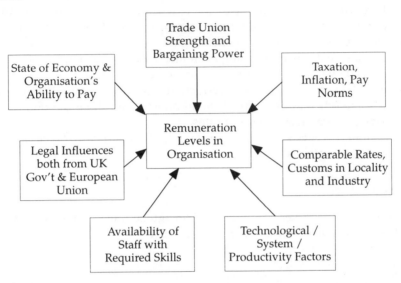

Figure 12.4: Influences on remuneration levels

Conventionally the term 'wages' is used for manual and production workers and 'salaries' for office workers, supervisors and managers. Although this distinction is breaking down because many organisations pay salaries to all employees, the convention is still widely used.

There are numerous pay systems for manual workers but they can be classified into those based on *time* and those based on *output*. These systems are briefly described below.

Time based wages

At the simplest, wages are paid at a basic rate per hour up to, say, 38 hours per week. Time worked above 38 hours would be classed as overtime and is usually paid at a higher rate, for example, 'time and a half' i.e. $1\frac{1}{2} \times$ basic rate per hour, depending on the number of hours worked and when the overtime was worked.

Time based wages are not dependent on the level of output but naturally output quantity and quality are still vital factors and it is normal for performance to be closely monitored. Time based systems are most appropriate where quality is all important or where output related schemes would be difficult or impossible to install.

Time based systems frequently also include bonuses and other payments. For example, timekeeping and shift bonuses, good housekeeping bonuses, safety bonuses and so on.

Output based wages

Schemes in which wages are dependent on output are usually known as *incentive schemes*. There are numerous types of these schemes, some apply to individuals, others to groups, some have minimum earnings guarantees and so on. Properly organised incentive schemes can benefit both the employee and the firm. The employee from the extra wages arising from increased production and the employer from the reduced overheads per unit of the increased production.

Incentive schemes can increase production and wages and thereby improve morale, but some schemes are difficult to administer and there can be problems in deciding upon performance levels and rates.

The commonest wages systems based on output are *Piecework Schemes* and *Bonus Schemes* which are explained below.

Piecework schemes

At their simplest, the worker would be paid an agreed rate per unit or operation, for the number of units produced or operations carried out.

Example

A machinist is paid on piecework at the rate of £1.80 per 100 components produced. During a week he produced 9,140 components of which 60 were rejected by inspection. What were his wages for the week?

Solution

Output for week	9,140	components
less rejects	60	
Net good output	9,080	

∴ Wages for week = 9,080 @ £1.80 per 100 = £163.44
Note that only good production is paid for.

Where, as in the example above, the same rate per unit is paid for all production, the system is known as *straight piecework*. On occasions, the rate is increased progressively at various output levels and this is then known as *differential piecework*.

Bonus systems

There is a great variety of these systems which usually combine a flat rate per hour with a bonus for achieving a given output level. Often the bonus is based on the savings made between the actual time taken and the target time for a job.

Example

A worker with a basic rate of £5 per hour receives a bonus of half the hours saved on each job. In a 38 hour week he completes 2 jobs as follows:

Job	Target time	Actual time
A	32 hours	23 hours
B	16 hours	15 hours
		38 hours

What are his wages for the week?

Solution

Bonus hours

Job A	$= \frac{1}{2}(32 - 23)$	$= 4\frac{1}{2}$ hours
Job B	$= \frac{1}{2}(16 - 15)$	$= \frac{1}{2}$ hour
Total Bonus Hours		5 hours
Total pay hours	$= 38 + 5$	$= 43$ hours
and wages	$= 43 \times £5$	$= £215$

A pay system which has elements of time and output is called *Measured Day Work* or *High Day Rates*. This is a system in which employees receive premium time rates provided that an agreed performance or output level is achieved. This system is widely used where piece-work is inappropriate and where there is a long job cycle. Measured day work is common in continuous process industries such as refining and chemical manufacture.

Another system which is being used in some manufacturing companies where flexible working and other modern production methods have been adopted is called *skills-based pay*. These systems link pay to the acquisition of skills and knowledge so that workers become multi-skilled and thus more flexible.

Salary systems

Salaries are paid to staff workers and sometimes to all employees. A salary system usually consists of a number of salary bands or grades applied to different levels of jobs.

Within a given salary band for a grade it is normal for there to be a number of pay points, called *increments*. Movement up the increments may depend on length of service or merit or some combination of the two. In the Public Sector, for example, Central and Local Government, Education etc. movement up the increments is normally based entirely on length of service whereas in the Private Sector merit increases are more common. However as more Civil Service functions are hived off into Agencies, which are charged with adopting commercial attitudes, it is likely that merit-based salary progression will become more common. In an attempt to be as fair and objective as possible in the assessment of performance in a job, many firms base merit awards on formal appraisal schemes, dealt with earlier sometimes called *merit rating*.

Especially in large concerns it is important that grades and salary levels are seen to be fair across the organisation. This means that jobs must be ranked according to the demands that the job makes on the person carrying out the job. A common way this is done is by the technique of *job evaluation*.

Job evaluation

This seeks to show in a reasonably objective manner the relative worth of jobs. It attempts to do this by analysing the content of each job under various categories, e.g. Training required, Degree of responsibility, Working conditions, Types of decisions involved and so on, and giving a points score for each factor. The total of the points' scores for each job is then used to establish the ranking of one job to another and, by reference to pay scales, the normal salary for the job.

Advantages:
   (a) Makes an attempt to be objective in ranking jobs.
   (b) Reasonably effective within an organisation at ranking jobs, particularly relatively low level ones.
Disadvantages:
   (a) Not suitable for ranking widely different jobs, particularly in different organisations.
   (b) Gives a spurious air of objectivity to job comparison. The Job Evaluation process itself contains many subjective elements.

Other elements of remuneration policy occasionally found are performance related pay and profit sharing, described below.

Performance related pay (PRP)

This is a pay system where a proportion of a person's pay is linked to their performance in achieving one or more performance targets. The targets may be expressed in terms of profitability, quality, cases handled, income raised or some other measure that can be quantified. In certain circumstances PRP can work well and is an important motivator. It works best when a clear cut unambiguous quantitative measure can be identified. A typical example is when a Managing Director's pay has an element related to profitaility targets for the organisation as a whole.

However it is less clear whether PRP works as well when there is no clear-cut single indicator which provides a reasonable measure of performance. PRP has been criticised for encouraging short-termism and distorting operations in pursuit of a simplistic objective.

For example the Chief Executive of the Child Support Agency is on performance-related pay judged on the amount the Agency saves the Government in the first year. In consequence it is alleged that the Agency has concentrated on easy targets of fathers already contributing to their childrens' maintenance whilst giving less attention to the much more difficult task of tracing absentee fathers who make no contributions.

Profit sharing

This can be defined as the payment to employees of a proportion of company profits. The amount received by individuals is related to salary level and/or length of service and may be given in the form of cash or shares in the company. Profit sharing is in effect a bonus above basic pay unlike PRP, described above, which forms part of normal pay.

Profit sharing schemes may help employees to identify with the company and promote a more profit-conscious attitude but in general such schemes seem to be regarded as a welcome but minor bonus too remote from the workplace to have any real incentive effect.

Employee benefits

In addition to wages and salaries organisations also provide a range of other benefits for their employees, often called *fringe benefits*. Some may be available to all employees, for example, pensions, whilst others are restricted to senior employees, for example, company cars.

The table below gives a list of benefits often provided by an organisation although all would not be available to every employee.

Possible employee or fringe benefits

Pensions	Company cars
Life and Health insurance	Entertainment allowances
Subsidised meals or vouchers	Parking facilities
Share Options	Creches and child care
Bridging loans for house purchase	Interest free loans for season ticket
Discount purchase facilities for the	purchase
organisation's goods or services	Prizes
Counselling schemes	Sabbaticals and so on

Until recently, employee benefits were considered a tax-efficient way of rewarding employees over and above their salaries. During the 1980's and 1990's successive Budgets have closed numerous loopholes and most benefits (e.g. Company Cars, Insurance Schemes, Allowances etc.) are now fully liable to tax in a similar way to wages and salaries.

We now turn to the final section on Personnel Management, that dealing with Employee Relations.

Employee relations

Employee relations deal with the individual and collective relationships between employer and employee but naturally others are concerned, in addition to the two key parties. Typically the following may have some interest or influence:

- Employees
- Employers
- Trade Unions
- Tribunals and Courts
- Arbitrators
- Government Departments
- Employers' Associations

Since the Conservatives came to power in 1979 and with the UK's growing integration with Europe the law has become much more important in employee relations. This has brought the UK more in to line with most other industrialised countries.

The most important single item in employee relations is the individual *contract of employment*.

Contract of employment

A distinction in law is made between a contract of service where the person is an employee and a contract for services - where the person is an independent contractor. In doubtful cases the courts apply various tests to determine whether the person is genuinely an employee. These include; who controls the work of the person, how is he/she paid, who is responsible for paying the tax due and so on.

On the assumption that the person is an employee, and freely enters into a contract of service a typical employment contract contains both explicit and implicit terms. Typical items are shown in Figure 12.5.

Employment contracts

Typical explicit features	Typical implicit features
☐ letter of engagement	☐ custom and practice
☐ job description and duties	☐ common law obligations
☐ terms and conditions of employment	☐ implicit features of organisation's rules
☐ relevant collective agreements between employer and trade unions	☐ implicit features of relevant collective agreements
☐ rule book of organisation	
☐ general personnel procedures relating to promotion, dismissal, grievances, disciplinary matters etc	

Figure 12.5: Explicit and implicit features of employment contracts

The Employment Protection Act (1978) requires a written statement of the key terms and conditions of employment to be supplied to each employee within 13 weeks of commencing employment. The main requirements of this written statement are:

☐ Title of job

☐ Rates of pay and payment periods

☐ Normal hours to be worked

☐ Sick pay and holiday arrangements

☐ Pension arrangements

☐ Terms of notice

☐ Specific rules relating to the job

☐ Grievance, redress procedures

Although employment contracts are individual they are often strongly influenced by collective agreements and the general activities of trades unions.

Trade unions

Trades unions are organisations of workers which seek to promote the interests of their members, mainly through what is called *collective bargaining*. This is defined by the Advisory Conciliation and Arbitration Service (ACAS) as:

'the process whereby procedures are jointly agreed and wages and conditions of employment are settled by negotiation between employers, or associations of employers and workers organisations.'

Trades Unions have numerous functions including the following:

- Protecting and improving the pay conditions of members
- Influencing the industrial, social and economic policies of government
- Increasing the participation of workers in decision-making at all levels
- Providing benefits, training, legal advice etc. to members
- Improving the information available to members about individual firms, industries, health and safety and so on.

There are numerous types of Unions. For example, Manual Unions (National Union Of Mineworkers, Transport and General Workers etc.), so called White Collar Unions (NALGO, UNISON etc.) Managerial and Professional Unions (British Airline Pilots Association, Association of University Teachers etc.). Currently about 45% of employees in Britain are members of trades unions but union membership varies widely. Some industries have high union density (e.g. central and local government, coal mining), others have a much lower density (e.g. agriculture, retailing, banking etc.).

In general union membership (and influence) has declined since 1980 partly caused by what unions see as restrictive and punitive legislation and partly by changes in economic and social factors. The main areas of legislation have been:

- Definition of trade dispute made tighter and 'Secondary action' outlawed (1980 and 1982 Employment Acts)
- Postal ballots for election of officials and sanctioning strikes (1984 Trade Union Act)
- Closed shops outlawed (1990 Trade Union Act)
- Picketing restricted to 6 official pickets at the employees place of work

Trades Union officials and the management of the organisation (or the Employers Association) try to settle any dispute or pay claim by discussion and negotiation. Sometimes the discussions fail and then the Union may ballot its members regarding strike action and attempt to gain its demands by a strike or work-to-rule. On occasions one or other side may call in the Advisory, Conciliation and Arbitration Service (ACAS).

ACAS

ACAS is publicly funded but is independent of Government. Its aim is to help the parties to resolve disputes and, in effect, offers three services:

Conciliation

i.e. ACAS brings the two sides together to reach a mutually acceptable solution but does not impose any solution.

Arbitration

i.e. a neutral arbitrator makes an award based on a fair assessment of the two positions. Traditionally the award would be a compromise between the opposing positions but compulsory, pendulum arbitration is becoming more usual. This means that a choice is made; either the managements or the unions claim is chosen. It is argued that pendulum arbitration encourages both sides to be reasonable.

Mediation

i.e. a compromise between conciliation and arbitration where the mediator tries to guide the two sides to a compromise agreement.

A further aspect of employee relation concerns *worker participation*.

Worker participation

This deals with the extent of worker participation in the management and decision-making processes. In theory this could range from informal consultation with employees to total worker control of the organisation. The main possibilities are summarised below:

- ☐ Various forms of informal and formal consultation including meetings, joint management-employee committees etc.

- ☐ Works Councils. A system widely used in Germany known as 'Betriebsrat'. A council of employees only has legal rights of access to a range of information and may exercise joint decision making over personnel matters. Little used in the UK.

- ☐ Representation on the Board of Directors. Where this occurs there is some participation in strategic discussions and decision. Again widely used in Germany but rare in the UK.

- ☐ Workers full or partial ownership. This is where employees, of all levels, own shares in the firm. This has been encouraged in various privatisation schemes and in management buy-outs e.g. National Freight Corporation. It is argued that it encourages commitment and efficiency.

To some extent it can be argued that the somewhat confrontational attitude to industrial relations in Britain has slowed progress to genuine worker participation even though it has had success in other industrial countries.

Disciplinary and grievance procedures

An important facet of personnel management is to produce and publicise clear-cut procedures and guidelines regarding disciplinary matters and how employees may seek redress for a grievance.

ACAS (mentioned earlier) has a Code of Practice on disciplinary matters which is a good guide for organisations. In outline ACAS suggest disciplinary procedures should

- [] be in written form and well publicised
- [] offer a speedy, fair means of dealing with disciplinary matters including; proper notification, fair hearings with support if required, thorough investigations and so on
- [] properly inform any employee penalised of the penalties imposed and reasons
- [] provide a right of appeal

Employees should be left in no doubt what constitutes unsatisfactory behaviour and what are the likely consequences of misconduct and gross misconduct. Gross misconduct e.g. theft, wilful damage may result in immediate dismissal but most forms of misconduct are likely to be punished, in the first instance by a formal warning. Only in cases of repeated misconduct would more severe sanctions be considered.

Under the Employment Protection Act (1978) employees must be informed within 13 weeks of commencing work of their conditions of employment, including disciplinary and grievance procedures. Normally if a person has a grievance it is raised with his/her immediate supervisor. If the problem is not resolved at that level the grievance may be referred to a more senior manager when a formal meeting is held consisting of the senior manager, the employee (and friend if required) and the organisation's Personnel Manager. If the employee is still not satisfied there should be an Appeals procedure to the the highest level in the organisation when a further formal meeting would be held, the results of which should be distributed to all the parties concerned.

Developments affecting the personnel function

Having now briefly described the main areas of Personnel Management the chapter is concluded by considering some of the trends and developments which are affecting organisations, especially relating to personnel matters. These include; the reduction in the number of full-time employees, the changes in trade-union activities, the ageing population, influence of modern methods.

Reduction in number of full-time employees

Many organisations have reduced the number of full-time employees, or are planning to do so. This is not simply due to increased efficiency, although that is a factor,
but is a conscious effort to become more flexible. Increasingly firms are combining a
relatively small nucleus of full-time employees with fluctuating numbers of part-time
staff or 'service providers'. In this way firms gain flexibility to deal with rapidly
changing conditions.

In general the part-time workers tend to be paid less and have little or no job security and many are women, especially in retailing. The tendency for there to be a core
of full-time employees supported by part-timers called up as required can be seen in
many industries including; construction, retailing, local government, security, industrial cleaning and many others.

Changes in trade union activities

The traditional trade union approach was collectivist rather than individualistic. This
suited older, mass-employment industries such as coal mining, steel-making, ship-
building, engineering and others. In such industries there might be as many as a
dozen different unions within one company each representing a different type of
workers.

Nowadays the older industries have declined and in some cases virtually disappeared. There has been a spectacular growth of employment in service industries and
smaller firms, which are much less unionised. Also, there is now a much higher
proportion of women workers, again less unionised.
As a consequence of these changes trade union influence and national wage
bargaining has declined. Local and company agreements, often on an individual
basis, are now much more common. Following the example of the recently built
Japanese factories, for example Nissan in Sunderland and Toyota near Derby, single-
union agreements are now much more common. These are where a single union acts
for all the employees in the factory allowing simpler bargaining without disruptive
demarcation problems.

Ageing population

Because of the declining birthrate, especially over the last twenty years, the population is ageing. There are numerous consequences of this; there will be fewer young
people entering employment, older people will have to be encouraged to stay at
work, a smaller working population will have to support pensioners, the Welfare
State will be under pressure.

There are clear implications for manpower planning and personnel practices as a
result of an ageing population. Evidence presented to the British Psychological
Society Occupational Conference in 1994 suggested that many Personnel Managers
were unaware that the supply of young people will decline and very few had considered what action will need to be taken.

Influence of modern methods

This broad heading encompasses numerous items. Examples include; the increased use of information technology, team-working, the reduction in the number of management levels, the need for employees to be multi-skilled and to undertake many different jobs in their working lives.

Training will have to become a continuous process and much greater attention given to employee development and flexibility all of which will radically change personnel practices.

Key point summary

- ❐ Personnel management is a specialist management function dealing with all aspects of the human resources of an organisation.

- ❐ Manpower planning deals with plans for the development of skills, training, etc. and numbers of people required.

- ❐ Personnel policies are behavioural guidelines on personnel matters.

- ❐ Recruitment is the process of attracting a number of suitable applicants.

- ❐ Selection is choosing the best candidate for a vacancy.

- ❐ Employee Development seeks to maintain and enhance the skills and and knowledge of all employees.

- ❐ Performance Appraisal is carried out; to identify training needs, for merit and pay awards, to assess suitability for promotion.

- ❐ Training is a job-oriented process focusing on present needs. Development seeks to improve employee potential.

- ❐ Welfare deals with Health and Safety, Stress Management and Social Activities.

- ❐ Wages are paid according to time or based on some form of output measurement including piecework and bonus systems.

- ❐ Job Evaluation seeks to rank jobs in an objective manner.

- ❐ Other aspects of remuneration policy include; Performance Related Pay, Profit Sharing, Fringe Benefits.

- ❐ Employees must have Contracts of Employment and be given a written statement of terms and conditions within 13 weeks of commencement.

❏ Trades Unions fulfil many functions for their members, especially concerned with the protection of pay and conditions.

❏ ACAS is an independent conciliation, arbitration and conciliation service.

❏ Worker participation may range from consultation through Works Councils and Representation on the Board, to Workers ownership.

❏ Organisations should have Disciplinary and Grievance procedures which are speedy and just.

❏ Numerous developments are affecting the Personnel function including; the use of part-time employees, changes in Trade Unions, the Ageing population, modern methods.

Self review questions

1. *What is Personnel Management?*

2. *How is Manpower planning carried out?*

3. *Give examples of Personnel policies.*

4. *What is Recruitment and Selection?*

5. *What are the typical contents of a Job Description?*

6. *What is Rodger's Seven Point Plan?*

7. *Describe the Selection process.*

8. *What are the typical contents of a Contract of Employment?*

9. *What is Employee Development?*

10. *Distinguish between Training and Development.*

11. *What factors must be considered in looking after the Welfare of employees?*

12. *What is stress counselling?*

13. *What is job depth?*

14. *What pay systems are commonly used for manual workers?*

15. *What is Job Evaluation?*

16. *What is Profit Sharing?*

17. *What topics are included under the term 'Employee Relations'?*

18. *What is ACAS?*

19. *What is Worker participation?*

20. *What factors and trends are affecting Personnel Management?*

13 Management functions: production

Objectives

After you have studied this chapter you will:

☐ *Know that production is a transformation process.*

☐ *Be able to describe the range of tasks undertaken by Production Management.*

☐ *Understand the characteristics of jobbing, batch, and flow production.*

☐ *Know the features of Just-in-Time systems and their benefits.*

☐ *Be able to describe the features of Advanced Manufacturing Technology.*

☐ *Know the features and objectives of Total Quality Control and Total Quality Management.*

☐ *Understand the elements of Stock or Inventory Control.*

☐ *Be able to describe the main features of Work Study.*

☐ *Understand what is meant by Value Analysis or Value Engineering.*

What is production and production management?

Production is a process which transforms various forms of *inputs* (materials, energy, skills, money etc.) into *outputs* or finished products using a range of *facilities* (machines, buildings, people, information etc.).

Note that outputs may be *physical products* such as; televisions, cars, barrels of beer or they may be in the form of *services* for example, a life assurance policy, a package holiday and so on.

Production management, sometimes known as operations management, is the specialist management function which deals with all aspects of the production process. In outline, this includes the following:

Longer-term planning and decision-making concerning:

☐ Product design.

☐ Factory location and layout.

☐ Work organisation and methods.

- Equipment design and selection.
- Job and method design.
- Supplier selection.
- Training and development of production personnel.
- Total Quality management.

Short-term and decision-making concerning:

- Purchasing and materials scheduling.
- Production and Stock control.
- Inspection and quality control.
- Factory and production scheduling.
- Cost and waste control.
- Maintenance.
- Provision of fittings, jigs, tools etc.
- Labour organisation and supervision.

Categories of production

Numerous factors influence the form of production. These include:

- Volume required
- Degree of repetition in the product/service demanded
- Amount of standardisation possible
- Type of product/service

The three most common production categories are; *jobbing production, batch production* and *flow production*. The main features of these three broad categories are given below.

Jobbing production

Job or jobbing production is common in civil engineering, building, printing, repair shops, small foundries, ship-building and numerous other industries. Items are produced usually to a customer's special order, either as 'one-offs' or in very small quantities. They may range in size from huge items such as a ship or a bridge to a small, hand-finished casting.

The key features of jobbing production include:

- Work is done to special order, usually 'one-offs'.

- General purpose tools, equipment and machinery are required to cope with the variety possible.

- Parts/materials cannot generally be stocked in advance because of unpredictable demands.

- Workers need to be highly skilled and versatile.

- Each job requires customised planning and sequencing of production.

- Job planning, materials ordering and production cannot be done in advance of orders.

- Workers and management need to be adaptable.

- Because of the special orders and variety possible some idle time is inevitable.

- Relatively expensive form of production with little or no opportunity for economies of scale.

Batch production

Batch production is commonly encountered especially in the footwear, clothing, light engineering and similar industries. It is the production of a quantity of the same basic product, often in different versions, finishes or colours. The product is sufficiently standardised and quantities sufficiently large to justify dealing with the batches in a systematic, sequenced series of operations. Normally each operation is completed before the batch is passed on to the next stage or operation.

The main characteristics of batch production are:

- General purpose machinery/processes still needed to cope with variety but typically machines of a like type are grouped together.

- Batches pass from one machine/process to the next as standardised operations are complete.

- More division of labour than in jobbing production so that less skill required by the individual operator.

- Need for efficient planning and control of production.

- [ ] Need for efficient facilities for transferring work-in-progress from operation to operation.

- [ ] Completed products may move into stock, go to several customers or occasionally go to a single customer.

- [ ] Forward planning and purchasing of materials is required.

- [ ] Continual problem of determining an optimum batch size particularly where there is generalised demand.

Batch production can be considered as occupying an intermediate position between jobbing production and flow production.

Flow production

This is a production system, usually on a large scale, where a single product or a restricted range of products are made on a continuous basis with an unbroken production flow from one operation to the next.

Flow production may be classified into two main categories:

Process production is where a single homogeneous product is made by a continuously operating fixed sequence of processes. Examples of continuous process industries include; chemicals, oil, paper, steel-making. Note that discrete units are not produced. Typically, liquids, powders, continuous lengths of wire, paper etc. are made using process production.

Mass production or *assembly-line production* is where individual, discrete products are made in a series of repetitive operations in a fixed sequence, usually on an assembly line. Mass production methods are used widely. For example; vehicles, televisions, domestic appliances, computers and so on. Assembly lines were first used in a crude form for the production of railway wagons in America. However it was their use and improvement by Henry Ford in the production of a restricted range of cars that led to their widespread adoption for the mass-production of virtually all types of discrete products.

The main features of flow production include:

- [ ] High capital investment required
- [ ] Specialised machines, tools and equipment arranged to facilitate continuous flow.
- [ ] Sufficient demand to maintain flows.
- [ ] Closely defined product and material specifications.
- [ ] Meticulously integrated production planning and control systems required.
- [ ] Continuous maintenance to avoid breakdowns.

- Detailed scheduling of material/parts/assemblies to avoid stoppages on the line.
- Traditionally, highly specialised and narrow range of skill required by workers leading to boredom.

Where the product is sufficiently standardised and volumes are high, flow production is cost-effective and it is possible to achieve striking economies of scale. Electronic monitoring and computerised control have enabled some process factories (e.g. chemical production, oil-refining, cement manufacture) to be run almost automatically with very low staffing levels.

Over the last decade or so there have been revolutionary changes in mass production. Some of the changes have been due to the greater use of computers, robots, and other electronic equipment. Some have been changes in the way production is organised, some have been made to improve quality and others relate to the way individuals work together.

A number of the key developments in production and production methods are dealt with below. These include; Just-In-Time systems, Materials Requirements Planning, Advanced Manufacturing Technology, Total Quality Control and Total Quality Management.

Just-in-time (JIT) systems

JIT systems were developed in Japan, notably at Toyota, and are considered as one of the main contributions to Japanese manufacturing success.

The aim of JIT systems is to produce the required items, of high quality, exactly at the time they are required. JIT systems are characterised by the pursuit of excellence at all stages with a climate of continuous improvement.

A JIT environment is characterised by:

- a move towards zero inventory
- elimination of non-value added activities
- an emphasis on perfect quality i.e. zero defects
- short set-ups
- a move towards a batch size of one
- 100% on time deliveries
- a constant drive for improvement
- Demand-pull manufacture

It is this latter characteristic which gives rise to the name of Just-in-Time. Production only takes place when there is actual customer demand for the product so JIT works on a pull-through basis which means that products are not made to go into stock.

Contrast this with the traditional manufacturing approach of production-push where products are made in large batches and move into stock.

There are two aspects to JIT systems, JIT Purchasing and JIT Production.

JIT purchasing

This seeks to match the usage of materials with the delivery of materials from external suppliers. This means that material stocks can be kept at near-zero levels. For JIT purchasing to work requires the following:

(a) Confidence that suppliers will deliver exactly on time.

(b) That suppliers will deliver materials of 100% quality so that there will be no rejects, returns and consequent production delays.

The reliability of suppliers is all-important and JIT purchasing means that the company must build up close working relationships with their suppliers. This is usually achieved by doing more business with fewer suppliers and placing long term purchasing orders in order that the supplier has assured sales and can plan to meet the demand.

JIT production

JIT production works on a demand-pull basis and seeks to eliminate all waste and activities which do not add value to the product. As an example, consider the lead times associated with making and selling a product. These include:

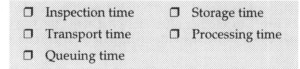

☐ Inspection time   ☐ Storage time

☐ Transport time   ☐ Processing time

☐ Queuing time

Of these, only processing time adds value to the product whereas all the othes add cost, but not value.

The ideal for JIT systems is to convert materials to finished products with a lead time equal to processing time so eliminating all activities which do not add value. A way of emphasising the importance of reducing throughput time is to express the above lead times as follows:

Throughput time = Value-added time + Non-value added time

The JIT pull system means that components are not made until requested by the next process. The usual way this is done is by monitoring parts consumption at each stage and using a system of markers (known as kanbans) which authorise production and movement to the process which requires the parts. A consequence of this is that there may be idle time at certain work stations but this is considered preferable to adding to work-in-progress (WIP) inventory.

Poor and uncertain quality is a prime source of delays hence the drive in JIT systems for zero defects and Total Quality Management. When quality is poor, higher WIP is needed to protect production from delays caused by defective parts. Higher inventory is also required when there are long set-up and changeover times. Accordingly there is continual pressure in JIT systems to reduce set-up times and eventually eliminate them so that the optimal batch size can become one. With a batch size of one, the work can flow smoothly to the next stage without the need to store it and schedule the next machine to accept the item.

JIT production implications

To operate JIT manufacturing successfully and achieve the targets of low inventories and on-time deliveries means that:

(a) The production processes must be shortened and simplified. Each product family is made in a work-cell based on flowline principles. The JIT system increases the variety and complexity within work cells. These contain groups of dissimilar machines which thus requires workers to be more flexible and adaptable.

(b) Using JIT the emphasis is on 'doing the job right first time' thus avoiding defects and reworking. JIT systems require quality awareness programmes, statistical checks on output quality and continual worker training.

(c) Factory layouts must be changed to reduce movement. Traditionally machines were grouped by function; all the drilling machines together, the grinding machines and so on. This meant a part had to travel long distances moving from one area of the factory to another often stopping along the way in a storage area. All these are non-value added activities which have to be reduced or eliminated.

(d) There must be full employee involvement. As an example it has been reported that the 60,000 employees of Toyota produced a total of 2.6 million improvement suggestions per annum. In most cases, after line management approval, the working groups simply get on with implementing their ideas. Arguably one of the most important behavioural implications of JIT is that the status quo is continually challenged and there is a never ending search for improvements.

Benefits from JIT

Successful users of JIT systems are making substantial savings. These arise from numerous areas:

(a) Lower investment required in all forms of inventory

(b) Space savings from the reduction in inventory and improved layouts

(c) Greater customer satisfaction resulting from higher quality, better deliveries and greater product variety

(d) The buffers provided by traditional inventories masked other areas of waste and inefficiency. Examples include; co-ordination and work flow problems, bottle necks, supplier unreliability and so on. Elimination of these problems improves performance dramatically.

(e) The flexibility of JIT and the ability to supply small batches enables companies to respond more quickly to market changes and to be able to satisfy market niches.

(f) The increase in efficiency and higher morale of the employees who are now organised in multi-skilled teams with no traditional trade or skill demarcations.

The lessons of Japanese 'lean production' methods are also being applied in Europe and the USA. For example:

Opel, a subsidiary of General Motors, manufactures cars at Bochum in West Germany, Zaragoza in Spain and at a purpose-built factory at Eisenach in East Germany. At Eisenach there has been an uncompromising application of Japanese methods with spectacular results. It takes just over 18 hours to make an Opel Astra or Corsa in Eisenach, compared with a time in the high 20s at the Bochum plant in western Germany and the low 30s at Zaragoza in Spain.

At the same time, Eisenach has set new quality standards, producing cars with an average of six to seven defects compared with about 20 at Bochum and more than 20 at Vauxhall. Workers operate in teams of six to eight. The division of labour between planning and production has been done away with or totally redefined.

Through agreements with the unions, production workers can do skilled trade work such as stopping and starting the line, changing weld tips and minor repairs. The result is just 10 maintenance staff per shift, compared with around 300 for the admittedly larger Bochum plant.

Overall, Eisenach's work space, workforce, storage space and transport capacity are around half of those in conventional plants.

Stocks next to the production line, in boxes meticulously placed within their designated spaces, are sufficient for two to three hours, with one to three days' worth in the warehouse. At Bochum the warehouse level is two to three weeks.

The Eisenach production cycle is closely linked to the railway timetable. There is also a 'buffer' of only 10 cars, or 20 minutes, between one production line and another, compared with 375 cars or six hours in Bochum. This means that any fault can be discovered in 20 minutes in Eisenach, and just 10 cars need looking at, as against six hour's worth at the western German plant. Absenteeism at Eisenach is down to 3 per cent, compared with the 10 per cent common in western German plants. The body works is 96 per cent automated, with GM robots changing their own tool heads depending on whether a Corsa or Astra is next on the same line.

Materials requirement planning (MRP)

MRP is a computerised information, planning and control system which has the objective of maintaining a smooth production flow.

It is concerned with:

- ☐ maximising the efficiency in the timing of orders for raw materials or parts that are placed with external suppliers
- ☐ efficient scheduling of the manufacture and assembly of the final product

The operation of an MRP System requires the following:

(a) A master production schedule showing the quantities and timings required for the finished product(s)

(b) A Bill of Materials (BOM) which shows the breakdown of each finished product into sub-assemblies, components and raw materials

(c) An Inventory file containing the balance on hand, scheduled receipts and numbers already allocated for each sub-assembly, component and type of raw material

(d) A parts manufacturing and purchasing file containing lead times of all purchased items and lead times and production sequences of all sub-assemblies and components produced internally.

MRP has evolved into MRPII which attempts to integrate material resource planning, factory capacity planning and labour scheduling into a single manufacturing control system.

Advanced manufacturing technology (AMT)

AMT is revolutionising the way products are designed and manufactured and how production is organised especially in what are termed World Class Manufacturers (WCM).

AMT can be defined as:

the use of computers and electronic equipment at appropriate stages in the manufacturing process. This includes; the planning and control of production, the scheduling and ordering of materials, product design, and product manufacture.

Companies need to compete in fast moving, sophisticated world markets. The use of AMT helps them to do this. It increases their capability to produce high-quality goods at low cost and thus provide high levels of customer satisfaction. Firms need to be innovative and flexible and to be able to deal with short product life cycles. They need to be able to offer greater product variety whilst maintaining or reducing their costs. They wish to reduce set-up times and inventories and have the greatest possible manufacturing flexibility. AMT helps them to do this.

Some of the key elements of AMT are dealt with below. These include Computer Aided Design (CAD), Computer-Aided Manufacturer (CAM) and Flexible Manufacturing Systems (FMS).

Computer aided design (CAD)

This is product/component design and testing using a computer terminal. The interaction between the designer, the computer and the database enables many more options and designs to be considered in order to achieve the greatest efficiency and simplicity at the lowest cost. An important facility is the interrogation of the CAD database to identify standard parts and methods thus simplifying product design, reducing the number of product parts, and thus helping to minimise inventories.

CAD enables skilled designers and draughtsmen to be much more productive and can produce automatically essential manufacturing information such as; parts lists, material requirements and so on.

Computer aided manufacture (CAM)

This is a wide ranging expression to cover the use of computers for the programming and control of production machines. It includes the use of robots, numerically controlled (NT) machines and computer numerically controlled (CNC) machines. Because of the ability to re-programme as required, CAM offers many advantages including;

- flexibility i.e. ability to perform a variety of operations and produce a range of parts
- greater control over manufacturing
- reduced set-up times
- better, more consistent quality
- fewer reworked items and less scrap
- less reliance on direct labour

In many companies CAD and CAM are integrated thus helping to reduce the lead time from the initial produce idea through to the market place.

Flexible manufacturing systems (FMS)

This is a highly-automated manufacturing system which is computer controlled and capable of producing a 'family' of parts in a flexible manner. The main essence is a mixture of CNC machines, robots and automated materials handling equipment to move the components from tool to tool.

The final stage in automation would be the complete automation of the whole factory, known as computer-integrated manufacturing (CIM). This stage has not been reached as even the most advanced of today's factories contain islands of automation (IA's) linked by human bridges.

In addition to the various AMT Systems mentioned above, most firms of any size use a variety of microprocessor-based measurement and control devices. These are used for measuring, counting, recording, testing and controlling production and machines. Circuits can be tested, materials analysed, parts counted, flows and pressures measured as required automatically by computer controlled devices.

Total quality control (TQC)

AMT and JIT systems have a total quality control philosophy in which the only acceptable quality level is zero defects. Prominence is given in JIT systems to all defects found so that the reason(s) for the defect can be discovered and put right. A defect found is a learning opportunity. This uncompromising attitude to quality has been accepted totally by Japanese manufacturers and is said to be one of the key elements in their success. It is ironic that the guiding forces behind the Japanese obsession with quality were a number of American Consultants, especially William Edwards Deming. For decades before the principle was even considered by the West Deming explained that if you improve quality at source productivity will rise and costs will fall. He also advocated team work and cooperation in the workplace.

With conventional Western thinking, activities and cost associated with poor quality are obscured by the common practice of including, in production costs a 'normal' allowance for scrap, waste and reworks. Thus as long as the production process turned out high volumes and kept within 'normal' scrap levels all was thought to be well.

The conventional wisdom was that there was an optimal percentage of defects with a quality: cost trade-off. This is shown in Figure 13.1

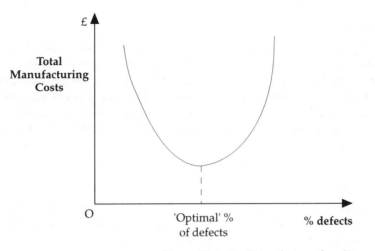

Figure 13.1: Traditional view of quality-cost trade off

Contrast this with the TQC view in Figure 13.2, which shows that as the percentage of defects rise, costs rise, and that the optimal percentage of defects is zero.

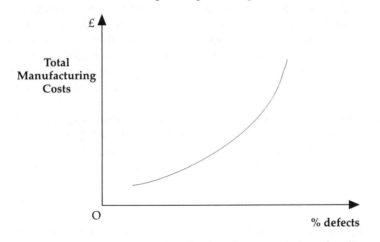

Figure 13.2: Total quality control view of quality-cost trade off

Moving towards TQC

Companies operating TQC measure defects not as a percentage of outgoing items but as a part-per-million (PPM) ratio of defects to items produced. They realise that many things have to be done correctly to achieve continual reductions in PPM defect rates.

The most important thing is to realise that quality has to be designed in, not inspected in. TQC has to be considered at every stage starting with the initial product idea. It is not something which is solely the concern of Inspectors at the end of the production line.

The following are the key points at which TQC must operate:

Product design

Probably the key stage. Product design should have price, performance, ease of manufacturing and quality in mind throughout the design stage. An important factor is simplicity; fewer parts preferably of standard design. Product designers should also liaise closely with manufacturing and process engineers. A well designed product not only works well, it is easy to manufacture. During the design stage the technique of value analysis is used extensively. This the systematic examination of cost factors in order to devise ways of achieving the specified purpose, most economically, at the required standard of quality and reliability.

Production engineering

This is the process of designing the methods for making a product to the design specification. This also includes the tools and processes to be used, the tolerances and finishes required, assembly sequences and so on.

Manufacturing

Manufacturing considerations must be part of product design because it is estimated that only 20% of quality defects can be traced to the production line. The other 80% being attributable to design factors or poor purchasing. In JIT systems the responsibility for defects has moved away from quality control inspectors to the operatives. Operators are expected to maintain their equipment and produce zero defect output. They are, of course, aided in this by CNC machines and automatic equipment which often incorporates computerised gauging and measuring devices. In addition there is extensive use of Statistical Process Control and Control Charts.

JIT systems emphasise in-process checks rather than waiting until the product is fully completed before it gets a final inspection. This was the traditional method and is still widely used even though it is a less efficient system.

(Note: Statistical Process Control and Control Charts are covered in detail in *Quantitative Techniques* by T. Lucey, DP Publications.)

Goods inwards

The quality of output depends on the quality of input materials. This means that Quality requirements are also imposed on suppliers to ensure quality and no inspection is performed on incoming supplies.

Output inspection

Final inspection is being replaced by in-process checking. Final inspection, based on sampling does still take place mainly to satisfy management that quality control in production is being maintained.

When TQC is properly applied and the incidence of defects decrease, total manufacturing costs, including warranty and service costs, decrease.

This is not surprising because if items are made correctly first time money is saved from the avoidance of detection, reworking, scrapping, repairing in the field and so on.

Higher quality means *lower costs.*

Total quality management (TQM)

TQM is where there is a defined culture of quality awareness and quality improvement in every process, in every department and at every level in the organisation. Organisations practising TQM have a long-term commitment to quality and consider quality to be a core value of the organisation. They take an *external* view of quality as compared with the traditional Western *internal* view.

The internal view of quality concentrates on ensuring that items produced conform to their specification within accepted tolerances. This view considers that quality costs money and, as production costs must be minimised, quality factors are always limited by their cost. On the other hand the external view, pioneered by the Japanese, places much more emphasis on the original design which the customer ordered. This view considers quality as the heart of the production process where every part will be fit for its purpose and will be right first time. With this philosophy there is emphasis on continual improvement of the product and *preventing errors* rather than relying on post-production inspection to reject faulty items and to correct mistakes. One of the American consultants who greatly influenced the Japanese acceptance of TQM, Joseph Juran, showed that over 80% of failures in production were attributable to management and stressed that management should deal with the *causes* of production problems rather than the short-term concentration on the *symptoms*, which is all too common.

William Edwards Deming, another of the pioneering Americans who advised Japanese industry, advocated a total quality approach as well as changes in other management practices - a number of which have still to be accepted fully in the West. Key points advocated by Deming include:

- ❏ the organisation, at all levels, must accept and practise their commitment continuously to improve customer satisfaction.
- ❏ Quality improvement must be embedded in the organisation's culture from top to bottom.
- ❏ Aim for constant improvement in products and processes.
- ❏ Provide adequate training and equipment and encourage pride in their own work and the product.
- ❏ Encourage cooperation and teamwork and develop trust throughout the organisation.
- ❏ Encourage self-improvement and education at every level.
- ❏ Choose suppliers for quality and reliability rather than price.

Deming had an enormous influence on Japanese industry and can be credited with much of its post-war success. Deming Awards for Quality are given each year in Japan and his portrait has pride of place in Toyota's headquarters. He died in December 1993.

Quality Circles are another facet of the total quality approach which originated in Japan and are spreading to the West. Quality circles are small groups which meet regularly to discuss matters such as productivity, safety, quality and so on. The idea is to develop and implement improvements directly at the work-place. The circles select their own leaders and are seen as a practical way of delegating real powers to employees and of achieving grass-roots participation.

The benefits of Quality Circles include:

- improvements in commitment, motivation and confidence.
- increased awareness of shop-floor problems
- improvements in quality, productivity and safety.

A feature of TQM is that closer links are forged between top management and shop-floor operators. Operatives are encouraged to take more decisions and accept more responsibility. As a consequence, middle management and the formal structures that go with layers of management are being reduced or eliminated.

Professor Handy estimates that over one million middle management positions have disappeared in the USA over the last ten years. The same process is also taking place in Europe.

In 1993 Herr Piech, Chairman of Volkswagen, Europe's largest car maker said that there were a mass of people in VW's Group Administration who had to ask themselves what they did to earn their keep and announced that it was VW's intention to reduce the number of management levels from nine to three.

Many forward looking organisations in the West are adopting a total quality approach. These include service and government organisations as well as manufacturers. As an example, consider Brent London Borough Council. Brent are carrying out a radical overhaul of their management practices. The operations of the Council are to be carried out by some 80 'business units' with substantial powers of decision-making devolved to the lowest possible level. Coupled with the authority to make decisions there is also the need to be accountable for the decisions. Integral to this radical overhaul is a Total Quality Programme which is shown in outline in Figure 13.3

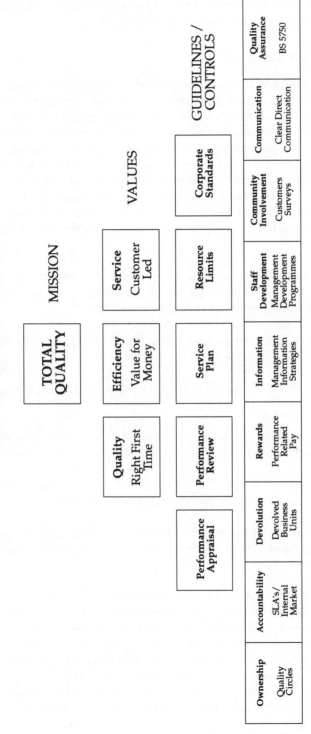

Figure 13.3 (Source: Certified Accountant, *March 1993)*

In the UK, national encouragement to improve quality systems is provided by the British Standards Institute, especially BS 5750.

British Standard 5750

BS 5750 applies to all types of organisation and a wide variety have obtained accreditation. These include; travel agents, solicitors, transport firms, tyre and exhaust fitters, local government as well as numerous manufacturers.

BS 5750 seeks to encourage organisations to develop quality management systems and its award provides public recognition that organisations have reached certain standards. BS 5750 is not a product or service testing system, nor does it set specific quality standards. It concentrates on checking whether there is a framework of procedures, systems and records throughout the organisation relating to quality.

To become accredited under BS 5750 the organisation has to satisfy external assessors that it has the main elements of a quality system. These include:

- There must be adequate documentation to support the quality systems across the whole organisation including; customer specifications, product routeing, control and test procedures etc.

- There must be a designated senior manager with the responsibility of ensuring BS 5750 requirements are met.

- Records are required to ensure that customer quality requirements are being met.

- There must be written control of the quality systems to be applied by suppliers and procedures for inspecting and testing incoming goods.

- there must be effective internal quality audit systems and appropriate statistical techniques for monitoring quality standards.

- Quality systems must be planned and developed across all functions in the organisation with adequate resources, equipment and training.

BS 5750 is clearly a major step in promoting the idea that quality is everyone's responsibility and increasingly Government suppliers are required to have accreditation. However it should be pointed out that the Standard, and the voluminous records and manuals associated with it, has received some criticism for being over-bureaucratic and encouraging 'paper-compliance'.The principles of BS 5750 are being adopted internationally under the standard ISO 9000.

The concluding part of this chapter describes some important techniques associated with production. These include; Stock Control, Work Study and Value Engineering.

Stock control

Alternatively known as *inventory control*, this is a system used to control the organisation's investment in stock. This includes; the recording and monitoring of stock levels, forecasting future demands and deciding when and how many to order. The overall objective of inventory control is to minimise, in total, the cost associated with stock. These costs can be categorised into three groups:

Carrying costs i.e. storage costs, interest on capital invested, handling, deterioration etc.

Ordering costs i.e. purchasing, transport, reception and, for internal manufacture, set-up and tooling costs.

Stock-out costs i.e. lost sales, lost goodwill, cost of production stoppages etc.

As with most techniques stock control has its own jargon. A number of the more common terms are illustrated in Figure 13.4 and defined below. The diagram shows a typical 'Saw-tooth' pattern with stocks gradually declining through usage and then being replaced by fresh deliveries.

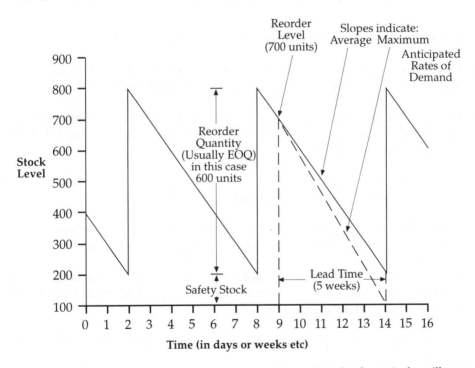

Figure 13.4: Stock terminology illustrated

The diagram shows a simple stock position with the following assumptions and values:

- Regular rate of demand of 100 units per week
- Fixed lead time of 5 weeks
- Re-order quantity 600 units
- Maximum rate of demand 140 units per week
- Safety stock 200 units
- Re-order level 700 units

Notes:

(a) It will be seen that the 200 safety stock is necessary to cope with periods of maximum demand during the lead time.

(b) With constant rates of demand, as shown, the average stock is the safety stock plus 1/2 reorder quantity

i.e. in example above average stock $= 200 + \dfrac{1}{2} (600)$

$$= 500 \; units$$

Definitions of the stock control features shown in Figure 13.4 follow.

(a) *Lead or procurement time.* The period of time between ordering (externally or internally) and replenishment, i.e. when the goods are available for use.

(b) *Economic Ordering Quantity (EOQ) or Economic Batch Quantity (EBQ).* This is a calculated reorder quantity which minimises the balance of cost between carrying costs and ordering costs.

(c) *Buffer Stock or Minimum Stock or Safety Stock.* A stock allowance to cover errors in forecasting the lead time or the demand during the lead time.

(d) *Maximum Level.* A stock level calculated as the maximum desirable which is used as an indicator to management to show when stocks have risen too high.

(e) *Reorder Level.* The level of stock (usually free stock) at which a further replenishment order should be placed. The reorder level is dependent on the lead time and the rate of demand during the lead time.

(f) *Reorder Quantity.* The quantity of the replenishment order, frequently, but not always, the EOQ.

Calculating control levels

Typical methods of calculating the major control levels: Reorder Level, Minimum Level, and Maximum Level, are illustrated below using the following data:

Average usage	100 units per day
Minimum usage	60 units per day
Maximum usage	130 units per day
Lead time	20–26 days
EOQ (previously calculated)	4000 units

Reorder level = Maximum usage × maximum lead time
$$= 130 \times 26$$
$$= 3380 \ units$$

Minimum level = Reorder level - average usage in average lead time
$$= 3380 - (100 \times 23)$$
$$= 3380 - 2300$$
$$= 1080 \ units$$

Maximum level = Reorder level + EOQ - minimum anticipated usage in minimum lead time
$$= 3380 + 4000 - (60 \times 20)$$
$$= 6180 \ units$$

Notes:

(a) These are the normal control levels encountered in basic inventory control systems. Each time an entry is made, a comparison would be made between actual stock and the control level.

(b) Reorder level is a definite action level; maximum and minimum levels are levels at which management would be warned that a potential danger may occur.

(c) The minimum level is set so that management are warned when usage is above average and buffer stock is being used. There may be no danger, but the situation needs watching.

(d) The maximum level is set so that management will be warned when demand is the minimum anticipated and consequently stock may rise above maximum intended.

(e) The calculation of control levels is done relatively infrequently in manual systems, but in a computer based system calculations would take place automatically to reflect current and forecast future conditions.

Economic ordering quantity (EOQ)

It will be recalled from above that the EOQ is a calculated order quantity which minimised the balance of cost between ordering and carrying costs. To be able to calculate a basic EOQ certain assumptions are necessary.

> ☐ That there is a known, constant stockholding cost.
>
> ☐ That there is a known, constant ordering cost.
>
> ☐ That rates of demand are known.
>
> ☐ That there is a known, constant price per unit.
>
> ☐ That replenishment is made instantaneously i.e. the whole batch is delivered at once.

The above assumptions are wide ranging and it is unlikely that all could be made in practice. Nevertheless the EOQ calculation is a useful starting point in establishing an appropriate reorder quantity.

The EOQ formula is given below.

$$\text{EOQ} = \sqrt{\frac{2.\text{Co}.\text{D}}{\text{Cc}}}$$

where: Co = Ordering cost per order
D = Demand per annum
Cc = Carrying cost per item per annum

Example

Find the EOQ where the forecasted demand is 1000 units per month, the ordering cost is £350 per order, the units cost £8 each and it is estimated that carrying costs are 15% per annum.

Here: Co = £350
D = 1000 x 12
= 12,000 units per annum
Cc = £8 x 15%
= £1.2 per item per annum

Thus: $$\text{EOQ} = \sqrt{\frac{2 \times 350 \times 1200}{1.2}}$$

= *2646 units*

It will be seen that it has been necessary to bring the factors to a common timescale, in this example, in annual terms.

Work study

The modern technique of Work Study evolved from the pioneering work of Taylor, Gantt and the Gilbreths in America during the early years of this century. Work Study consists of two complementary techniques, Method Study and Work Measurement. It is a systematic method of examining work and working methods in order to reduce waste and costs and to increase productivity. Normally, method study takes place first followed by work measurement. These two techniques are described below.

Method study

This is a detailed analysis of work in order to improve cost-effectiveness and increase productivity. It can cover a variety of production problems including; the detection and elimination of unnecessary or difficult operations and movements, the way materials and parts are handled and transported, the design of tools, jigs and fixtures, the design and layout of the work-place, the design of the product and so on.Method Study is only worthwhile for repetitive operations and volume production where a fraction of a penny saved per item becomes significant if millions are produced.

Standard Symbol	Meaning
◯	Operation (ie carrying out work)
➜	Transportation (ie moving something)
▢	Inspection
D	Delay (or temporary storage)
△	Pemanent storage

Figure 13.5: Standard method study symbols

There are a number of steps in a typical Method Study which are outlined below:

Select   process, product operation to be studied. Typically this is on the basis of potential cost savings and/or bottleneck and/or volume.

Record   in detail, all relevant facts of the current or proposed methods. Typically the record is a specialised form of flow chart or diagram (see below).

Analyse   critically all data gathered asking questions such as; why is this done? Are there unnecessary operations, movements? How could it be improved? and so on.

Develop   an improved method/tool/sequence etc.

Install   the improved method ensuring full guidance and training is provided.

Monitor   the progress of the new method in order to resolve problems, make adjustments and so on.

As mentioned above it is normal to use flowcharts to record the work done, movements, delays, timings etc. and standard method study symbols are used, as shown in Figure 13.5

Other types of diagrams used in Method Study include; String diagrams (mainly to show movements) Multiple Activity Charts (where several workers/machines are recorded on the same chart) and Flow Diagrams. In addition, photography using still or video cameras, is used extensively especially where there are rapid movements or operations.

Work measurement

When the job or method has been precisely defined by Method Study, Work measurement takes place in order to establish a standard time for the operation(s). Standard times are required for numerous purposes including; payment and incentive schemes, product costing, production planning and scheduling, machine and labour scheduling and so on.

Standard times are established using a technique called *Time Study*. Based on the method or job as defined by Method Study procedures (described earlier) Time Study uses the following steps to arrive at a standard time.

Sub-divide   job into various short elements.

Measure   performance of person carrying out the job elements (usually by stopwatch).

Rate   observed performance in terms of 'average' performance levels to establish a *basic time*.

Add   allowances for fatigue, relaxation etc. to basic time to arrive at the *standard time*.

The last two steps outlined above require judgement to be exercised by the time study analyst, hence it should be remembered that there is an element of subjectivity in all standard times.

Rating means that the analyst has to judge whether the person being observed is working below or above or at 'average' pace. Average pace is denoted by 100 so a person judged to be working *below average* may be rated at 85 whilst another, judged to be working *above average*, may be rated at 120. Using the Rating a basic time is calculated using the formula:

$$\text{Basic time} = \text{Observed time} \times \frac{\text{Rating}}{100}$$

For example, an operative is timed for a particular work element at 24 seconds and is judged to be working below average pace at a rating of 90.

$$\text{Basic Time} = 24 \text{ seconds} \times \frac{90}{100}$$

$$= 21.6 \text{ seconds}$$

The Basic Times for each one of the elements in the whole operations are added together to form the Basic Time for the entire operation or job. To this Basic Time is added various allowances for tool and material collection, personal needs, unavoidable delays etc. to arrive at the Standard Time.

The above outline deals with *direct* Time Study i.e. where a job is already in existence so can be directly studied and timed. Sometimes direct timing is not possible because times are required for new jobs or new designs. In these cases *indirect* Time Study is used. There are two main methods; *Synthetic Timing* which uses records of similar parts or operations which have been directly studied in the past and *Predetermined Motion Time Study* which uses previously determined universal times for the smallest basic hand, eye and other movements which are required for any job element.

Value engineering (or value analysis)

This is a technique used extensively in volume production. It is a searching examination of the function of a product or component in order to find ways to fulfil the function at the least possible cost without any decline in quality or reliability. Its overall aim is to optimise the value of the product to the customer.

Value analysis tries to get away from conventional approaches and solutions by applying lateral thinking to problems. It is normally undertaken by multi-disciplinary teams (e.g. designers, engineers, accountants, buyers, production personnel) in order to approach the problem from many directions with many different types of expertise. The Japanese apply value engineering as a matter of routine throughout the design stage of a product and the technique has been credited with numerous successes.

Key point summary

☐ The Production process transforms inputs into outputs using facilities.

☐ Production Management deals with longer-term and shorter-term planning and decision making and includes; product design, job design, quality management, production and stock control etc.

☐ Jobbing production is work done to special order using general purpose machinery and equipment.

☐ Batch production is the production of a quantity of the same basic item using a sequenced series of operations.

☐ Flow production means that items are made on a continuous basis with a flow from one operation/process to the next.

☐ Flow production consists of both process production and mass or assembly-line production.

☐ Just-in-Time systems aim for zero stocks, perfect quality, constant improvement and production on demand.

☐ Materials Requirements Planning is a computerised information, planning and control system.

☐ Advanced Manufacturing Technology is the use of computers and electronic equipment at all stages of the production process.

☐ Computer Aided Design and Computer Aided Manufacture are extensively used.

☐ Total Quality Control aims for zero defects and operates at all stages of production.

☐ Total Quality Management means that quality awareness and improvement permeates the whole organisation at every level.

☐ Quality Circles seek to develop and implement improvements directly at the work-place.

☐ British Standard 5750 is awarded to organisations who satisfy external assessors that they have the procedural elements of a quality system.

☐ Stock or Inventory Control is used to minimise the total of carrying, ordering and stock-out costs.

❐   The Economic Ordering Quantity formula is $\sqrt{\dfrac{2.Co.D}{Cc}}$

❐   Work Study is a systematic method of examining and improving work. It comprises Method Study and Work Measurement.

❐   Value Engineering or Value Analysis examines the function(s) of a product in order to find alternative, cheaper ways of achieving the function(s).

Self review questions

1.   *What is Production Management?*

2.   *What are the features of jobbing, batch and flow production?*

3.   *What is process production?*

4.   *What are the characteristics of Just-in-Time (JIT) systems?*

5.   *What is Materials Requirements Planning?*

6.   *Describe Advanced Manufacturing Technology.*

7.   *What is Total Quality Control?*

8.   *What are the characteristics of Total Quality Management?*

9.   *Why does Total Quality Management affect organisation structures?*

10.   *What is BS 5750?*

11.   *What is Stock Control?*

12.   *How is the EOQ calculated?*

13.   *What is Work Study?*

14.   *What is Time Study?*

15.   *Describe Value Analysis.*

14 Management functions: finance and accounting

Objectives

After you have studied this chapter you will:

☐ *Know that Financial Accounting mainly deals with external matters.*

☐ *Understand the meaning of key terms such as; debtors and creditors, fixed and current assets etc.*

☐ *Know that Profit and Loss is a summary of the costs, revenues and profit/loss for a period.*

☐ *Be able to describe Gross and Net Profit, Retained Profit and Reserves.*

☐ *Understand that a Balance Sheet is a snapshot view of the assets and liabilities of the business.*

☐ *Know that Cash Flow Statements show the causes of the cash changes from period to period.*

☐ *Understand the principles and objectives of Ratio analysis.*

☐ *Be able to describe cost analysis and cost ascertainment.*

☐ *Understand the general principles of cost behaviour.*

☐ *Know the objectives and methods of budgeting for planning and control.*

☐ *Be able to calculate budgetary and standard cost variances.*

☐ *Understand what is relevant information for decision making.*

☐ *Know what is meant by Marginal costing.*

☐ *Be able to describe the working capital cycle and understand its importance.*

☐ *Understand how to draw up Cash Forecasts.*

☐ *Understand the principles of investment appraisal and the techniques of payback and discounted cash flow.*

The scope of finance and accounting

Finance and accounting is the specialist management function responsible for collecting, recording and analysing financial data and for presenting financial statements and financial information of all types to managers and others inside the organisation and/or to people outside the organisation.

For convenience of study the whole subject is divided into three sections as shown below but it should be emphasised that there are many overlaps between the three sub-divisions and in practice they are often all dealt with by one department. The three main sub-divisions of finance and accounting are:

Financial accounting

includes the stewardship function, external relationships, record keeping using ledger accounting, preparation of the key statutory financial statements, tax computations etc. The main emphasis is on recording, analysing and reporting on past activities.

Management accounting

includes product costing, cost control through budgets and standards, provision of financial information for planning, control and decision making. The main focus is on the production of relevant information for internal purposes.

Financial management

includes working capital and cash management, raising finance, dividend policy, investment appraisal.

The three sections are dealt with in more detail below.

Financial accounting

Modern accounting evolved out of management's stewardship function and this remains a key role of financial accounting. Stewardship means accounting for and taking care of the financial resources entrusted to the management of the organisation by the owners, for example, by the shareholders.

There are many definitions of financial accounting and a comprehensive one is:

The classification and recording of monetary transactions of an entity in accordance with established concepts, principles, accounting standards and legal requirements and presentation of a view of the effect of those transactions during and at the end of an accounting period.

from the Terminology, Chartered Institute of Management Accountants.

The various elements in the above definition are expanded below:

❏ All financial transactions are recorded using *double-entry accounting* in *ledgers*. (Note: the same terms and principles are used whether the system is manual or computerised).

❏ The different classes and types of transactions are separately identified and recorded. For example; cash sales and sales on credit, purchases of assets used permanently in the business i.e. *fixed assets* and temporary assets such as goods for resale i.e. *current assets*, amounts owed by the business to *creditors* and amounts owed to the business by *debtors* and so on.

❏ The records are summarised in such a way that the owners and others can see the overall effect of all the transactions. The two key summary statements are the *Profit and Loss Account* (which shows the profit or loss made over a period) and the *Balance Sheet* (which shows the assets and liabilities and capital employed of the business at the end of the period).

❏ Companies are the main form of business organisation and the records they must keep and the information they must make public are defined by Statute in great detail in the Companies Act 1985 (Amended 1989). In addition to statutory requirements the Accounting Profession specifies what is regarded as 'best practice'; through Statements of Standard Accounting Practice (SSAP's) and Financial Reporting Standards.

The key statements that must be published are: the Balance Sheet, the Profit and Loss Account, the Directors' Report, the Auditors' Report and Notes to the Accounts. In addition, a Cash Flow Statement is usually published although this latter statement is not a statutory requirement.

Because of their special importance in financial accounting the Profit and Loss Account and the Balance Sheet are described in more detail below.

The profit and loss (P & L) account

The P & L account is a summary statement of the revenues and costs of the organisation and resulting profit or loss for a past period. The Companies Act specifies that a P & L account must be published annually although for internal management purposes P & L accounts are often prepared on a monthly basis. The P & L account shows what happened in the period covered and is based on a number of accounting conventions of which some key ones are shown below.

Key accounting conventions

Realisation – profit is deemed to be earned at the time of sale not at the time of payment.

Accruals – revenues and costs are recognised and included in financial statements as they are earned or incurred not as they are received or paid.

Conservatism or Prudence – known liabilities or losses are provided for in current statements but gains or profits are only included when they have been realised.

> *Going Concern* – it is assumed that the business will continue in operational exis-
> tence for the forseeable future.
>
> *Consistency* – there should be consistent accounting treatment of like items from
> period to period.
>
> *Business entity* – the business is seen as separate from the owner(s).

For internal purposes most firms prepare a Trading and Profit and Loss account although only an abbreviated version of this usually is published for outsiders. Below is shown a typical Trading and P & L account for internal use.

ABC Limited – Wholesalers

Trading and Profit and Loss account for the year ending 31st December 19x4.

			£000	See Note
	Sales		11,162	
less	Cost of Goods Sold	£000		
	Opening stock	1,291		
+	purchases	10,702		
		11,993		
–	Closing stock	1,648	10,345	(a)
=	Gross Profit		817	(b)
less	Expenses			(c)
	Wages and salaries	329		
	Rents and Rates	52		
	Depreciation	28		
	Vehicle costs	61		
	Insurance	17		
	Heating	14		
	Maintenance	32		
	Sundry expenses	19	552	
=	Net profit before tax		265	(d)
	less Corporation Tax due		87	(e)
=	Net profit after tax		178	
	less Proposed dividends		100	(f)
	Transferred to General Reserve		78	(g)

(a) From the sales (both for Cash and on Credit) is deducted the cost of goods sold to arrive at the Gross Profit. The cost of goods sold is found from the simple formula:

Value of Stock at beginning of period (i.e. 1st January 19x4)
+   All purchases during period of goods for resale
−   Value of stock at end of period (i.e. 31st December 19x4)

=   Cost of Goods Sold during the period (i.e. the year ending 31 Dec 19x4)

(b) The gross profit is the margin between the cost of goods and what they are sold for. The part of the account that finds the Gross Profit is the Trading account.

(c) The expenses (or overheads) are the running costs of the business. Only a few typical items are shown; most businesses have many more. In published P & L accounts all the various expenses are usually summarised under two or three headings such as Administration, Distribution, Financial expenses etc.

(d) Net profit is; gross profit − expenses. Note that all the items in the account (sales, purchases, expenses) use the accruals convention i.e. they are included when they are earned or incurred not when the cash is received or paid. For example it is highly likely that ABC Limited have not received all the cash due to them for the sales on credit which are included. Conversely they may not yet have paid for all the purchases included.

(e) Limited companies pay Corporation Tax on their profits. This is at varying rates dependent on the size of the company and the amount of profit. Note that ABC's tax, as at 31st December 19x4, has not been paid.

(f) A dividend is the return from the company that the owners (i.e. the Shareholders) receive. ABC have an Issued Share Capital of 1,000,000 £1 shares so the proposed dividend is at the rate of 10p per £1 share i.e. 1,000,000 x 10p = £100,000. Note that this dividend has not yet been paid so is owed by ABC Ltd to its Shareholders at the Balance Sheet date.

(g) The net amount of profits after deducting the tax due and the proposed dividend is to be retained within ABC Ltd. The residual amount of profit is transferred to the General Reserve.

Balance sheets

Unlike P & L accounts which cover a period, balance sheets are a 'snapshot' view of the business on a particular date, usually the last day of the financial year. A balance sheet is a summarised statement of the organisation's assets (i.e. things it owns), liabilities (i.e. what it owes to its creditors) and capital employed (i.e. the shareholders' capital and reserves). The Balance Sheet of ABC Ltd as at 31st December 19x4 is shown below.

ABC Limited – Wholesalers

Balance Sheet as at 31st December 19x4

Notes

(a) FIXED ASSETS

	Cost	Accumulated Depreciation	Written down Value
	£000	£000	£000
Fixtures and Fittings	1800	750	1050
Vehicles	310	134	176
	2110	884	1226

(b) Current Assets

Stock	1648	
Cash and Bank	113	
Debtors	983	
	2744	

(c) less Creditors due within 1 year

Tax due	87	
Proposed dividend	100	
Trade creditors	1240	1427

(d) = Net Current Assets   1317

(e) = Net Assets   2543

Represented by

(f) Issued Share Capital

1,000,000 £1 Ordinary Shares   1000

(g) General Reserve B/F   1465

+ Transfer for current year   78   1543

2543

Notes

(a) Fixed assets are those assets bought and retained for use within a business. They
are shown at original cost less all the depreciation that has written off to date.
This gives their written down or book value. Note that part of the accumulated
depreciation is the depreciation charged in this year's P & L account. Fixed assets
arise from *Capital expenditure.*

(b) Current assets are the temporary, fluctuating assets which are acquired during
normal trading e.g. stocks of goods for resale, amounts owed by credit customers
i.e. the debtors. Current assets arise from *revenue expenditure* and sales.

(c) These are amounts that ABC owe and which will have to be settled fairly soon.
Trade creditors arise from purchases on credit by ABC Ltd. Note that the tax due
of £87,000 and the proposed dividend of £100,000 are the values from the P & L
account shown earlier.

(d) Net Current Assets is the amount by which Current Assets exceed Current Liabilities. This figure is considered an important test of a firm's ability to pay its way.

(e) This is the net value of all assets (Fixed and Net current) used in the business. It could also be called the balance sheet *Net Worth* or *Capital Employed*.

(f) This is the share capital of ABC owned by the shareholders. An alternative term for Ordinary Shares is *Equity Shares*. Ordinary shares are the ultimate risk bearing shares and are not guaranteed any dividend although businesses prefer to pay dividends as consistently as possible. Some firms also have *Preference Shares*. These are shares with a fixed rate of dividend (e.g. 8%) which must be paid before any dividend is paid to the Ordinary Shareholders.

(g) The General Reserve is the cumulative amount of profits which have been retained in the business over the years. Equally, this could be called *Revenue Reserve* or *Unappropriated Profit*. Note that this is not a sum of cash; the Reserve is already represented by the various assets shown in the Balance Sheet.

Cash flow statements

Each year, in addition to a P & L account and a Balance Sheet most businesses produce a Cash Flow Statement as specified by Financial Reporting Standard 1 (FRS 1). The Statement shows in some detail the causes of the change in cash and cash equivalents between last year's Balance Sheet and this year's.

A full FRS 1 statement is a complex document usually prepared by a qualified accountant but an outline is shown below.

Outline of FRS 1 cash flow statement for year ending XXX

	£
Net Cash Flow from operations	XXX
+ or – Returns on investment and servicing of finance	
(i.e. interest and dividends paid and received)	XXX
– Tax paid	XXX
+ or – Purchase/Sales of Fixed Assets	XXX
= Net Cash Flow before financing	XXX
+ or – Financing cash flows	
(i.e. share issues, receipt/repayment of loans)	XXX
= Increase/Decrease in Cash and Cash Equivalents	XXX

Interpretation of accounts and ratio analysis

The main financial statements (the P & L account and Balance Sheet) present historical information using various conventions and judgements. As a consequence there are many problems in using them to assess company or management performance and it is quite possible to come to wrong conclusions. This point should be borne in mind whilst studying what follows.

In general, absolute values by themselves provide little useful information when analysing accounts. For example, in a year a firm made £50,000 profit. Is this good or bad? Without more information we cannot tell. It may be excellent for a street corner shop but would be a disaster for Marks and Spencers. Accordingly it is normal to relate one figure to another using *ratio analysis* in order to provide more relevant information. For example we could relate *Profit* to the *Sales* required to make the profit.

Before considering particular ratios we must first examine some factors which make ratio analysis more useful.

Trends

A single ratio is of little value so it is normal to prepare ratios for several years to see if there is an upward or downward trend.

Comparisons

It is useful to compare the ratios for one company with other similar companies. However, companies differ so care is needed. Like must be compared with like.

Industry averages

Where averages for the whole industry are available (e.g. from Trade Associations, Inter-Firm comparisons etc.) these are useful for comparison.

Basis of ratios used

When making any type of comparison it is essential that the same basis is used both for the information and the ratio itself. For example, there would be little point in comparing Gross Profit:Sales ratio of one firm with the Net Profit:Sales ratio of another.

Types of ratios

Literally hundreds of different ratios may be prepared if thought useful but we shall only consider a few key ones to show general principles.

Ratios may be separated into two broad categories thus:

Performance ratios to assess the firm's profitability, how it uses its capital and so on.

Liquidity ratios to assess a firm's solvency, cash flows and so on.

Performance ratios are considered first.

Performance ratios

Three key ratios are shown below:

Ratio 1   Return of Capital Employed (ROCE) = $\dfrac{\text{Net Profit}}{\text{Capital Employed}}$

(also known as the Primary Ratio. Note there are many variants of this ratio.)

Ratio 2   Profit to Sales Ratio = $\dfrac{\text{Net Profit}}{\text{Sales}}$

(this ratio gives the Percentage profit on sales)

Ratio 3   Rate of asset turnover = $\dfrac{\text{Sales}}{\text{Capital Employed}}$

(this shows how intensively the assets are used)

NB   Ratio 1 = Ratio 2 × Ratio 3

Based on the P & L account and Balance Sheet of ABC Limited shown earlier, worked examples of the three Performance ratios are shown below.

$$\text{ROCE} = \dfrac{\text{Net Profit}}{\text{Capital Employed}}$$

$$= \dfrac{£265,000}{£2,543,000}$$

$$= 10.4\%$$

(Note that Net Profit before tax and Net Assets (i.e. equivalent to Share Capital + Reserves) have been used. Other definitions of profit and capital employed are, of course, possible).

$$\text{Profit: Sales} = \dfrac{\text{Net Profit}}{\text{Sales}}$$

$$= \dfrac{£265,000}{£11,625,000}$$

$$= 2.37\%$$

$$\text{Rate of Asset Turnover} = \dfrac{\text{Sales}}{\text{Capital Employed}}$$

$$= \dfrac{£11,162,000}{£2,543,000}$$

$$= 4.39 \text{ times}$$

and ROCE = Percentage on Sales × Asset turnover

i.e.   10.4% = 2.37% × 4.39

Thus it will be seen that the Return on Capital is dependent on both the profit on sales and how intensively the assets are used to make sales.

Liquidity ratios

Five commonly used ratios are shown below although many others are possible.

$$Current\ ratio = \frac{Current\ assets}{Current\ liabilities}$$

(This ratio effectively assesses the Working Capital of the firm. Traditionally a value of 2:1 has been thought to be desirable but considerable variation is encountered.)

$$Acid\ Test\ ratio = \frac{Current\ assets - Stock}{Current\ liabilities}$$

(also known as the 'Quick Ratio' it concentrates on the immediate liquidity and solvency of the firm)

$$Stock\ turnover\ ratio = \frac{Cost\ of\ goods\ sold\ in\ period}{Average\ stock\ in\ period}$$

(this measures the conversion of stocks into Sales. In general the faster the rate, the better)

$$Average\ collection\ period\ in\ days = \frac{Debtors}{Credit\ Sales} \times 365$$

(this measures how well the firm collects its debts)

$$Average\ payment\ period\ in\ days = \frac{Creditors}{Credit\ purchases} \times 365$$

(the measure of how long it takes, on average, for the firm takes to pay its debts).

Again using the figures from the ABC Limited Statements given earlier worked examples of the above ratios are given below.

$$Current\ Ratio = \frac{Current\ assets}{Current\ liabilities}$$

$$= \frac{£2,744,000}{£1,427,000}$$

$$= 1.92$$

$$Acid\ Test = \frac{Current\ assets - Stock}{Current\ liabilities}$$

$$= \frac{£2,744,000 - 1,648,000}{£1,427,000}$$

$$= 0.77$$

$$\text{Stock turnover} = \frac{\text{Cost of goods sold}}{\text{Average Stock}}$$

$$= \frac{£10,345,000}{£1,469,500^*}$$

$$= 7.04 \text{ times}$$

*The average stock has been calculated as follows. (Opening Stock + Closing Stock) ÷2 i.e. (£1,291,000 + 1,648,000) ÷2 = £1,469,500.

$$\text{Average collection period} = \frac{\text{Debtors}}{\text{Credit Sales}} \times 365$$

$$= \frac{£983,000}{£11,162,000^*} \times 365$$

$$= 32.14 \text{ days}$$

*It has been assumed that all sales were on credit. If this was found not to be the case clearly some adjustment would be required.

$$\text{Average payment period} = \frac{\text{Creditors}}{\text{Credit purchases}} \times 365$$

$$= \frac{£1,240,000}{£10,897,000^*} \times 365$$

$$= 41.53 \text{ days}$$

* It has been assumed that purchases of goods for resale and expenses (excluding Wages, Salaries and depreciation) were all on credit.

To gain the maximum information from the Performance and Liquidity Ratios calculated above it would be normal to calculate the same ratios for several years to assess trends and to compare the calculated ratios and trends with those from similar companies, if available.

Having briefly outlined some important features of Financial Accounting we now turn to what is known as *Management Accounting*.

Management accounting (MA)

MA is that part of accounting which is concerned with identifying, presenting and interpreting information to management. MA deals mainly with internal matters and provides vital financial information to management in three inter-related areas.

- ❏ Cost analysis and cost ascertainment
- ❏ Planning and control
- ❏ Decision making and performance appraisal

These three areas are developed below.

Cost analysis and cost ascertainment

The foundation of MA is a well developed cost analysis system. At a minimum every item of expenditure is classified in two ways; by *type of expenditure* and the *location or use of the expenditure*. Types of expenditure include; wages, materials, salaries, electricity, rates, insurance etc. etc. The location or use may include; expenditure going directly into the product, that spent by the Advertising Department, the Personnel Office etc. etc. This primary analysis is necessary to be able to answer questions such as; 'What did it cost to run the Drawing Office last year?' or 'How much did we spend on materials?' or 'How much did it cost to produce component x?'

All costs may be classified as either *direct* or *indirect*.

Direct costs are those that can be directly identified with a product or service i.e.

☐ Direct Material – the materials incorporated into the finished product.

☐ Direct Labour or Wages – the wages of the people who make the product

☐ Direct Expenses – Any other expenses directly associated with the product e.g. royalties

The total of direct costs is known as the PRIME COST

All costs which are not direct are indirect, and are usually known as overheads. There are many more types of overheads than direct costs; in large organisations there may be thousands of different types of expenditure which make up the total of overheads. Naturally, overheads form part of the total costs of the organisation so it is necessary for each product made (or service provided) to carry an appropriate share of overheads. Thus, in outline, a product cost is found as follows:

Outline product cost

	£
Direct Labour	xxx
Direct Materials	xxx
Direct Expense	xxx
= Prime Cost	xxx
+ Share of overheads	xxx
= Total Cost	xxx

On the whole, direct costs are readily identifiable with the product but several steps are required to deal with overheads.

Dealing with overheads

Using the two-way expenditure analysis mentioned earlier, overhead items are charged to the various departments, known as *cost centres*. Some expenditure items are *general costs* not identifiable with a specific cost centre so the cost has to be spread over all cost centres. This process is known as *apportionment*. For example, the total charge for Business Rates is apportioned (or spread) over all the cost centres on the basis of their floor areas; the larger the cost centre, the more Rates are charged to it.

Having arrived at the total of overheads for a cost centre there remains the problem of ensuring that each unit of the product or service that goes through the cost centre carries an appropriate share of those overheads. This is done by the process known as *overhead absorption* or *overhead recovery*. Typically, the amount of overheads per labour or machine hour (known as the Overhead Absorption Rate – OAR) is calculated and then applied to the products according to the number of labour or machine hours that the product takes. This is shown in outline in Figure 14.1

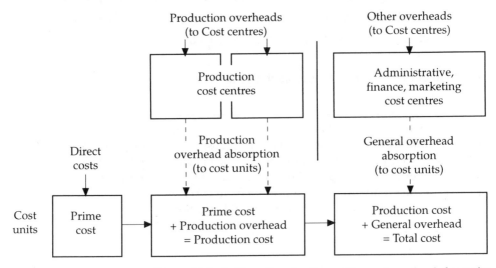

Figure 14.1: Outline of production costing and overhead absorption

An example of a typical Product cost calculation follows:

Example

A batch of 150 control units was made with the following details recorded

	£
Direct Materials	2591
Direct Wages	4328

The panels were made in two departments, Machining and Assembly and the following details recorded for the batch:

Machining Department   64 machine hours
Assembly Department   93 labour hours

The previously calculated Overhead Absorption Rates are

Machine Department   £25 per machine hour
Assembly Department   £11 per labour hour

Administrative overheads are recovered at 20% of total production cost.

What is the cost per control unit?

Solution

Batch Cost – 150 Control Units

	£
Direct Materials	2591
Direct Wages	4328
= Prime Cost	6919
Production Overheads	
Machining dept (64 hrs @ £25 per hr)	1600
Assembly dept (193 hrs @ £11 per hr)	2123
= Production Cost	10642
+ Administrative Overheads (20% × 10642)	2128
= Total Batch cost	12770

$$\therefore \text{Cost per unit} = \frac{12770}{150} = £85.13$$

Note: The choice whether to absorb overheads on machine hours or labour hours depends on the type of department and overheads. A department which is heavily mechanised with most overheads related to the machinery would use machine hours. Less machine dependent departments are likely to use labour hours.

The type of product costing outlined above is known as *absorption costing* or *total absorption costing*. It is the traditional method and is widely used. An alternative method which is becoming more popular is *Activity Based Costing (ABC)*. ABC treats direct costs in exactly the same way but absorbs overheads into the product according to the usage of what are known as cost drivers, rather than machine or labour hours. Cost drivers are the activities which cause overheads, for example, the number of set-ups, the number of orders and so on. The reasoning behind ABC is that the level of support overheads is greatly influenced by the range and complexity of production rather than simply volume which is the assumption underlying traditional absorption costing. Accordingly it is claimed that product costs using ABC are more realistic.

Cost behaviour

Another important way of classifying costs is by their behaviour especially in response to changes in the level of activity. Three broad categories are possible:

Fixed cost

A cost which remains the same when the activity level changes e.g. Rates, Salaries.

Variable cost

A cost which varies in proportion to changes in activity e.g. direct materials

Semi-variable cost (or semi-fixed cost)

A cost with both fixed and variable elements e.g. telephone charges contain a fixed element – the standing charge, and a variable element which changes with activity – the call charges.

Analysis of costs according to behaviour is used frequently in management accounting. For example in the provision of information for planning, control and decision making.

Information for planning and control

As explained previously planning is the managerial process of deciding in advance *what* is to be done and *how* it is to be done. Control is the process of ensuring that operations proceed according to plan. Naturally cost, revenues and profits are essential elements in planning and control and management accounting is a major supplier of information for these purposes.

There are two key management accounting techniques associated with planning and control: *budgeting* and *standard costing*. These are described below.

Budgeting

Budgeting is a short-term planning and control technique widely used in industry, commerce and government. A budget is a financial expression of a plan. For example, the plan may be to produce 10,000 units. A budget is then developed showing , in detail, the types and amounts of expenditure necessary to produce 10,000 units. This is the *planning* side of budgeting. During and after production *control* is exercised by comparing actual expenditure with that budgeted. The procedures of budgetary planning and control are shown in Figure 14.2.

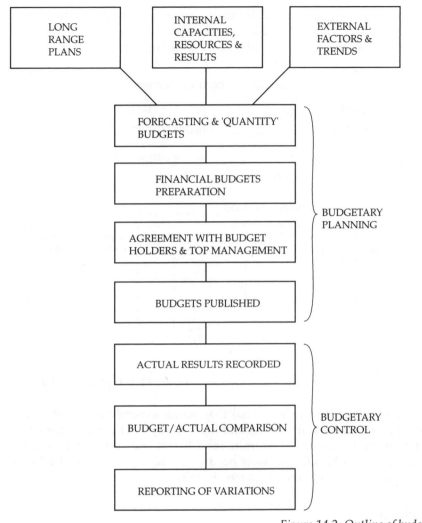

Figure 14.2: Outline of budgeting

Budgeting is usually done for the year ahead divided for control purposes into months. As will be seen from Figure 14.2 budgeting works best within the framework of long range plans.

Properly carried out, budgeting aids *coordination* between departments, improves *communication*, assists *control* and may *motivate* staff to achieve targets.

Budgetary control

Typically, each month every manager receives a budgetary control report showing actual expenditure for each expense item for which he/she is responsible compared with its budgeted amount. The difference betwen the budget and actual is known as a *budget variance*. If an item is broadly in line with budget it can be assumed to be in accordance with the plan. Thus the manager is able to concentrate on the few items not going to plan, as identified by their variances. It is this feature which makes budgetary control a good example of *management by exception*.

Figure 14.3 shows a typical Budgetary Control report.

BUDGETARY CONTROL REPORT NO

BUDGET CENTRE _____   DATE PREPARED _____

BUDGET HOLDER _____   BUDGETED ACTIVITY LEVEL _____

REPORT RELATIONSHIP   UP _____   ACTUAL ACTIVITY LEVEL _____

                       DOWN _____

ACCOUNTING PERIOD _____

BUDGETED ITEM		CURRENT PERIOD			YEAR TO DATE			TREND OF VARIANCE	SIGNIFICANT? (Yes/No)	COMMENTS
CODE	DESCRIPTION	BUDGET	ACTUAL	VARIANCE	BUDGET	ACTUAL	VARIANCE			

Figure 14.3: Typical budgetary control report

For control to be effective it is vital that actual expenditure for the activity level achieved is compared with a budget for that activity level. It is pointless, for example, to compare the budgeted expenditure for a 10,000 unit production level with actual expenditure when 11,000 units were produced. Like must be compared with like.

The way this is done is to use *flexible budgets*.

Flexible budgets

Flexible budgets are budgets designed so that permitted cost levels can be adjusted to suit the level of activity that actually occurred. The key to this flexibility is knowledge about the way the various items of cost are expected to behave, some will remain the same i.e. *fixed*, some will vary proportionately i.e. *variable* and some are a combination of fixed and variable elements, known as *semi-variable*.

The following example shows the main principles of flexible budgeting and budget variances.

Example

The following information is available relating to the overheads of a department.

Cost item	Cost behavioural Characteristics	Budget for average production of 5000 units
		£
Indirect Wages	Semi-variable(£3000 + £1 per unit)	8,000
Consumables	Variable(£3 per unit)	15,000
Maintenance	Semi-variable(£6500 + £2.5 per unit)	19,000
Rates	Fixed	11,500
		53,500

During a period 4650 units were produced and actual costs were

	£
Indirect Wages	7900
Consumables	13250
Maintenance	18750
Rates	11500
	51,400

Required: Calculate the budget variances for the period.

Solution

To calculate the budget variances it is necessary to derive a budget for 4650 units and then compare this with the actual costs. The flexible budget for 4650 units is found using the cost behavioural characteristics shown above.

Cost item	Flexed budget for 4650 units	Actual Costs	Variances
	£	£	£
INDIRECT WAGES (1)	7650	7900	250 (ADV)
CONSUMABLES (2)	13950	13250	700 (FAV)
MAINTENANCE (3)	18125	18750	625 (ADV)
RATES	11500	11500	—
	51,225	51,400	175 (ADV)

The budgeted values are found as follows:

(1) Indirect wages	=	£3000 + 4650 (£1)	=	£ 7650
(2) Consumables	=	4650 (£3)	=	13950
(3) Maintenance	=	£6500 + 4650 (£2.5)	=	18125

Note

An adverse (ADV) variance shows an *overspend*

A favourable (FAV) variance shows an *underspend*

The calculated variances direct attention to possible inefficiencies/efficiencies and are used to try to improve future performance.

Standard costing

Standard costing is a cost control technique similar in principle to budgeting but at a more detailed level. It is best suited to repetitive manufacture and is applied to individual products and operations.

A *standard cost* is developed for a product based on detailed technical estimates for material price and usage, labour rates and efficiency and for overheads. This serves as a target cost for the period ahead against which actual costs are compared and variances calculated. It will be noted that this is similar to budgeting but is carried out in more detail especially with regard to the variance analysis.

Before considering individual variances it is worthwhile emphasising some general principles thus:

☐ Price variances are always extracted first, subsequently all calculations use standard price.

☐ The basis of most variances is the following comparison

| *Actual cost* | is compared with | *Standard Cost* |
| *of Actual Quantity* | | *of Actual Quantity* |

☐ If the variance is sufficiently large it would be thoroughly investigated.

An example follows which illustrates the calculation of some typical variances for material and labour.

Example

The standard cost per unit for material and labour of Part No 226 is:

	Standard Cost Part No 226
	£
Material 12 kgs @ £6.50 kg	78
Labour 4.5 hours at £7.25 hour	33.75
	111.75

During a period 89 units were made and 1124 kilos of material at a cost of £7190 were used. 380 labour hours were worked at a cost of £3040 wages.

Required: Calculate the material and labour variances and comment on their meaning.

Solution

Material Variances

		£	VARIANCE
Actual cost		7190	Price variance
Material			= £116 FAV
less Actual quantity at standard price			
(1124 kgs × £6.50 kg)		7306	
			Material usage
less Std. Qty. for Actual Production × Std. Price			variance
(12 × 89) kgs × £6.50 kg)		6942	= £364 ADV

∴ Total Material Variance = £116 FAV + 364 ADV = £252 ADV

Labour Variances

		£	VARIANCE
Actual cost		3040	Labour Rate
			variance
less Actual hours at Std. Rate			£285 ADV
(380 hrs × £7.25 hour)		2755	
			L'br Efficiency
less Std. hours for Actual Production × Std. Rate			Variance
((4.5 × 89) hours × £7.25)		2904	£149 ADV

∴ Total Labour Variance = £285 ADV + £149 FAV = *£136 ADV*

Note how in each case the calculations move from all at actual to all at standard.

Comments on variances

Material Price, £116 Favourable. This may reflect good purchasing, or may be because of buying inferior material.

Material Usage, £364 adverse. This represents a substantial excess usage which may be because of poor working or using a sub-standard material. Further investigation needed.

Labour Rate, £285 adverse. May be due to paying higher rates or using a higher grade labour than planned.

Labour Efficiency £149 favourable, may be due to the standard labour working more efficiently or the effect of a higher grade of labour.
In each case the variances are not an end in themselves but are a trigger for action.

Decision making and relevant information

Decision making is a vital management task and the management accounting system is an important provider of financial information for decision making purposes. The information supplied must be relevant for the purpose and relevant information for decision making has the following characteristics:

Future costs and revenues

Decision making relates to the future so it is expected future costs and revenues that are important. Costs already spent, known as sunk costs, are irrelevant.

Differences in costs and revenues

If a cost or revenue, remains constant for all the options being considered it can be ignored; only the differences are relevant.

For many short-run decisions the principles of marginal costing are used.

Marginal costing

The key elements of marginal costing are the separation of costs into fixed and variable and the calculation of the amount of *contribution* as follows:

$$\text{Contribution} = \text{Sales} - \text{Marginal Cost}$$

Marginal cost is the variable cost of the product or option and a typical marginal cost statement is as follows:

		£
	Sales	xxx
less	Marginal Cost	xxx
=	Contribution	xxx
less	Fixed cost	xxx
=	Profit	xxx

The importance of marginal costing in short-run decision making is that, over the short-term, fixed costs are likely to remain the same and the only costs that will alter, and are thus relevant, are the variable or marginal costs. Accordingly the option which produces the most contribution is likely to be the best choice.

In many situations a *limiting factor* can be identified. This is a factor which constrains actions. It could be a shortage of skilled labour or materials or sales or finance or some other limitation. Where a single key factor can be identified the general objective of maximising contribution is achieved by selecting the option which *maximises contribution per unit of the limiting factor*.

Some examples follow illustrating the above principles.

Example

Morning Start Ltd. manufacture a breakfast cereal which they sell for 50p per packet. Current output is 200,000 packets per period which represents 80% of capacity. They have the opportunity to use the surplus capacity by selling their product at 30p per packet to a supermarket chain who will sell it as an 'own label' product.

Total costs for last period were £70,000 of which £20,000 were fixed. This represented a total cost of 35p per packet.

Should the supermarket order be accepted even though the selling price is below total cost?

Solution

The key point is that the price of 30p offered by the supermarket should be compared with the marginal cost of production, not with total cost (assuming fixed costs do not change).

The present position is:

	£	
Sales (200,000 × 50p)	10,000	
less marginal cost	50,000	(i.e. 25p per packet)
= Contribution	50,000	
less Fixed cost	20,000	
= Profit	30,000	

The supermarket order would produce the following extra contribution:

	£	
Sales (400,000 × 30p)	12,000	
less marginal cost	10,000	(i.e. 25p per packet)
= Contribution	2,000	

Thus, assuming fixed costs do not alter, the supermarket order seems worthwhile financially although numerous other factors would have to be considered before a final decision was taken.

The following example deals with problems where a limiting factor can be identified.

Example

A company is able to produce four products and is planning its production mix for the next period. Estimated cost, sales, and production data are:

PRODUCT	L	M	N	O
	£	£	£	£
Selling price per unit	60	90	120	108
less variable costs				
Labour (at £6 per hour)	18	12	42	30
Material (at £3 per kg)	18	54	30	36
= Contribution per unit	24	24	48	42
Resources per unit				
Labour (hours)	3	2	7	5
Materials (kgs)	6	18	10	12
Maximum demand (units)	5,000	5,000	5,000	5,000

Based on the above information what is the most profitable production mix if labour hours are limited to 50,000 hours in a period?

Solution

It will be seen that all the products show a contribution so that there is a case for their production. However, because a constraint exists, the products must be ranked in order of contribution per unit of the limiting factor so that overall contribution can be maximised. Accordingly, the contribution per unit of the inputs must be calculated.

PRODUCT	L	M	N	O
	£	£	£	£
Contribution per unit	24	24	48	42
Contribution per labour hour	8	12	6.85	8.5

When labour hours are restricted to 50,000:

To make all products to the demand limits would need $(5,000 \times 3) + (5,000 \times 2) + (5,000 \times 7) + (5,000 \times 5) = 85,000$ hours. As there is a limit of 50,000 hours in a period the products should be ranked in order of attractiveness judged by contribution per labour hour i.e. M,O,L and N

Best production plan when labour is restricted:

Produce	5000 units M using	10,000	labour hours
	5000 units O using	25,000	labour hours
	5000 units L using	15,000	labour hours
	and no units of N		
which uses the total of		50,000	hours available

Thus when labour hours are restricted the maximum possible contribution is $(5000 \times £24) + (5000 \times £42) + (5000 \times £24) = £450,000$.

Where the decision concerns costs and revenues over a number of years ahead *long-term decision-making techniques* are required. These are dealt with in the section on Financial Management.

Break-even charts

The principles of marginal costing are also used to prepare what are known as *break-even charts*. These are charts which show the interaction of costs, revenues and profits at various activity levels. The charts are simple to draw and whilst they provide only an approximate overview of results they are useful as a means of visual presentation and often serve as a summary of more detailed numeric information.

Two forms of break-even chart are shown below both illustrating the following details.

A company makes a single product with a total capacity of 35,000 units. Costs and sales are as follows:

Selling price £7 per unit   Marginal cost £4 per unit   Fixed costs £50,000

Show the profit at an expected production of 27,000 units using
(a) a Traditional Break-Even Chart. (See Figure 14.4).
(b) a Contribution Break-Even Chart (See Figure 14.5).

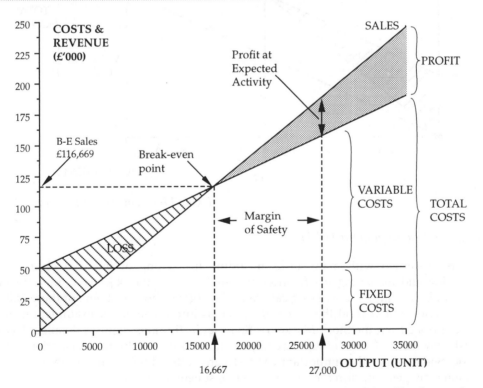

Figure 14.4: Traditional break-even chart

The margin of safety is the difference between the expected production level and the break-even point. In this case, 27,000 – 16,667 = 10,333 units.

Note that in the Traditional B-E Chart, fixed costs are plotted *first* then variable costs.

The Contribution B-E chart uses the same axis and data as that for the traditional chart. The only difference is that variable costs are drawn *before* fixed costs. This produces a 'wedge' (X,O,Y) showing the contribution earned at various activity levels as well as the other information shown on the traditional chart.

Although the above charts have numerous limitations they are commonly used to add visual appeal to management reports.

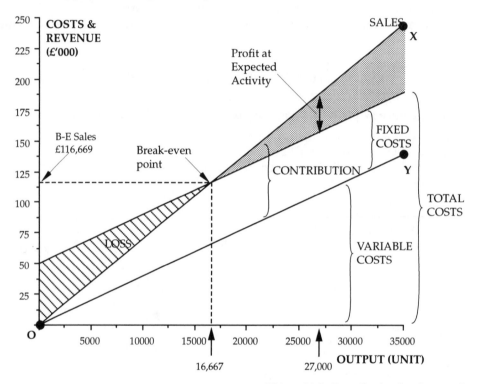

Figure 14.5: Contribution break-even chart

Financial management (FM)

FM is concerned with many tasks including the setting of financial objectives, acquiring and managing the finances required to meet the objectives, investment appraisal, managing the working capital of the organisation etc. Some of these tasks are complex and beyond the scope of this short introduction. For example, raising extra finance from the Stock Market or financial institutions requires detailed, technical knowledge of matters such as company law, taxation, actuarial calculations and so on. Some of the other important FM tasks are outlined below including: working capital management, cash forecasting and investment appraisal.

Working capital management

As previously explained the value of working capital at any one time is found thus

> Current Assets – Current Liabilities = Working Capital

Whilst the above calculation is correct at any one time it fails to emphasise that working capital fluctuates constantly as the firm makes and sells its products, pays wages, settles its debts and so on. Working capital movements and the resulting increases and decreases in cash, need to be considered as constantly changing circulating flows and need to be continually monitored.

Figure 14.6 shows cash flows in a typical working capital cycle.

For completeness the main long-term cash movements are also shown on Figure 14.6 i.e. purchase and sale of fixed assets, increases or decreases in loans and share issues.

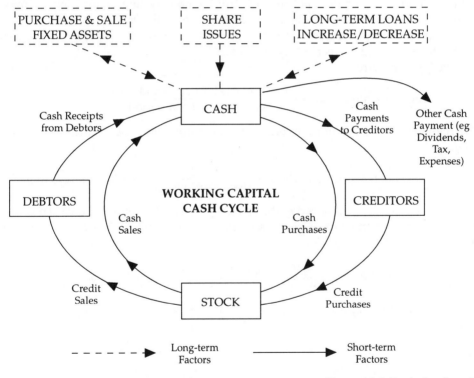

Figure 14.6: Typical cash cycle

There are some external ways of increasing working capital; for example, issuing more shares, raising loans, debt factoring (i.e. selling your book debts at a discount) and these are sometimes used. However even if one or other of these external ways of increasing working capital are used it remains essential to monitor and control the key internal factors. These are:

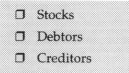

The three factors are dealt with below.

Stocks

For most organisations a certain level of Stocks (raw material, work-in-progress and finished goods) is necessary to service production and to be able to supply customers without delay. However it remains true for all organisations that stocks should be at the minimum level possible.

To do this it is essential that there is proper recording of all stock movements and an appropriate stock control system. It will be recalled that Stock Control was dealt with in Chapter 13, *Production* Stock control includes setting control levels (maximum, minimum, re-order level) and calculating Economic Order Quantities.

To monitor stocks it is normal to calculate various ratios on a regular basis so as to be able to detect, and correct, adverse trends.

Two key ratios are

$$\text{Stock Turnover Ratio} = \frac{\text{Cost of goods over period sold}}{\text{Average Stocks in period}}$$

The higher the ratio the more intensively stocks are being used which assists cash flow.

$$\text{Stock in terms of sales days} = \frac{1}{\text{Stock Turnover Ratio}} \times \text{No. of days in period}$$

The lower the number of sales day the stock represents the better for the cash flow.

For example, if the cost of goods sold in a 30 day period was £2m and average stocks were £400,000 then:

$$\text{Stock turnover} = \frac{£2m}{£400,000} = 5 \text{ times}$$

and Stock represents 6 days sales (i.e. $\frac{1}{5} \times 30$)

Debtors

Some businesses are able to sell most items for cash e.g. retailers, but many firms have to sell on credit. As a result collecting debts is a never-ending chore common to most businesses. It is essential that debtors are kept as low as possible because this has a direct effect on cash flow. Some of the ways that may help are:

(a) Raise and post invoices promptly.

(b) Send monthly statements on time.

(c) Follow up slow payers, send reminders, chase debts by letters and by telephone, and, as a last resort, take legal action.

(d) Offer discounts for prompt payment. Although common this can be expensive for the firm.

In many firms debtors are monitored on a daily basis with various statistics collected including:

❑ analysis by age of debt.

❑ analysis by size of debt.

❑ reminder schedules showing actions taken.

❑ regular calculation of the collection time ratio i.e $\dfrac{\text{Debtors}}{\text{Sales}} \times 365$ to watch for lengthening credit periods.

Creditors

To take excessive credit seems an easy way to ease a firm's cash flow but is not recommended for the following reasons.

❑ suppliers may refuse further credit and insist on cash with order.

❑ there will be a loss of prompt payment discounts.

❑ a supplier may take legal action for debt recovery. If other suppliers hear of this and do likewise it may lead to liquidation.

In general it is good business practice to pay creditors promptly which helps to improve relationships with suppliers.

Overtrading

One of the objects of monitoring working capital and cash flow is to avoid *overtrading* and its consequences. Overtrading is caused by increasing sales at too fast a rate without adequate cash resources. The main indicators are:

(a) Rapidly increasing sales

(b) Increasing stocks

(c) Increasing debtors

(d) Taking longer to pay creditors

To increase sales is normally an excellent thing for an organisation but care must be taken that there is sufficient cash to support the inevitable increases in stocks and debtors and to pay creditors on time.

Cash forecasts

To assess the likely movement of cash over the near future it is normal to prepare *cash forecasts*, alternatively called *cash budgets*, for several periods ahead. These projections are prepared on a rolling basis. For example in January, cash forecasts may be prepared for February, March and April and in February, forecasts would be made for March, April and May and so on.

Cash forecasts enable the organisation to assess whether operations can proceed as planned, whether they need to be curtailed, whether there is the need to approach the bank for a loan and so on. The forecast must include every type of cash outflow and cash receipt. In addition to the *amounts*, the *timings* of all receipts and payments must be forecast.

A typical format for a Cash Forecast is shown in Figure 14.7.

CASH FORECAST

	Period 1	Period 2	Period 3	Period 4
Receipts:	£	£	£	£
OPENING CASH BALANCE b/f	ZZZ	AAA	BBB	CCC
+ Receipts from Debtors + Sales of Capital Items + Any Loans Received + Proceeds from Share Issues + Any other Cash Receipts				
= TOTAL CASH AVAILABLE				
Payments:				
- Payments to Creditors - Wages and Salaries - Loan Repayments - Capital Expenditure - Dividends and Taxation - Any other payments				
= TOTAL CASH PAYMENTS				
= CLOSING CASH BALANCE c/f	AAA	BBB	CCC	

Figure 14.7: Typical layout of cash forecast

Note how the closing balance of cash for one period becomes the opening balance for next period.

Investment appraisal

Investment appraisal is an example of long-run decision making. It is usually applied to capital expenditure decisions i.e. the purchase of assets for use within the organisation e.g. a new machine, launch of a new product, buying a factory and so on.

As in short-run decision making there is the need to consider *future* costs and revenues and changes in costs and revenues. In addition because costs and revenues are being considered over several years ahead, the *time value of money* must be allowed for. This means that costs and revenues are reduced to their equivalent value at a common date. The date invariably chosen is *now* i.e. the present time. Two commonly used investment appraisal techniques are described below; *payback* and *discounted cash flow*.

Payback

Payback is probably the most widely used investment appraisal technique – it is simple and understandable. Payback is the period, usually in years, which it takes for the cash inflows of a project to equal the initial cash outflow. The project with the shortest payback period is normally chosen.

Example

Three projects are being considered and estimates of the cash flows are as follows:

	Project X		Project Y		Project Z	
Years	Annual Cash Flow	Cumulative Cash Flow	Annual Cash Flow	Cumulative Cash Flow	Annual Cash Flow	Cumulative Cash Flow
Now	−£5,000	−£5,000	−£5,000	−£5,000	−£5,000	−£5,000
1	+2,100	−2,900	+400	−4,600	+900	−4,100
2	+1,800	−1,100	+700	−3,900	+800	−3,300
3	+700	−400	+1,800	−2,100	+1,100	−2,200
4	+400	-	+2,100	-	+1,000	−1,200
5	-	-	-	-	+1,200	—
6	-	-	-	-	+950	+950

Solution

Payback periods: Project X = 4 years
                   Project Y = 4 years
                   Project Z = 5 years

Note: Each project requires an initial investment now of £5,000 which is an outflow, denoted by a negative sign. The positive signs denote cash inflows after 1 year, 2 years and so on.

Features of Payback

(a) It is based on cash flows not profits and thus is more objective.

(b) It is a measure of liquidity not of wealth. Judged on Payback alone, Projects X and Y would be preferred to Z even though Z carries on earning after the payback period.

(c) Payback does consider the timing of cash flows but only in a crude manner. Projects X and Y are ranked equally yet there are clear timing differences.

(d) Payback is simple and easily understood and is widely used either by itself or in conjunction with other investment appraisal techniques.

Discounted cash flow (DCF)

DCF is based on cash flow estimates and converts them to equivalent values at a common date, typically now. This enables them to be compared directly and a net value to be calculated for the project as a whole. Monies received earlier are worth more than those received later and this is known as their *time value*. The discounting process automatically reduces future sums to their equivalent present day value. The amount of the reduction depends on the *discounting rate* used which itself depends on prevailing interest rates and other financial factors.

The most important DCF method is known as Net Present Value (NPV).

Net Present Value (NPV)

To calculate the NPV of an investment the expected cash inflows and outflows are discounted (reduced) by a discount factor (or Present Value factor) from Table A. Table A shows the discount factors for discount rates 1% to 30% and for periods, normally years, from 1 to 25. For example what is the present value of £500 received in 3 years at 10%?

From Table A the discount factor for 3 years at 10% is 0.751 thus the present value of £500 received in 3 years is:

$$£500 \times 0.751 = £375.50$$

An example follows.

Example

A company with a cost of capital of 10% is considering a project with the following estimated cash flows:

Now	After 1 year	2 years	3 years	4 years
–£5,000	+£900	+£1,800	+£2,400	+£1,600

(minus represents an outflow, positive represents an inflow)

What is the NPV of the project?

Should it be accepted?

Solution

From Table A the discount factors for 10% are

1 year	2 years	3 years	4 years
0.909	0.826	0.751	0.683

NPV $= -£5,000 + (0.909 \times £900) + (0.826 \times £1,800) + (0.751 \times £2,400) + (0.683 \times £1,600)$
 $= -£5,000 + £818 + £1,487 + £1,802 + £1,093$
 $= +£200$

As the NPV of the project is positive, at the company's cost of capital, it should be accepted. The £200 represents the increase in wealth that could be gained by the project, measured in present day values.

Note: The initial outlay of £5,000 does not need discounting because it is already at the present day value.

Key point summary

☐ Finance and Accounting can be sub-divided into Financial Accounting, Management Accounting and Financial Management.

☐ Financial accounting deals mainly with external matters and recording past transactions.

☐ The Profit and Loss account is a summary Statement showing the revenues, costs and profit(or loss) for a past period.

☐ The Balance Sheet is a snapshot view of the assets, liabilities and capital of the business.

☐ Cash Flow Statements, as specified by FRS 1, support the P & L account and Balance Sheet.

☐ Ratio analysis is widely used as an aid to interpreting accounts.

☐ Ratios can be sub-divided into those relating to Performance and those relating to Liquidity.

☐ Management Accounting deals mainly with the provision of information to management.

☐ Costs may be sub-divided into Direct and Indirect (or Overheads).

☐ Overheads are absorbed into products by means of overhead absorption rates based usually on labour or machine hours.

❑ Costs may be analysed according to behaviour into Fixed, Variable or Semi-Variable.

❑ Budgeting is a short-term planning and control technique.

❑ The difference between budgeted and actual expenditure is known as a variance.

❑ Standard costing uses the same general principles as budgeting but is applied to production.

❑ Relevant information for decision making concerns the future and the differences between alternatives.

❑ Marginal costing principles are useful for short-run decision making.

❑ Break-even charts show the interaction of costs and revenues in a simple, visual manner.

❑ Working capital is the excess of current assets over current liabilities.

❑ The key elements in the working capital cycle are; stocks, debtors and creditors.

❑ Cash forecasts show the results of the expected cash movements over the periods ahead.

❑ Investment appraisal deals with long-term decision making.

❑ Two important techniques are Payback and Discounted Cash Flow.

Self review questions

1. *Distinguish between Financial Accounting, Management Accounting and Financial Management.*

2. *What are; fixed assets, current assets?*

3. *What is the Profit and Loss account?*

4. *What is the Balance Sheet?*

5. *What is the difference between Gross and Net Profit?*

6. *What is capital employed?*

7. *What is a Cash Flow Statement?*

8. *What is Ratio Analysis?*

9. *What are the main two categories into which Ratios can be separated?*

10. *What is Return on Capital Employed?*

11. *What is the Acid Test ratio?*

12. *What are direct costs? overheads?*

13. *How is a product cost calculated?*

14. *What is Activity Based Costing?*

15. *Distinguish between Fixed and Variable costs.*

16. *What is budgeting?*

17. *What are variances?*

18. *What is marginal costing and why is it useful for decision making?*

19. *What are break-even charts?*

20. *What is working capital management?*

21. *How are cash forecasts prepared?*

22. *What is Discounted Cash Flow?*

Assessment and revision section

Assignments

1. Find examples of branding applied to service industries. How do the firms use branding? Can you find any examples of branding applied to non-profit seeking organisations?

2. The product life cycle consists of 6 phases. Try to find examples of actual products you consider to be at each stage of the cycle.

3. Select a low-value consumer product and analyse all the ways it is promoted. Do the same for a high value industrial product. Why are there differences?

4. Choose a local organisation; public or private sector and try to find what personnel policies it has.

5. Try to find a real Job Description and suggest ways it could be improved.

6. A woman of 30 with several GCSE's and two 'A' levels has just commenced work as a supervisor in one of the stores of 'Tesburys', a large retail chain.
   Design a training programme for her and also a management development programme.

7. Find examples of jobbing, batch and flow production firms and compare as many of their characteristics you can discover (size, structure etc.).

8. Total Quality management is being applied in manufacturing and service organisations. Find an example of each that practises TQM and contrast the differing approaches.

9. Using standard Work Study symbols flow chart the process of getting into and starting a car. Start from the point of standing by the car door.

10. Obtain the published accounts of two companies in the same type of business. Contrast the financial performance of the two companies in as much detail as you can.

11. Find examples of management by exception being used in practice. How are exceptions recognised? Does the procedure aid management control?

12. A college is considering whether to launch a course aimed at business executives. List all the financial factors which you think should be considered. What period of operation do you think should be considered in the appraisal?

Mini-Case 1 – The Davill Group

As part of the Davill Group's Management Development programme John, a young graduate was put in charge of a small warehouse which had been established some years ago to act as a central supply source for the Group.

The programme called for John to have three-monthly review meetings with the Group Personnel Officer. At his first meeting John was very enthusiastic and confident and described in detail the numerous developments and improvements he had already initiated and his ideas for the future. When asked about problems John mentioned the 'stick-in-the-mud' attitude of the staff and the lack of co-operation he had received.

Enquiries among the staff by the Personnel Officer discovered that there was dissatisfaction about John's leadership. The staff felt that he was in too much of a hurry and they were a litle apprehensive about what they considered to be risky and ill-thought out decisions that John had taken. They thought that he had little interest in them and they were not sure whether their work was up to his requirements. One thought that a Group decision had already been taken to close the warehouse and John had been sent to do a hatchet job. The Personnel Officer knew that this fear was quite unfounded.

Task 1 *What managerial problems are revealed by the above case?*

Task 2 *What should the Personnel Officer do?*

Task 3 *What should John do to improve the present position?*

Task 4 *How do you think the situation should have been handled from the beginning?*

Mini-Case 2 – Diamond Pickles Ltd

Diamond Pickles Ltd have an established range of pickles, chutneys and sauces marketed under the well known slogan 'Pickles with the cutting edge'. The company is considering launching a range of pre-cooked convenience meals. The meals would be complete and would only need warming before consumption. The company thinks that their existing reputation in the convenience food industry and their well known brand image would help to establish their proposed new products.

Task 1 *Choose three possible ways that the company could assess consumers' reactions to the meals and give their advantages and disadvantages.*

Task 2 *Discuss the key factors that the company will have to consider under each element of the Marketing mix.*

Task 3 *Try to think up a slogan for the new range of meals.*

Examination questions with answers

A1 The process of effective departmental management implies the effective training and development of all grades of staff, whether managerial, professional, administrative or clerical.

By what means may training and development needs be identified, and how may staff training and development be implemented by the organisation?

ACCA – Effective Management

A2 George has been appointed to take charge of the management accounting department of a manufacturing plant of a large national company. The plant has been producing a product which is at the end of its life cycle. Profits have been declining and the outgoing manager of the department has been tightening capital budgets and raising performance targets to reduce costs.

A new product is gradually being brought into production and one of George's first tasks is to introduce the relatively small changes in data collection and data processing associated with controlling the costs of the new product.

Any changes he asks for are met by groans from his staff, with comments such as:

'That is not the sort of work I am supposed to do.'
'I don't know how to do this.'
'I have not been trained for such work.'
'I have got far too much to do already.'
'John has hardly anything to do – give it to him.'
'William is the expert on this – he will find it easy.'

In relation to the last two comments, George finds they have no basis in fact. He also finds that some staff are sitting around only pretending to be busy although they have finished their immediate work, while others are resentful of having to stay late to finish their work. George cannot rely on messages being passed on, and finds that his staff are unhelpful to each other. Although they try to ingratiate themselves with George, they are reluctant to try out any new equipment even if it is obviously better than the old.

You are required to analyse the situation and recommend, with reasons, what George can do to improve personnel matters.

CIMA – Management

A3 What is total quality management (TQM)? How may it be implemented?

ACCA – Management

A4 A stock turnover ratio is calculated for a Company as follows:

$$\frac{\text{Annual cost of goods sold during previous year}}{\text{Average amount of stock at end of year}} = \frac{£2,600,000}{£460,000} = 5.6$$

(a) How would you decide if this ratio is too high?

(b) If you were to conclude that it required reduction how would you seek to improve performance?

IAM – Financial & Quantitative Methods

A5 WZ Foods plc had developed a range of convenience meals. (A convenience meal is one that requires little preparation, by the consumer, and can be used at any time.)

It now has to decide on a strategy for the introduction of the foods to consumers.

(a) You are required
   (i) to list and explain the benefits that WZ Foods plc could expect from test marketing the range,
   (ii) to indicate what other options are available, should WZ Foods plc decide that test marketing is not appropriate,
   (iii) to describe one on the options you have indicated in (ii).
(b) When selecting products for development, describe the screening processes that could appropriately be employed to increase the chances of eventual success.

CIMA – Management Accounting – Strategic Planning & Marketing

A6 Sales of ABC cosmetics have recently fallen following a campaign by an animal-rights pressure group against the methods used by the firm in testing its products.

Requirements

(a) Explain what is meant by the term pressure group.
(b) Discuss how the firm might use a marketing campaign to restore the sales of ABC cosmetics to their previous level.

CIMA – Business Environment and IT

A7 The new manufacturing environment is characterised by more flexibility, a readiness to meet customers' requirements, smaller batches, continuous improvements and an emphasis on quality. In such circumstances, traditional management accounting performance measures are, at best, irrelevant and, at worst, misleading.

You are required

(a) to discuss the above statement, citing specific examples to support or refute the views expressed,
(b) to explain in what ways management accountants can adapt the services they provide to the new environment.

CIMA – Management Accounting Techniques

A8 Describe Just-in-Time systems, and their effect on organisation and management.

CIMA – Management

Examination questions without answers

B1 L Ltd is a firm which undertakes road reconstruction and maintenance. The work is carried out by teams which operate independently of each other. The team members have worked together for years and are well integrated. Each team includes a salesman who is responsible for getting additional work, ideally in the area where the team is already working. The teams draw their materials and road-surfacing and other machinery from the company pool, and obtain information on potential customers from a central sales office.

   Although the firm's performance has been satisfactory, a new operations manager has decided to try to improve productivity by introducing competition between the teams. This will be done by drawing half of the wages of each team member from a single bonus pool for which all the teams compete.

   You are required to explain how such a policy is likely to affect the behaviour of these groups.

CIMA – Management

B2 Your company has operated a staff appraisal scheme for a number of years, with apparently mixed results. You have been asked by the board of directors to carry out a review of this staff appraisal scheme.

   Write a review for the board (i) identifying the objectives of a staff appraisal scheme; and (ii) outlining criteria by which the success of a company staff appraisal scheme might be evaluated.

ACCA – Effective Management

B3 'Accounting ratios only repeat information already contained in the Balance Sheet and the Profit and Loss Account, therefore they tell you nothing that you did not already know;. Examine the truth of this statement, illustrating your answer with reference to various types of accounting ratio.

IAM – Financial & Quantitative Methods

B4 Describe the main types of production and give illustrative examples of each type.

   In what ways is the effectiveness of the purchasing function relevant to achieving the desired output of products or services for sale in the markets served by the enterprise?

ACCA – Effective Management

B5 RUS plc operates a chain of hotels. Its strategy has been to provide medium-priced accommodation for business people during the week and for families at weekends. The market has become increasingly competitive and RUS plc has decided to change its strategy. In future, it will provide 'a high-quality service for the discerning guest'.

   You are required

   (a) to explain the relevance of a programme of 'total quality management' for RUS plc in the implementation of its new strategy;

(b) to summarise the financial and organisational implications of RUS plc's new strategy;

(c) to discuss the contribution that RUS plc's Management Accountant could make to the new strategy.

CIMA – Management Accounting, Strategic Planning & Marketing

B6 PQ Limited has two production departments – machining and assembly. Two of its main products are the Major and the Minor, the standard data for which are as follows:

	Per unit	
	Major	*Minor*
Direct materials:		
Material @ £15 per kg	2.2 kgs	1.4 kgs
Direct labour:		
Machining department @ £6 per hour	4.8 hrs	2.9 hrs
Assembly department @ £5 per hour	3.6 hrs	3.1 hrs
Machining time	3.5 hrs	0.9 hrs

The overhead rates for the period are as follows:

Machining department	*Assembly department*
£16.00 per machine hour	£9.50 per labour hour

Requirement

(a) Calculate the standard production cost for each product showing clearly, as a sub total, the standard prime cost.

(b) During the period, actual results for labour were as follows:

	Major	*Minor*
Production	50 units	842 units
Direct labour:		
Machining department	2,990 hrs costing £18,239	2,480 hrs costing £15,132
Assembly department	2,310 hrs costing £11,700	2,595 hrs costing £12,975

Requirement

Calculate the direct labour total variance and the rate and efficiency variances for each product and each department.

(c) Explain briefly what information the above variances provide for management.

CIMA – Cost Accounting & Quantitative Methods

B7 (a) What is market segmentation and why is this done?

(b) Discuss how a manufacturer of fast moving consumer goods may segment the market and contrast this with a manufacturer of capital equipment for industrial markets.

Additional reading

Elements of Marketing, A. R. Morden, DP Publications.

Personnel Management, G. A. Cole, DP Publications.

Production and Operations Management, R. Wild, Cassell.

Foundation Accounting, A. H. Millichamp, DP Publications.

Management Accounting, T. Lucey, DP Publications.

The Japanese Industrial System, C. J. McMillan, de Gruyter.

15 *Information and communications*

Objectives

After you have studied this Chapter you will:

☐ *Be able to distinguish between data and information.*

☐ *Understand how information becomes valuable.*

☐ *Be able to describe the characteristics of good information.*

☐ *Know the main channels of communication within organisations.*

☐ *Be able to describe the communication process.*

☐ *Understand encoding, decoding, and noise.*

☐ *Know the main communication methods.*

☐ *Be able to describe the main types of meetings.*

☐ *Understand the functions of the Agenda, the Chairman (Chair) and the Minutes.*

☐ *Know the distinction between routine and special reports.*

☐ *Be able to describe the typical format of a report.*

☐ *Know the key guidelines for drafting reports.*

Information and management

In all but the smallest organisations management rarely observe operations directly. They attempt to make decisions, prepare plans and control activities by using *information*. There are two main sources of information; *formal* and *informal*.

Formal sources include; reports, statements, files, manuals, operating procedures, notices and the various forms of output from the organisation's management information system (MIS). Informal sources include; conversations, telephone calls, observation, social contacts and so on. Before looking at these sources in detail it is necessary to examine the characteristics of information itself.

Data and information defined

The terms 'data' and 'information' are often used interchangeably in everyday speech as meaning the same thing. However, the terms have distinct meanings:

(a) Data are facts, events, transactions and so on which have been recorded. They are the input raw materials from which information is produced.

(b) Information is data that have been processed in such a way as to be useful to the recipient.

In general terms basic data are processed in some way to form information but the mere act of processing data does not of itself produce information. This is an important distinction which is developed later.

Data characteristics

Data are facts obtained by observation, counting, measuring, weighing etc. which are then recorded. Frequently they are called *raw* or *basic data* and are often records of the day to day transactions of the organisation. For example; the date, amount and other details of an invoice or cheque, payroll details of pay, National Insurance and tax for a person, the output for a machine or shift, the number of vehicles passing a road monitoring point and so on.

Data are derived from both external and internal sources and whilst most external data are in readily usable and concrete forms – for example, bank statements, purchase invoices – internal activities require appropriate measuring and recording systems so that facts can be captured. Data may be produced as an automatic by-product of some routine but essential operation such as the production of an invoice or alternatively a special counting or measuring procedure must be introduced and the results recorded. Much of cost accounting, stock control, production control and similar systems would fall into this latter category.

What is information?

Information is data that have been interpreted and understood by the recipient of the message.It will be noted that the *user* not just the sender is involved in the transformation of data into information. There is a process of thought and understanding involved and it follows that a given message can have different meanings to different people.

It also follows that data which have been analysed, summarised or processed in some other fashion to produce a message or report which is conventionally deemed to be 'management information' only becomes information if it is understood by the recipient. It is the *user* who determines whether a report contains information or just processed data.

In summary, information is knowledge and understanding that is usable by the recipient. It reduces uncertainty and has surprise value. If a message or report does not have these attributes, *as far as the recipient* is concerned, it contains merely data not information. This is a crucial point not always fully appreciated.

The value of information

Information has no value in itself; its value derives from the value of the change in decision behaviour caused by the information being available minus the cost of producing the information. There is a tendency to assume that more information, earlier or more up to date information, more accurate information etc. is all better information. It may be better information but only if it improves the resulting decisions, otherwise it has no value. It will be seen that, once again, the user is all important.

Data capture, handling, recording and processing – by whatever means – incur costs and do not produce value. It is only when data are communicated and understood by the recipient and are thus transformed into information, that value may arise – providing that the information is used to improve decision making or some other management action.

To ensure that information does have value means considering both the *user* and the *problem* or *decision* being dealt with. Figure 15.1 shows the typical trade-off between costs and value of the information.

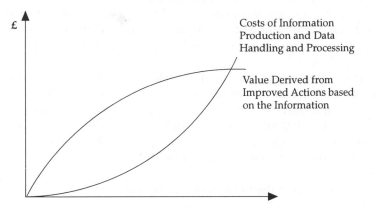

Figure 15.1: Information – cost and value

Characteristics of good information

Good information is that which is used and which creates value. Experience and research shows that good information has numerous qualities as follows:

Good information is:

(a) relevant for its purpose
(b) sufficiently accurate for its purpose
(c) complete enough for the problem
(d) from a source in which the user has confidence
(e) communicated to the right person
(f) communicated in time for its purpose
(g) that which contains the right level of detail
(h) communicated by an appropriate channel of communication
(i) that which is understandable by the user

Of these characteristics, relevance is the over-riding quality. In addition care must be taken that the user is not swamped by excessive detail or that information is delayed in the search for greater accuracy. There should be the least amount of detail that suits the intended purpose and the level of accuracy must be related to the decision involved.

Channels of communication

To be usable information must be transmitted by means of a communication process. Communication involves the interchange of facts, thoughts, value judgements and opinions and the communication process may take many forms; face-to-face conversations, telephone calls, informal and formal meetings, conferences, memoranda, letters, reports, tabulations, V.D.U. transmissions and so on.

Whatever the process, good communication results where the sender and receiver are in accord over the meaning of a particular message. Although this sounds like a modest objective, it is proving to be, in Peter Drucker's words 'as elusive as the Unicorn.'

The channel of communication should be selected having regard to such things as; the nature and purpose of the information, the speed required and, above all, the requirements of the user. The typical output of formal information systems is a printed report or tabulation. These have their uses, of course, but there is research evidence that many managers, specially at senior levels, obtain most of their information aurally. They use written reports merely to confirm or reinforce information they already have.

Communication within the formal organisation may be:

Vertical: downwards (i.e. superior to subordinate) e.g. instructions and orders, assigning duties and tasks, guidance and advice etc.

upwards (i.e. subordinate to superior) e.g. reporting results, suggestions, performance statistics, grievances etc.

Horizontal or lateral: informal and formal contacts between people of same grade e.g. sharing information, resolving conflicts, assisting with problems etc.

Communication may be in one direction only e.g. a notice to all staff about time-keeping or it may allow feedback and discussion and thus becomes two-way communication. Clearly two-way communication is essential for most matters especially concerning detailed or complicated subjects or those of a personal nature.

The communication process

Communication can be said to be successful if:

(a) the message is received and

(b) the receiver derives from the message the same meaning that the sender intended.

Regrettably these apparently simple conditions are not always met and communication failures are commonplace. A general outline of features common to all communication systems is shown in Figure 15.2

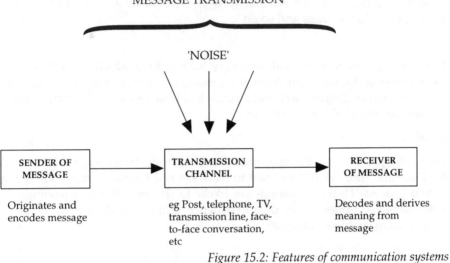

Figure 15.2: Features of communication systems

A brief explanation of the communication terminology shown in Figure 15.2 follows.

Encoding

All messages originate in a person's mind and the process of encoding is the way that the message is written down or spoken in order to be able to communicate with another person. Variation in word connotation by different people can alter the meaning of a message and voice emphasis and/or facial expressions and/or gestures all play a part in the encoding process when conversation is used. It will be realised that the way we convey meaning by the written word, figures, diagrams, speech and so on is an individual, often idiosyncratic process.

Encoding problems include:

- ◻ distortion or omission of information by the sender
- ◻ use of unexplained terminology/jargon.
- ◻ verbose, badly phrased messages
- ◻ unclarified or unstated beliefs and assumptions

Channel

The means by which the information is carried, e.g. the internal mail system, external postal services, telephone and telecommunication networks, television, radio, satellite links and so on. Channels are not perfect because distortion, losses and delays may occur. Care must be taken that the correct type of channel is used having regard to such matters as urgency, sensitivity, need for security and accuracy, type of information, cost effectiveness and so on.

Noise

The term used in communication theory for anything which causes the message at the receiver to be different from the message that went into the transmitter. For example, poor or illegible writing, accents, bad form design, poor picture quality, loss or damage, actual physical noise etc.

Decoding

This is the process of achieving understanding from the message. In general, people read, see and hear what they want to read, see and hear so that decoding is an individual process. Different people are likely to derive different meanings from the same message, influenced by their experience, attitudes and value systems.

Decoding problems include:

- ◻ information overload
- ◻ lack of training in subject matter
- ◻ carelessness and uninterest
- ◻ differences in age, social or racial background create barriers to understanding

A variety of methods are used to ensure that messages are properly received and understood, particularly if they contain urgent or important items.

Examples include:

(a) repetition of important words or figures

(b) confirmatory letters following meetings or telephone calls

(c) multiple copies of the message

(d) repeated V.D.U. screening at intervals, and so on.

Communication methods

Various channels of communication are used by organisations. These include:

Face-to-face communications	Written communications
❑ interviews	❑ external mail by letter
❑ formal meetings	❑ internal mail by memoranda
❑ informal contacts	
❑ talks and discussion groups	❑ booklets and manuals
❑ video telephones	❑ reports
Visual communications	❑ statements and tabulations
❑ films and slides	❑ video displays using electronic mail (Email)
❑ videos	
❑ charts	❑ company magazines, newsletters and bulletins
❑ posters	❑ notice boards
Oral communications	❑ Fax
❑ telephone	
❑ public address systems	

Formal, written communications have the advantage of completeness and regularity and are the only feasible methods of communicating much of the routine mass of data which flows through an organisation. In addition written matter can be filed and referred to as required without the ambiguity than can occur when recalling a conversation. On the other hand formal written communications may not always cover the current problem and may not be produced on time. Hence the importance of informal contacts through telephone calls, conversations and casual meetings. The informal network, often called the 'grape vine', is flexible and can deal with nuances that are lost in formal communication.

There is research evidence that at higher levels of management informal channels, particularly concerned with external information, are of greater importance than the formal MIS. The information specialist is prone to exaggerate the importance of written information compared to face-to-face conversations even though research evidence confirms its importance.

Studies by Mintzberg, and Ives and Olson found that as much as 80% of a chief executive's time was spent in verbal communication.

The formal and informal channels should not be viewed as competitors but as complementary facets of the total information network in the organisation.

Because of their importance two important means of communication are dealt with below in more detail; *meetings* and *reports*.

Meetings

This brief section does not deal with those special formal meetings which have legal functions e.g. the Annual General Meeting of a company or Local Council Meetings. These types of meetings have closely defined rules regarding; notice, attendance rights timings, etc.

Rather, the section deals with meetings held within organisations to discuss problems and to make decisions. Such meetings are very common within most organisations and take place at every level. Typical of the types of meetings are the following:

Briefing meetings – held to inform, relay instructions and decisions

Decision-making meetings – held for groups to come together to make decisions. May be directors, managers, local government officials etc.

Problem solving meetings – held to discuss and consult with interested parties

Working-party meetings – held to deal with some task or implement a decision

Brainstorming meetings – held to exchange views and generate new ideas

Liaison meetings – held to communicate and maintain formal links between groups/departments/interests etc.

and so on.

Badly organised and poorly targeted meetings are a waste of time but a well focused, controlled meeting can be extremely effective. Some guidelines on how to plan and organise meetings follow; i.e. the Agenda, the Chairman, and the Minutes. These apply mainly to the more formal meetings held within an organisation. More informal ad-hoc meetings take place all the time without formality or rules or any prior organisation.

The agenda

The agenda is the programme of business planned for a meeting and is normally sent out in advance. The agenda helps to focus the meeting and gives the intended participants time to prepare themselves, if required. Where correspondence, reports or more detailed material is referred to in the agenda it is normal for copies to be sent out with the agenda so that participants will have time to study them.

A typical agenda for a monthly departmental meeting is shown in Figure 15.3

```
┌─────────────────────────────────────────────────────────────────┐
│                 PRODUCTION CONTROL DEPARTMENT                     │
│                                                                   │
│          Meeting:  Friday 30th January at 9.30 am in Room 292     │
│                                                                   │
│                            AGENDA                                 │
│                                                                   │
│     1.    Apologies for absence                                   │
│                                                                   │
│     2.    Minutes of meeting of 29th December (attached) to be read│
│           and confirmed                                           │
│                                                                   │
│     3.    Matters arising from minutes                            │
│                                                                   │
│     4.    Budgetary Control Statement for December (attached)     │
│                                                                   │
│     5.    Progress of new Quality Control System (A Smith to report)│
│                                                                   │
│     6.    Delivery and production schedules for February (attached)│
│                                                                   │
│     7.    Liaison Committee (B Jones to report)                   │
│                                                                   │
│     8.    Any other business                                      │
│                                                                   │
└─────────────────────────────────────────────────────────────────┘
```

Figure 15.3: Example of an agenda

The agenda acts as a framework for the meeting and indicates what matters are of primary importance and have to be dealt with.

Chairman (or Chair)

The Chairman is arguably the most important person at 'a meeting'. The Chairman, ideally, should have; a sound knowledge of the appropriate rules governing the meeting, communication skills and be fair and impartial.

The main tasks of the Chairman are:

Before the meeting starts: ensuring that it has been properly convened by notice and that there is a quorum (minimum number required to hold the meeting, as specified by the rules)

During the meeting: maintaining order, guiding the meeting through its business, giving everyone an opportunity to speak, ensuring no one dominates discussions, dealing with amendments and points of order, at the end of debates ascertaining the sense of the meeting, where necessary putting motions to the vote and, on occasions, using a casting vote.

After the meeting: arranging for the minutes to be prepared, signing the minutes, ensuring their distribution. (Minutes are dealt with in detail below.)

Minutes

The minutes are a written record of the business done at a meeting. Minutes are essential for all formal meetings and have the following functions:

- [ ] a record of events and attenders for reference
- [ ] evidence of decisions taken
- [ ] precedent and authority for future proposals
- [ ] an aid to compiling future agendas

The minutes are a formal and complete record, in abbreviated form, of work done and decisions taken at a meeting. They do not usually attempt to record the debate about various issues merely the decisions reached. On occasions, participants may request that their views are recorded in the minutes. This is usually done when the participants wish to disassociate themselves with some view or decision of the majority at the meeting.

The exact form of the minutes varies greatly. However they should all contain the following:

Heading including; Name of meeting, date and place held, names of people present, apologies for absence, meeting duration (Note that some minutes record the names of those 'in attendance' i.e. those that were at the meeting but who did not have an automatic right to be there.)

Body of minutes This should follow the sequence of the agenda and should be divided into paragraphs, numbered for reference. Decisions, but not discussions, should be given in full. It is normal to record the proposer and seconder of motions and the numbers voting for and against and abstaining.

Chairman's Signature the last item should be the Chairman's signature certifying that the minutes are a true record of proceedings.

It is common practice to note in the margin of minutes who is to be responsible for any action to be taken. Normally that person then reports on progress at the next meeting.

Minutes should be impersonal and impartial and written in the past tense. They should be concise but sufficiently detailed to make the sense of the meeting clear.

Reports

The term 'report' is widely used in business. It may be used to describe a routine, regularly produced statement dealing with operational matters. Examples include; production reports, sales reports, budgetary control reports. These reports fulfil specific functions and are produced in a style and format agreed by the users and producers of the information. Generally they consist almost entirely of numeric information.

Alternatively, the term may be used to describe written reports specially prepared to deal with a particular problem or situation. In general such reports summarise the background and facts relating to the problem, analyse the facts in relation to the organisation's objectives and current position, draw relevant conclusions and make practical recommendations regarding decisions/actions that should be taken. These reports vary greatly in length and are largely narrative in form although the narrative is often supported by detailed numeric or statistical information, contained in appendices.

Many organisations specify the format and sequence of the contents of internal reports. Naturally where these guidelines exist they must be followed. However where there are no such rules Figure 15.4 shows a typical report format.

TITLE OF REPORT / INTRODUCTION
including: title/subject of report, who has prepared it, for whom it is intended, date of completion.

TABLE OF CONTENTS
giving sections, sub-sections, page numbers.

TERMS OF REFERENCE
specifying the scope and purpose of report, exactly what instructions the writer was given, whether recommendations are to be made etc.

SUMMARY OF RECOMMENDATIONS
Concise statement of the recommendations the writer makes cross-referenced to the terms of reference. For a simpler report, this may be a summary of action taken.

PROCEDURE OR METHOD
Outlines the steps taken, investigations made, files and people consulted. Sometimes this section is combined with the section below.

FINDINGS/ARGUMENT
The main body of report showing how the conclusions were reached. It should be complete, structured but as concise as possible.

CONCLUSIONS
This summarises the main findings and argument. There should be a clear relationship between the conclusions and recommendations.

APPENDICES
Typical contents: statistical tables and summaries, any form of detailed information. May also include minority reports where there is not unanimity between the writers of the report.

Figure 15.4: Typical report contents

Drafting reports

It is not easy to write clear, informative reports yet it is a skill well worth developing. Reports should be written using simple words and straightforward sentences. The subject matter should develop in a logical sequence and extraneous or irrelevant material excluded. Adherence to the following guidelines will help to produce good reports.

- ❏ Keep the terms of reference in mind and do not stray from the subject.

- ❏ Avoid emotional or otherwise loaded words.

- ❏ Avoid colloquialisms and slang.

- ❏ Make sure you know the meaning of every word you use.

- ❏ Try to write grammatically correct English. If in doubt, check it.

- ❏ Where it is necessary to use technical words, provide a terminology so that there will be no doubts over meanings.

- ❏ Make the report as attractive as possible: e.g. proper headings, the judicious use of capitals, italics, figures and diagrams.

- ❏ Keep the target readership in mind. If it is a known, small group familiar with the subject matter, jargon and abbreviations may be in order, otherwise they should be avoided.

- ❏ Use positive rather than negative sentence construction.

- ❏ Unless it is a short, informal report use the more formal third person sentence construction e.g. 'It was found' rather than 'I found'.

Key point summary

- ❏ Information is derived from formal and informal sources.

- ❏ Data are facts, information is processed data useful to the recipient.

- ❏ Information has no value in itself, value comes from using information.

- ❏ Good information is that which is relevant, on time, understandable and sufficiently accurate for the purpose intended.

- ❏ Communication may be vertical or horizontal; one-way or two-way.

❐ Successful communication means that the sender and receiver are in accord over the meaning of a message.

❐ Noise is anything which causes the message at the receiver to be different from the message that went into the transmitter.

❐ Communication methods include; written, oral, visual and face-to-face.

❐ Meetings are of various types; briefing, decision-making, brainstorming, liaison etc.

❐ The Agenda is the programme of business planned for the meeting.

❐ The Chairman's task is to run the meeting fairly, deal with amendments, put motions to the vote, arrange for minutes to be taken.

❐ The minutes are a formal record of the business of a meeting, decisions taken, participants.

❐ Reports may be routinely prepared or specially commissioned.

❐ The main parts of a report are: Terms of Reference, Recommendations, Findings and Conclusions.

❐ Reports should be written in a simple, straightforward manner avoiding irrelevant material. Care must be taken with grammar and the language used.

Self review questions

1. *What is the difference between data and information?*

2. *How does information derive value?*

3. *What are the characteristics of good information?*

4. *What types of communication exist in organisations?*

5. *What are the basics of the communication process?*

6. *Give examples of communication methods used in organisations?*

7. *What types of meetings are used?*

8. *What are the duties of the meeting's Chair?*

9. *What are Minutes and what are typical contents?*

10. *What is a typical Report format?*

16 Information technology: office support systems

Objectives

After you have studied this chapter you will:

☐ *Know what is meant by Information Technology (IT).*

☐ *Be able to distinguish between: Office Support Systems, Data Processing and End User Computing.*

☐ *Understand the main features of Word Processing, Photocopiers and Desk-Top Publishing.*

☐ *Know the characteristics of microfilm and microfiche.*

☐ *Understand the features of teletext and viewdata systems.*

☐ *Know the importance of telecommunication links including Electronic Mail and Networks.*

☐ *Be able to describe the various forms of data transmission including Fax and Electronic Data Interchange.*

What is information technology?

There are few aspects of life nowadays which are unaffected by IT. In the office, factory or at home, visiting a bank, supermarket or garage and in many other places IT is used to carry out transactions, provide information, record data, make decisions and perform an ever increasing range of tasks.

A useful definition of IT is given by the Department of Trade and Industry:

> 'the acquisition, processing, storage and dissemination of vocal, pictorial, textual and numeric information by a micro-electronics based combination of computing and telecommunications'

Because this book concentrates on the business aspects of organisations, emphasis will be given to the administrative use of computers and telecommunications. This means that some major and important applications of IT are outside the scope of this book. Examples include; robotics, industrial process control, computer aided design and manufacture (CAD/CAM), scientific uses of IT and so on.

Background computer knowledge

The next two chapters are about the use of computers and IT in information systems and are not about computers themselves. Accordingly there will be no attempt to explain what computers are, the ways that they work, the nature of their component parts or how they process and store data.

It is assumed that teachers will be familiar with the more common terms associated with computers. Examples include; hardware, software, files, VDU, disk storage, terminal, program, packages, printers, on-line and so on. Readers unfamiliar with these terms or who wish to study computers in more detail are advised to study a comprehensive book on the subject, for example, *Data Processing and Information Technology*, C.S.French, DP Publications.

Are computers essential for information systems?

The short answer to this question is, not essential but they can be very useful. The study of information systems is not about the use of computers, it is about the provision and use of information relevant to the user. Computers are one – albeit important – means of producing information and concentration on the means of production rather than the needs of the user can lead to expensive mistakes. There is undoubtedly an important and growing role for computers and IT in information systems but the technology must be used with discretion.

Computers can help to overcome some of the limitations people have when processing data. These include:

☐ Slowness in reading and calculating.

☐ Only a low volume of data can be stored in the human brain.

☐ Difficulties in following a complex sequence of instructions repetitively.

☐ Boredom/inefficiency resulting in errors.

☐ Data in one brain not accessible to others without some form of written or verbal communication.

Computers are good at rapid and accurate calculations, manipulation, storage and retrieval but less good at unexpected or qualitative work or where genuine judgement is required. It has been suggested that computers can be used to best advantage for processing information which has the following characteristics:

(a) a number of interacting variables

(b) speed is an important factor

(c) there are reasonably accurate values

(d) accuracy of output is important

> (e) operations are repetitive
>
> (f) large amounts of data exist

These characteristics can be related to the needs of the various management levels as shown in Figure 16.1.

Information Characteristics	Presence in Management Information		
	Operational Level	Tactical Level	Strategic Level
Interacting Variables	Frequent ─────────────────────────►		Always
Speed Important	Usually ─────────────────────────►		Rarely
Data Accuracy	High ─────────────────────────►		Low
Output Accuracy	Always ─────────────────────────►		Rarely
Repetition	Usually ─────────────────────────►		Rarely
Data Volume	High ─────────────────────────►		Low

Resulting Application of Computers

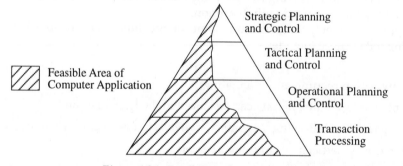

Feasible Area of Computer Application

Strategic Planning and Control

Tactical Planning and Control

Operational Planning and Control

Transaction Processing

Figure 16.1: Feasibility of computer application by management level

The unshaded area of Figure 16.1 represents unstructured problems and decisions where human involvement is essential. The division between computer and human tasks is constantly changing. As software and hardware develops and organisations gain more skill in using computers, tasks previously requiring managerial expertise and judgement become worthwhile computer jobs.

An example is the now widespread use of 'credit scoring' in banks. An applicant for a loan fills in a detailed questionnaire and the answers are input into a computer. The program carries out a series of checks and tests and decides whether or not the loan should be granted. Previously all loan applications required a managerial decision which is now needed only for unusual requests, large loans or industrial applications.

Despite some well publicised success stories it remains true that IT has had the greatest impact at operational and tactical levels. A survey by PA Management Consultants on New Information Technology (NIT) found:

firms largely ignoring NIT other than at operational levels e.g. 45% reported that NIT had made little or no impact on their activities and that 39% had no defined strategy for innovation or application of NIT in the next 5 years.

IT and information systems

Although the boundaries between them are blurred it is possible to distinguish three major areas of application of IT in information systems. These are

☐ Office Support Systems

☐ Data Processing (or transaction processing)

☐ End User computing

These categories overlap and inter-relate and are summarised in Figure 16.2. Office Support Systems are covered in this chapter and Data Processing and end user computing in the next.

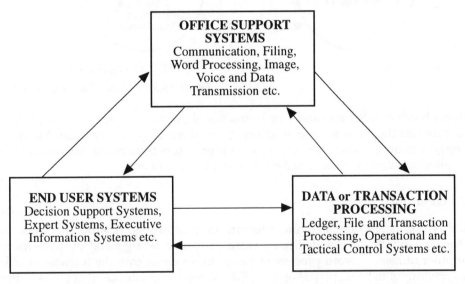

Figure 16.2: IT and information systems

Office support systems

Micro-electronics and telecommunications are in the process of transforming office work. In turn this is influencing the availability and type of information that managers use.

Figure 16.3 provides an overview of the main developments in Office Support Systems which are then briefly outlined in the paragraphs which follow.

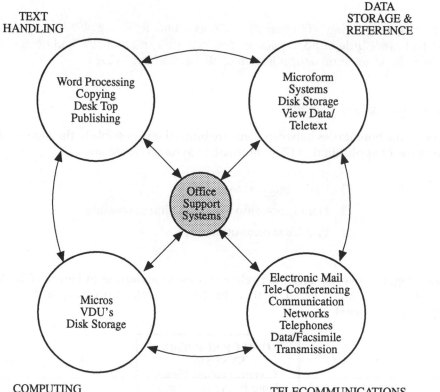

TEXT
HANDLING

DATA
STORAGE &
REFERENCE

Word Processing
Copying
Desk Top
Publishing

Microform
Systems
Disk Storage
View Data/
Teletext

Office
Support
Systems

Micros
VDU's
Disk Storage

Electronic Mail
Tele-Conferencing
Communication
Networks
Telephones
Data/Facsimile
Transmission

COMPUTING

TELECOMMUNICATIONS

Figure 16.3: IT based office support systems

Although sub-divided into areas for instructional purposes there is no real dividing line between the systems. For example, several micro-computers may be linked through a communication network which allows access from numerous points to the organisation's records maintained on disk storage and so on.

Text handling

Word processors are now a common feature in most offices. A word processor can either be a stand-alone or dedicated word processor or a general purpose micro-computer utilising a word processing program. In either case the software enables the typed input to be displayed on the VDU, altered or manipulated at will and then transferred to the printer any number of times or stored on disk for future use.

Word processors are invaluable for producing 'individualised' standard letters or for lengthy reports which require extensive editing and revision, but less necessary for short one-off letters. They can improve productivity dramatically whilst at the same time improving quality. More modern systems have numerous editing, indexing and referencing features and can be linked with the organisation's computer system.

Photocopiers have become more flexible and in addition to the routine copying of office paperwork, the more modern machines have become miniature printing systems whereby high quality reports and booklets, including colour and graphics, can be produced within the office. The ease with which multiple copies can be made can lead to waste so proper supervision is required. Most machines nowadays can copy on to plain paper, transparencies or duplicating masters. Forms may be produced by overlaying originals with headed and ruled transparencies thus producing composite copies, double sided if required.

Developments in software and laser printers have enabled the growth of *Desk-Top Publishing (DTP)*. DTP systems are versatile word processors with extensive layout and graphic facilities which enable good camera ready copy to be produced using high definition laser printers. Traditional type setting is thus eliminated. This means that professional quality sales literature, reports, books and other documentation can be produced 'in-house'.

DTP Systems combine text and graphics from other programs. The finished page can be made to resemble any magazine, book or brochure with rulings, boxes and frames emphasising blocks of text. DTP systems require high quality graphics software, the use of a mouse for ease of relocating text and diagrams round a page and a good quality laser printer. It is essential that WYSIWYG (What you see is what you get). This means that what appears on the VDU screen should exactly represent the page being made up.

Data storage and referencing

The ability to store and access vast volumes of data is an undoubted benefit of IT in organisations. Routinely the organisation's files, maintained on disk backing storage, are accessed using desk top VDU's and terminals. This facility is invaluable for current operations and for internal information, but where there is the need for repeated reference to information in a visual form then many organisations use *computer output on microform* (COM).

Computer output on microform (COM)

Microforms are photographically reduced information on files of which there are two main types:

(a) microfilm – 16mm roll film

(b) microfiche – sheet film

Computer output on tape or disk is fed into a machine called a microform recorder which reads the tape or disk and copies the data onto microforms. The information can subsequently be seen using a viewer which projects the contents of the microform onto a screen. Full size copies can be printed if desired. Reference and archive material is ideally suited to COM; examples being the systems used in libraries, garages, stores and so on.

Teletext/Viewdata

Teletext is a system for supplying commercial and other information through existing television networks. It is a form of electronic reference manual whereby 'pages' of information can be called onto the screen. There are two systems in the UK – CEEFAX (BBC) and TELETEXT (ITV) which are receive-only i.e. no interaction is possible. The systems contain largely general interest material of limited value within organisations.

Viewdata is somewhat similar to teletext in that it provides electronic reference to material but there are two main differences. Firstly, it is available to subscribers only and secondly it is interactive. This means that users can interrogate the data held in the system and also supply information to it. The information contained in the system is more specific and relevant to commercial users and the system uses a combination of telephones, computers, television and communication networks.

British Telecom operate a viewdata service known as PRESTEL and there are a growing number of private systems i.e. specific to a particular group. One example of a private viewdata system is that operated by Rover who have a system whereby their dealers can find a car of a required specification if held by another dealer. The dealers can access the system and also input changes to the information contained for example, when a particular car is sold. Another example is the information provided by airlines which can be accessed by travel agents to check flight times and availabilities and to book seats.

In the UK there are currently over 60,000 PRESTEL users many of whom are associated with the Stock Exchange, and the insurance and travel industries. The international name for viewdata is *videotex*.

Prestel has had only limited takeup in Britain but elsewhere similar systems have achieved spectacular success:

A viewdata system called Minitel was launched in France in the early 1980's. Today there are 5.5 million Minitel terminals in French homes and Offices and over 15,000 enterprises selling services on Minitel. These include: electronic banking, travel and holiday reservations, permanent news access, games, shopping, access to databases and so on. The success of the system is largely due to two early marketing decisions; to present it as a logical extension of the telephone (its original use was France Telecom's directory enquiries service) and to distribute thousands of Minitel terminals free to telephone subscribers.

Telecommunications

The power and flexibility of IT in organisations derives from a combination of the capabilities of the individual machine and from the ways that machines are linked and combined. Some of the more important facilities which can be classed under the general heading of telecommunications are electronic mailing, networks, tele-conferencing, data/facsimile transmission and electronic data interchange (EDI).

Electronic mail (E-mail)

This is a system in which messages are communicated by electronic means rather than by paper based communication. Messages are displayed on a desk top terminal and incoming and outgoing messages are filed electronically, if required. Obviously there is a considerable time saving and there is the inherent safeguard of certain delivery. A form of electronic mailing, the telex, has existed for many years but is less flexible than the newer systems for internal purposes. Electronic mail facilities are increasingly being combined with computing, word processing and telephone capabilities in one integrated work station.

Networks

Networks are communication systems which link together computers, storage devices, word processors, printers and even the telephone system of the firm. Within the one organisation, especially on one site, networks are known as Local Area Networks (LAN) and these networks allow interconnections between numbers of micro/mini-computers or between micro/mini-computers and the main processor. LAN form the vital links which allows distributed processing to take place whilst at the same time allowing users to share resources such as disks, printers and files. Network connections are essential if electronic mailing is to be used.

The key feature of a LAN is that the systems are linked by direct cables rather than by general telecommunication lines. In consequence LAN's do not need *modems*. A modem is a device to convert digital signals, as used in computers, to analogue or wave form signals used in the telephone network.

When networks are extended they are known as Wide Area Networks (WAN's). WAN's are usually larger than LAN's, cover a wider geographic area and use the general telecommunications network. They thus require modems between the terminals and computers and the telephone lines. Newer systems, sometimes known as Long Haul Networks (LHN) exploit optical fibre and satellite transmission.

Tele-conferencing and video-conferencing

An extension of conventional one-to-one telephone conversation has been the development of tele-conferencing facilities. These systems allow numerous people to be simultaneously connected so that discussion can take place even though they do not meet. This can take place either within the organisation or externally and even on an international basis. The importance of discussion and informal contact, especially for senior management, has been stressed earlier in the book so that these newer telephone facilities could have a significant impact on management's ability to gather and assess information.

Sound only conferencing is inexpensive but has limitations e.g. identification of speakers and so on. Video-conferencing overcomes these problems but is far more expensive and with present levels of technology requires specialist studio equipment.

In the USA over 80% of the Fortune 500 companies (i.e. the 500 largest) have or are planning to install tele and video conferencing and there is little doubt that this will become an increasingly important aspect of office automation.

Data transmission

In the UK most data transmitted between different locations is transmitted over ordinary telegraph and telephone circuits which are capable of carrying data as well as speech. Data can be transmitted over the ordinary public telephone circuits or a private line can be hired.

Transmission is possible in three modes:

(a) *Simplex*

transmission is possible in one direction only.

(b) *Half Duplex*

transmission is possible in both directions but not simultaneously.

(c) *Duplex*

transmission is possible in both directions simultaneously.

Where the telephone circuits are used a MODEM (MODulator/DEModulator) is required to convert digital signals (used by computers:) into analogue signals (used for transmission) at each end of the line.

Facsimile transmission or fax

Fax allows the transmission of an exact copy of an original document including diagrams, pictures, text and so on. It can be thought of as long distance photo-copying. Fax is a reliable, speedy method of sending duplicates and is widely used in business, government and the professions. There have been a number of problems with Fax systems including their speed, use of special paper and so on but newer systems are much faster and produce high definition copies on plain paper. Many facilities are now available including; simultaneous two-way transmission, automatic transmission from a buffer store, transmission direct from a computer i.e. no hard copy and so on.

Electronic data interchange (EDI)

EDI is computer-to-computer data interchange and so is a form of electronic mail. An important application is direct communication between the computers of different companies thus replacing traditional paper based communication via orders, invoices and so on. EDI is widely used in retailing e.g. Marks and Spencers use the Tradanet system. There is little doubt that the use of EDI will increase but at present there are compatibility problems between different computers.

A specialised application of EDI called Electronic Funds Transfer (EFT) is well established. EFT means that the computer user sends electronic data to his bank giving instructions to make payments or to transfer funds between accounts. EFT is used for paying suppliers, paying salaries and so on. There is an international fund transfer system known as SWIFT (Society of Worldwide Interbank Financial Telecommunications) and within the UK, interbank settlements are also made by EFT using CHAPS (Clearing House Automated Payment System).

The greater use of IT and of data transmission is affecting not only how work is done but where it is done. In America it is estimated that over 8m people now work at home using computers and data links. Alvin Tofler has coined the phrase 'electronic cottage industries' to describe this trend.

An illustration of IT in practice

Properly selected IT systems and computers can improve the efficiency of single administrative tasks. However, even greater gains can be made when there is integration of various aspects of IT, data transmission and computing.

As an illustration of such integration consider the 1991 Population Census in Britain. A Census is conducted every 10 years and has been done since 1801. Twenty three million forms were completed on 21st April 1991 with two types of answers. 'Tick Box' answers for items such as sex and marital status and statement answers for less defined information.

Figure 16.4 provides an overview of the census operation.

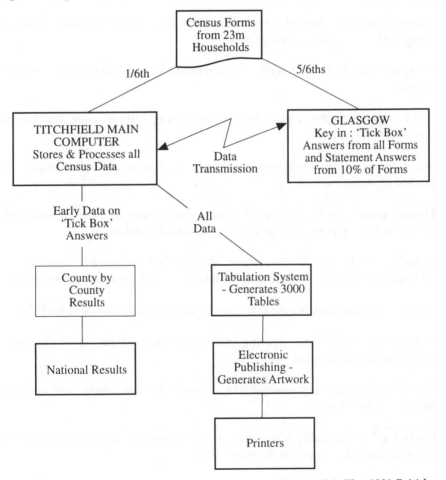

Figure 16.4: The 1991 British census

The system used electronic data transmission via the Government's own data network enabling data entered in Glasgow to be transmitted directly to the large, mainframe computer at Titchfield. This was speedier and more secure than the system used in 1981 which involved the physical transfer of magnetic discs.

However the main time saving came from the technology used to speed up publication of the 3000 tables generated by the Census. The table layouts were programmed well in advance using electronic publishing awaiting only the entry of the census data. When this was available high quality camera ready copy was sent straight to the printers.

Overall the system integrated numerous aspects of IT, computing, electronic publishing and data transmission to deal with a massive operation efficiently and speedily.

Key point summary

☐ Information Technology (IT) is information processing using micro-electronics, computers and telecommunications.

☐ Computers can help to overcome human limitations including; slowness, errors, fatigue etc.

☐ Office Support Systems include; Text Handling, Data Storage and reference, Telecommunications.

☐ Word-processors enable typed input to be displayed, altered as required and printed or stored on disk.

☐ Photo-copiers have become much more versatile and facilities include; colour, double-sided copying, enlargement and reduction and so on.

☐ Desk-Top Publishing (DTP) systems are, in effect, advanced word-processing packages including extensive graphic facilities and high quality laser printers.

☐ Reference and archive material is often stored on microfilm or microfiche.

☐ Teletext is a system for supplying information through the television network. No interaction is possible.

☐ Viewdata (or videotex) systems are available to subscribers only and permit two-way interaction.

☐ Electronic mail (E-mail) is a system where messages are communicated electronically, usually on personal computers.

☐ Local Area Networks (LANS) are communication systems which link together computers, printers, word processors etc. usually on the same site.

❐ Networks over a wider area are known as Wide Area Networks (WANS) or Long Haul Networks (LHNS).

❐ Facsimile Transmission or FAX enables an exact copy of a document to be transmitted. Newer machines are much more versatile.

❐ Electronic Data Exchange (EDI) is computer-to-computer data interchange and is widely used in retailing, banking etc.

Self review questions

1. *Define IT.*

2. *What are the features of information processing which makes computer use feasible?*

3. *What are the three main areas of IT application in information systems?*

4. *What main developments could be described as office support systems?*

5. *What are word processors?*

6. *What are the two types of COM?*

7. *Distinguish between teletext and viewdata.*

8. *What is electronic mail?*

9. *What is a LAN?*

10. *What is simplex and duplex transmission?*

11. *What is EDI?*

17 Information technology: computers and data processing

Objectives

After you have studied this chapter you will:

☐ *Understand the distinction between transaction (or data) processing and end user computing.*

☐ *Know that all data processing systems consist of input, processing, file maintenance and output.*

☐ *Be able to define a database.*

☐ *Understand the functions of a Database Management System (DBMS).*

☐ *Know the meaning of end-user computing.*

☐ *Understand that Decision Support Systems support managers in dealing with semi-structured problems.*

☐ *Be able to describe the main types of Decision Support Packages.*

☐ *Understand the key features and uses of Spreadsheets.*

☐ *Know what is meant by an Expert System.*

☐ *Be able to describe the features and uses of Executive Information Systems.*

Computers and information systems

The previous chapter outlined the role of IT in Office Support systems. It is now time to examine in more detail the use of computers in organisations.

The mere fact of using a computer does not of itself mean that work is done more efficiently or that better information is produced. Too often computers are introduced in an attempt to solve a technical problem when the real problem is one concerned with management, or lack of clear objectives, or poor coordination, on one caused by environmental change or some other factor. To gain the maximum advantage from using computers it is essential that problems are clearly identified before a computer system is introduced. This means that there must be considerable investigation into management's requirements, problems, information needs and so on before there is any attempt to design a computer system.

Before deciding what computer system will be used or even whether a computer is needed it is first necessary to find out what the system must do.

The passive view says; 'We have a system, it needs improvement: lets see how this can be done'. The more radical view says; 'Never mind how we do it now, let's sort out what we want to do and see if we can develop a system to do it'. Too often an existing manual system is transferred on to a computer without sufficient thought being given to its real purpose. This approach tends to produce information systems which perpetuate existing deficiencies and swamp managers with reports they rarely use.

The preferred approach recognises that an information system is part of a wider management system. It must provide support and assistance to management for planning, control, decision making and other functions. The preferred approach is a top down one concentrating on what first, then how, and moving to successive levels of detail. The development of an information system can be likened to the stages by which an architect designs a building.

Firstly, he receives a design brief which spells out what the building is expected to do. He then considers how to fulfil the objectives and produces a high level plan showing the overall perspective of the building. Lower level plans are then drawn each giving progressively more detail. This is a hierarchically structured approach which is also used for the design of information systems.

Applications of computers

We now turn to the use of computers in organisation. Although in practice there is no clear cut dividing line between the areas of application, for clarity, the use of computers will be outlined in two broad categories.

☐ the routine processing of day-to-day transactions, known as *data processing* or *transaction processing* or *file processing*.

☐ the use of computers *by the end-users* themselves. The end-users include; managers, accountants, office staff, sales people, executives and others.

Both data processing and end-user computing produce management information. The key difference is that data processing systems supply pre-determined outputs and reports so there is less flexibility. This means that great care must be taken in analysing and determining management's real information needs before the system is designed.

On the other hand with end-user computing there is more flexibility and interaction so that the emphasis becomes one of supporting the end user rather than the production of a specified report.

Data processing systems

These systems perform the essential role of collecting and processing the daily transaction of the organisation, hence the alternative term, *transaction processing*. Typically these include; all forms of ledger keeping, accounts receivable and payable, invoicing, credit control, rate demands, stock movements and so on.

These types of systems were the first to harness the power of the computer and orig-inally were based on centralised mainframe computers. In many cases this still applies, especially for large volume repetitive jobs, but the availability of micro and mini computers has made *distributed data processing* feasible and popular. Distributed data processing has many variations but in essence means that data handling and processing are carried out at or near the point of use rather than in one centralised location.

Transaction processing is substantially more significant in terms of processing time, volume of input and output than say, information production for tactical and strategic planning. Transaction processing is essential to keep the operations of the organisation running smoothly and provides the base for all other internal informa-tion support. This is shown in Figure 17.1.

Figure 17.1: Transaction processing as a base for the organisation's information system

Characteristics of data processing systems

These systems are 'pre-specified': that is their functions, decision rules and output formats cannot usually be changed by the end user. These systems are related directly to the structure of the organisation's data. Any change in the data they process or the functions they perform usually requires the intervention of informa-tion system specialists such as system analysts and programmers.

In outline, all data processing systems contain four inter-related elements; INPUT-PROCESS – FILE MAINTENANCE – OUTPUT. These four elements are shown in Figure 17.2 related to a payroll system.

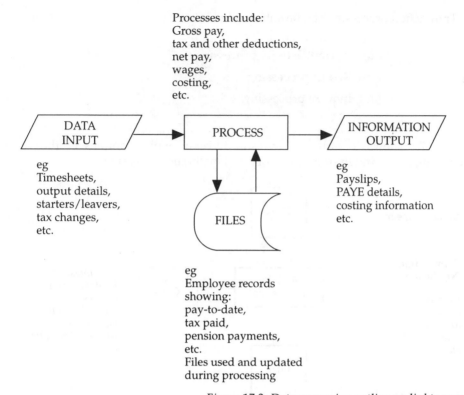

Processes include:
Gross pay,
tax and other deductions,
net pay,
wages,
costing,
etc.

DATA INPUT

PROCESS

INFORMATION OUTPUT

eg
Timesheets,
output details,
starters/leavers,
tax changes,
etc.

FILES

eg
Payslips,
PAYE details,
costing information
etc.

eg
Employee records
showing:
pay-to-date,
tax paid,
pension payments,
etc.
Files used and updated
during processing

Figure 17.2: Data processing outline applied to payroll

Some data processing systems have to cope with huge volumes and a wide range of data types and output formats. As an example consider the Electricity and Gas Board Billing and Payment Handling systems, the Clearing Bank's current Accounting systems, the Motor Policy handling systems of a large insurer and so on. The systems and programming work required for these systems represents a major investment. For example the development of a large scale billing system for a public utility represents something like 100 man years of effort.

Of course, data processing also takes place on a more modest scale and the ready availability of application packages – i.e. software to deal with a particular administrative or commercial task – means that small scale users have professionally written and tested programs to deal with their routine data processing. The better packages provide for some flexibility and the user can specify – within limits – variations in output formats, data types and decision rules.

Scope of transaction processing

Transaction processing is necessary to ensure that the day-to-day activities of the organisation are processed, recorded and acted upon. Files are maintained which provide both the current data for transactions; for example the amount invoiced and cash received during the month for statement preparation, and which also serve as a basis for operational and tactical control and for answering enquiries.

Transaction processing can be sub-divided into:

a) Current activity processing

(b) Report processing

(c) Inquiry processing

Figure 17.3 shows in outline these sub-divisions with examples of the various processing types drawn from inventory and materials processing.

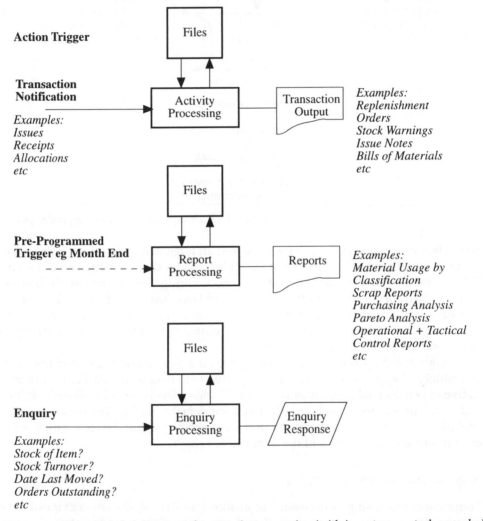

Figure 17.3: Subdivisions of transaction processing (with inventory control examples)

An illustration follows of transaction processing. It is in outline only and shows the main system flowcharts, main files and the outputs produced.

Illustration of sales order processing

Central Spares Ltd. are based in Birmingham and supply shops and workshops with a range of spare parts for televisions, video recorders and domestic appliances. A range of approximately 2000 items is stocked and there are approximately 500 customers. Virtually all orders are received by telephone or fax and the company prides itself on its 24 hour delivery service. In general orders are processed and accumulated during the day and a twilight shift makes up the orders which are delivered the next day if the items requested are in stock.

The company uses a mini-computer, disk storage and VDU's

The System

Figure 17.4 shows the Order Handling System.

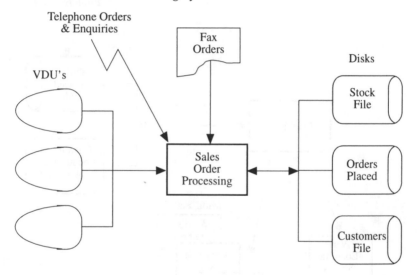

Figure 17.4: Central spares: order handling

An order clerk calls up information on the screen and, interacting with the customer, processes the order as follows:

Screen information	Customer
Customer's name and address and account no.	Confirms
Delivery address	Confirms
Order number	Supplies
Credit position	Makes payment arrangements
Product name, stock number and quantity	Orders
Price and any delivery charge	Accepts/rejects
Alternative products and -promotions	Considers
Stock position	Advised of shortages
Expected delivery date	Accepts/rejects

Assuming that the customer's credit position is satisfactory and the customer accepts the price/delivery/alternatives offered the order is accepted and the customer orders placed and stock files are updated.

Figure 17.5 shows the Invoice/Despatch Note printing. A multi part set, including address labels is printed in bin number sequence on a printer located in the warehouse.

After the close of order taking for the day the computer prints out a load sheet for each delivery van.

The load sheet takes account of delivery addresses and economic journeys and is used to obtain delivery signatures from customers.

Finally there is an Accounting Run shown in Figure 17.6 which deals with despatched orders, shortages, cash received and so on.

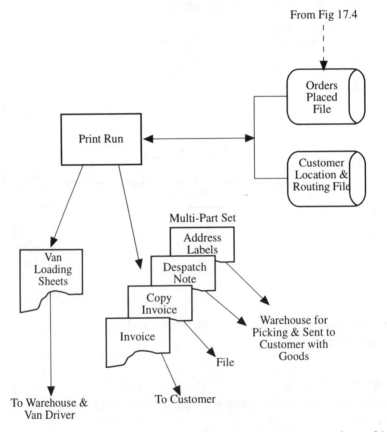

Figure 17.5: Central spares: despatching process

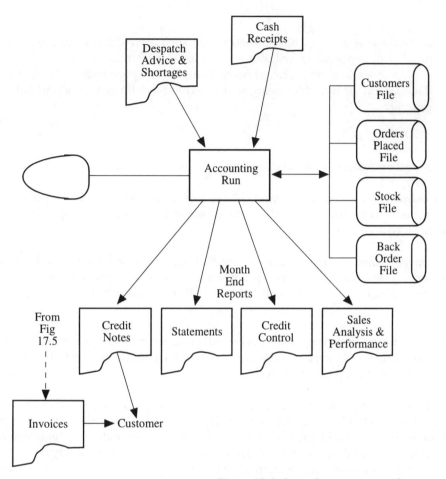

Figure 17.6: Central spares: accounting processes

Databases

In the early days of computerisation it was normal to maintain specific files for individual applications. Data were processed centrally in archives and there was little or no on-line interrogation of files.

This approach meant that there was duplication of data, inflexibility, concentration on the needs of the computer system rather than the user, and difficulties of accessing files by on-line users. To overcome these problems *data bases* were developed.

A database can be defined in various ways, for example:

A database is a collection of structured data. The structure of the data is independent of any particular application.

British Computer Society

> A database is a file of data structured in such a way that it may serve a number of applications without its structure being dictated by any one of those applications, the concept being that programs are written round the database rather than files being structured to meet the needs of particular programs.
>
> *CIMA*

The important features of a database are:

Data independence means an item of data is stored for its own sake and not for one specific use. Thus the use of the data is generalised and is independent of the programs which use it.

Data integrity means the avoidance of conflicting, duplicated data by only showing one copy. If, for example, a stock balance alters, only one update is needed and all programs which access the stock balance will automatically be given the correct figure.

Flexibility means that data can be accessed in many different ways and for many different purposes. These can range from routine accesses for transaction processes to one-off queries by the Chief Executive.

The database can grow and change and is built up stage by stage within the organisation.It will actually comprise several databases, each providing the anticipated information for several logically related management information systems where the data can be accessed, retrieved and modified with reasonable flexibility.

The data structures and relationships require highly technical software – known as the Data Base Management System (DBMS) – to deal with them. Fortunately the user is shielded, to a large extent, from the complexity and is able to access the data base with the minimum of technical knowledge.

When the only form of data storage possible was unrelated, unique files for each application, this engendered a narrow, parochial view of information. The reality is that management need information which crosses functions, applications and levels and the flexibility of databases and the linkages possible make the concept a powerful one and essential for end user systems.

An organisation is not confined to its own internal database. There are companies which sell access to databases dealing with matters which an individual organisation would find expensive to collect. Examples of these public databases include those providing; Stock Exchange and financial data, environmental data, legal matters including EU treaties and legislation, consumer research and marketing data and so on. In 1994 over 8000 external databases were available and the numbers are continually growing.

End user computing

Traditionally, the only people who had direct contact with computers were the systems professionals (programmers, systems analysts etc.). The introduction of personal computers, terminals, networks, user-friendly software, databases etc. has altered the position dramatically and has led to the growth of end-user computing.

This may be broadly defined as

> the direct, hands-on approach to computers by users – not indirect use through systems professionals. Users include; managers, office staff, sales people, production workers and others.

End-user computing is a large and growing field and some of the applications are listed below:

- ☐ Decision Support Systems
- ☐ Expert Systems
- ☐ Executive Information Systems
- ☐ End-user programming
- ☐ Computer based training
- ☐ Search and retrieval of information
- ☐ Text handling and publishing

and so on

Because of our emphasis on management and information this book concentrates on the first three applications shown above i.e. Decision Support Systems, Expert Systems and Executive Information Systems.

Decision support systems (DSS)

The objective of DSS is to support managers in their work, especially decision making. DSS tend to overlap both data processing systems and office support systems. They acquire much of their basic data from routine transaction processing and the results of analyses performed on such data may be included in reports prepared by the office support system, for example, on a word processor.

DSS tend to be used in planning, modelling, analysing alternatives and decision making. They generally operate through terminals operated by the user who interacts with the computer system. Using a variety of tools and procedures the manager (i.e. the user) can develop his own systems to help perform his functions more effectively. It is this active involvement and the focus on decision making which distinguishes a DSS from a data processing system. The emphasis is on support for decision making not on automated decision making which is a feature of transaction processing.

DSS are especially useful for semi-structured problems where problem solving is improved by interaction between the manager and the computer system. The emphasis is on small, simple models which can easily be understood and used by the manager rather than complex integrated systems which need information specialists to operate them.

The main characteristics of DSS are:

(a) The computer provides support but does not replace the manager's judgement nor does it provide pre-determined solutions.

(b) DSS are best suited to semi-structured problems where parts of the analysis can be computerised but the decision maker's judgement and insight is needed to control the process.

(c) Where effective problem solving is enhanced by inter-action between the computer and the manager.

Where to apply DSS

DSS are man/machine systems and are suitable for semi-structured problems. The problem must be important to the manager and the decision required must be a key one. In addition if an interactive computer-based system is to be used then some of the following criteria should be met.

(a) *There should be a large data base.*
A data base is an organised collection of structured data with a minimum duplication of data items. The data base is common to all users of the system but is independent of the programs which use the data. If the data base is too large for manual searching then a computer-supported approach may be worthwhile.

(b) *Large amount of computation or data manipulation.*
Where analysis of the problem requires considerable computation or data manipulation, computing power is likely to be beneficial.

(c) *Complex inter-relationships.*
Where there is a large data base or where there are numerous factors involved it is frequently difficult to assess all the possible inter-relationships without computer assistance.

(d) *Analysis by stages.*
Where the problem is an iterative one with stages for re-examination and re-assessment it becomes more difficult to deal with manually. The computer-based model can answer the questions, 'What if?' quickly and effectively.

(e) *Judgement required.*

In complex situations judgement is required to determine problem and solution. Unaided, no computer system can provide this.

(f) *Communication.*

Where several people are involved in the problem solving process, each contributing some special expertise, then the co-ordinating power of the computer can be of assistance.

It follows from the above criteria that DSS are inappropriate for unstructured problems and unnecessary for completely structured problems because these can be dealt with wholly by the computer and man/machine interaction is unnecessary.

In outline DSS require a database, the software to handle the database and decision support programs including, for example, modelling, spread sheet and analysis packages, expert systems etc.

Decision support packages

The existence of the database and a DBMS to handle it means that the manager can interrogate and access a mass of data at will. He then needs to be able to use this data in exploiting alternatives and making decisions. To do this there is an enormous range of packages available. These include packages for:-

(a) Modelling and simulation

(b) Spread sheets

(c) Forecasting

(e) Non-Linear and Linear Programming

(f) Regression modelling

(h) Sensitivity and risk analysis

(i) Expert systems

and so on

It is clearly beyond the scope of this book to describe all these types of packages in detail but two of the more relevant ones are briefly described below, namely, spread sheets and expert systems.

Spreadsheet packages

The basis of a spread sheet package is an electronic worksheet whereby data can be stored and manipulated at will. The spread sheet is a matrix of locations which can contain values, formulae and relationships. The key feature is that all elements in the matrix are changed automatically when one or more of the key assumptions are changed. This means that a spread sheet can be used to show the results of different actions or assumptions which is a form of modelling.

For example, a series of interlocking departmental operating statements culminating in an overall projected profit and loss account may have been prepared on the spread sheet. If one or more of the variables (rates of pay, output levels, sales, absorption rates and so on) needs to be altered then the new value needs only to be entered once and the whole of the matrix is recalculated virtually instantaneously with all relationships, sub-totals and totals automatically catered for. This facility allows a series of outcomes to be explored, providing answers to the 'what if' questions which are so essential to the manager. For example, what would be the effect on profit of a change in inflation rate/cost per unit/contribution margin/scrap rates or whatever factor need to be explored. Used in this way spread sheet packages perform a modelling function and this facility is greatly expanded in the latest spread sheet packages.

Spreadsheets and budgeting

One of the important tasks of tactical level management is concerned with budgeting. Spread sheets can be of great assistance in exploring the effect on a budget of different values and assumptions so that the manager can make more effective decisions. As one example, consider the Credit Controller dealing with cash budgeting.

Cash budgets are examples of routine but highly essential reports which need frequent updating to reflect current and forecast conditions, changes in credit behaviour, anticipated gains or expenditures and so on. Each period (weekly, monthly, quarterly, as required) changes and up-to-date information are input and, in combination with the brought forward file data, the cash budget will be automatically projected forward by the spread sheet program with highlighted surpluses and/or deficiencies, balances carried forward from one period to another and all the usual contents of a cash budget. The budget could be shown in both an abbreviated and detailed format and could also be displayed in a graphical form.

Figure 17.7 shows the possible output of a Summary Cash Budget and a corresponding graphical display, the facility for which is increasingly being included in modern spread sheet packages such as Lotus 1-2-3.

Summary Cash Budget (Ref Detail Budgets A–E)									
	Jan £'000	Feb £'000	Mar £'000	Apr £'000	May £'000	Jun £'000	Jul £'000	Aug £'000	Sep £'000
Opening Balance	−2850	−2900	−2925	−2850	−3100	−3450	−3375	−3425	−3625
Add Total Receipts	3250	2900	2700	3100	3300	3200	2900	2700	2650
Less Total Payments	3300	2925	2975	3350	3650	3125	2950	2900	2450
Closing Cash Balance C/F	−2900	−2925	−2850	−3100	−3450	−3375	−3425	−3625	−3425
Current Overdraft Limit	3000	3000	3000	3000	3500	3500	3500	3500	3500
Warning Indicator				★				★	

Figure 17.7(a): Tabular cash budget

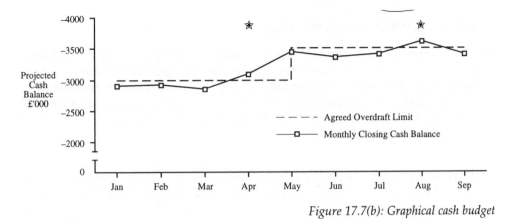

Figure 17.7(b): Graphical cash budget

Expert systems

At the present time, Expert Systems represent the most advanced stage of decision support systems. An Expert System is a computer system which embodies some of the experience and specialised knowledge of an expert or experts. An Expert System enables a non-expert to achieve comparable performance to an expert in the field. It uses a reasoning process which bears some resemblance to human thought.

The unique feature of an Expert System is the *knowledge base,* which is a network of rules which represents the human expertise. These rules and linkages are derived from discussions with experts and analysis of their decision making behaviour. Attempts are made to include the effects of uncertainty and judgement and clearly such an approach is likely to be costly and time consuming. Expert Systems are much more sophisticated and powerful that simply automating a typical structured decision but conversely, they are very much more difficult to implement.

As an example a doctor might supply a Medical Diagnosis Expert System with a particular set of symptoms. The program searches its knowledge base of symptoms and possible causes then, at certain stages, begins an interactive exchange with the doctor to find out more information or to suggest further tests that might be carried out. Thus, the user is not surrendering his judgement but is using the system to enhance his judgement and improve his decisions.

Expert Systems have been developed in a number of fields of which the following are examples:

- ❑ Medical diagnosis
- ❑ Personal tax planning
- ❑ Product pricing
- ❑ Selection of selling methods

- ❑ Statutory Sick Pay Entitlement and Claims
- ❑ Credit approval in banking
- ❑ Air crew scheduling

and so on.

Executive information systems (EIS)

These are forms of data retrieval systems that provide selected and summarised information for senior executives. They assist top management by providing information on critical areas of the organisation's activities drawn from both internal and external databases. EIS are becoming more widely available and organisations such as British Airways, ICI, BP, Glaxo and others are enthusiastic users.

The key features of an EIS are:

☐ Easy to use. The system must be fast and extremely simple to use as it will be used by busy executives. The use of touch screens, mice and icons, pop-up menus etc. is normal.

☐ Access to data. There must be unhindered rapid access to data permitting vertical and horizontal exploration. This is known as *drilling down the data*.

☐ Data analysis. Having obtained the data the EIS should provide facilities for such things as; ratio and trend calculations, data integration, forecasts and so on.

☐ Quality presentation. The system should provide interesting and understandable formats using colour, graphs, diagrams and so on.

A typical way that an EIS works is by exception reporting and drilling down to investigate the causes. For example a director may be alerted that a particular department is well over budget. (An exception to budget or target is known as a 'hot-spot' and would be highlighted by the EIS). The manager would then drill down the data by pursuing lower and lower levels of detail. He might first seek a breakdown of the departmental budget and actual expenditure into broad categories such as; Material, Labour and Overheads. If he discovered that the major overspend was in overheads he would access the detailed expenditure on the various items of overhead cost such as; Salaries, Depreciation, Telephones, Insurance and so on. In this way the executive can explore at will and is thus provided with better assistance in planning and controlling.

EIS are used personally by managers and it is thus essential that the system reflects their requirements. The managers must be involved in the development and implementation of the system. By their nature top level information and data requirements are difficult to specify precisely in advance and are subject to change, consequently the closest possible collaboration is necessary.

Key point summary

☐ Transaction processing systems are pre-specified and changes require the intervention of system specialists.

☐ The basis of all transaction or data processing systems is: INPUT, PROCESS, FILE MAINTENANCE, OUTPUT.

❏ Transaction processing comprises: activity processing, report processing and enquiry processing.

❏ A database is a collection of data, available to all, which is independent of individual programs.

❏ A Data Base Management System is the software which controls the database and which acts as a link between the users and the database.

❏ A DBMS comprises software for organising data, retrieving data and handling enquiries.

❏ Decision support systems are operated by the end user and supplement human judgement in semi-structured decision making.

❏ Decision support packages include: modelling, spread sheets, forecasting, linear programming, statistical analysis, expert systems and so on.

❏ Spread sheet packages can be used for transaction processing and for modelling in decision support systems.

❏ Expert Systems aim to incorporate human judgement and experience into a knowledge base.

❏ Executive Information Systems are easy to use data retrieval systems in which the executive can drill down for data.

Self review questions

1. Describe data processing systems and their characteristics.

2. What are the sub-divisions of transaction processing?

3. What is a database?

4. What is a DBMS?

5. What is end-user computing?

6. What are DSS?

7. Where should DSS be applied?

8. What are the main types of DSS?

9. What types of packages can be of assistance in support of decision making?

10. What is a spread sheet package and how can it be used?

11. What are expert systems?

12. What are the features of Executive Information Systems?

18 *Office organisation and management*

Objectives

After you have studied this chapter you will:

☐ *Know the main functions of offices which are mainly concerned with information handling and communication.*

☐ *Be able to define Administrative or Office Management.*

☐ *Be aware of IT developments which are changing the location where office work is done.*

☐ *Understand the key features of centralisation and decentralisation.*

☐ *Know the factors to be considered in planning offices.*

☐ *Be able to describe the features of private, cellular, open plan and landscaped offices.*

☐ *Know the main legal requirements regarding health and safety at work.*

☐ *Understand how to make offices more productive.*

☐ *Know the main objectives and principles of Organisation and Methods (O & M).*

☐ *Be able to describe the main steps in an O & M investigation.*

☐ *Understand the objectives and principles of form design.*

The key functions of the office

The office deals with the clerical work of the organisation. Traditionally this work was almost entirely paper-based but the increase in usage of information technology, computers and telecommunications means that major changes are taking place in the way that office work is dealt with. Nevertheless, it remains true that much office work is still concerned with paper-based activities e.g. dealing with correspondence, filling in forms, preparing reports and so on.

The functions of an office include:

☐ Gathering, processing, filing, sorting and retrieving information.

☐ Communicating information by typing, telephoning, posting, copying, printing, faxing etc.

- ❏ Originating information by writing reports, editing, re-arranging, collating, cross-referencing etc.
- ❏ Control activities including checking and audit, inspection, safeguarding assets, personnel evaluation.
- ❏ Ensuring that legal requirements are met.

It will be noted how many of the activities above deal with information and this emphasis is reflected in the Institute of Administrative Management's definition of administrative management (an alternative term for office management).

'Administrative Management is that branch of management which is concerned with the services of obtaining, recording and analysing information, of planning and of communicating, by means of which the management of a business safeguards its assets, promotes its affairs and achieves its objectives.'

(The Institute of Administrative Management)

The office can be considered in system terms – input, process and output – as shown in Figure 18.1

INPUTS	PROCESSING	OUTPUTS
eg	eg	eg
Correspondence,	Analysing,	Messages,
orders,	summarising,	correspondence,
invoices,	calculating,	memos,
telephone calls,	filing,	forms,
messages,	interpreting,	minutes,
cheques,	generating,	reports,
telex,	editing,	invoices,
fax,	controlling,	orders,
E-mail,	etc.	faxes,
etc.		E-mail,
		etc.

Figure 18.1: System's view of the office

Because of the primary importance of information and communication in offices a sound grasp of the characteristics of information and the various communication methods is essential. These have already been covered in Chapter 15 – Information and Communications.

Where is office work done?

Traditionally all office work was carried out in the organisation's own premises either in large, centralised offices or dispersed throughout the organisation. This is still largely true but developments in information technology and communication networks mean that an increasing number of people are able to work from home at least for part of the week. The use of faxes, E-mail and personalised telephone numbers which enable a subscriber to be tracked down anywhere in the world mean that, with the right facilities, a person can always be in two-way contact. In the UK this is known as tele-working and is defined by British Telecom (BT) as

'working in a location that is remote from an employer or from the normally expected place of work either on full-time or part-time basis. The work generally involves the electronic processing of information, the results of which are communicated remotely to the employer, usually by a telecommunication link'.

Other changes which are occurring are known as *hotelling* or *hot-desking*.

Some companies have found that 30 to 40 per cent of desks are vacant at any one time. In consequence expensive office space is being wasted. One approach to overcome this problem has been adopted by Arthur Andersen, the management consultants. Each work position, known as a carrel, is assigned to employees according to the task being performed that day. This is temporarily 'personalised' with name plates, re-routed telephone calls and any files required being made available. This is known as hot-desking. Although undeniably space saving, the process does strip workers of their own fixed desks and offices.

As yet teleworking and desk sharing schemes affect only a minority of office workers but it is inevitable that the proportion will grow as communication systems become cheaper and more efficient and firms strive for greater flexibility.

When office work is carried out within the organisation, which is still the norm, consideration must be given to obtaining the right balance of centralised and decentralised services.

Centralisation and decentralisation

The question of whether or not to centralise services is an important one for large organisations. As an example should the organisation have a central reprographics service using sophisticated and efficient equipment or would it be better for each of the departments to have their own less efficient equipment which would however be available as and when required?

The choice depends on a careful study of volumes, costs, service requirements, degree of control and other factors and each organisation must choose the best compromise to suit its own requirements. The advantages and disadvantages of centralisation are given below.

Advantages of centralisation:

☐ Greater control of costs and standards

☐ Enables higher skilled, specialist staff to be used

☐ Possible economies of scale through higher volumes, bulk purchasing etc

☐ Greater utilisation of expensive equipment

☐ Easier to ensure company guidelines and policies are followed

Disadvantages of centralisation:

☐ May not be responsive to local requirements

☐ Delays and inflexibility

☐ Loss of personal contact and convenience

☐ More communication and transport become necessary

In certain areas of work there has been more decentralisation over recent years. For example, data processing was at one time almost exclusively dealt with by centralised, main frame computers chiefly because of their high cost. Nowadays the availability of powerful, low cost mini and micro-computers means that distributed data processing is commonplace. A similar process has taken place with other office machines e.g. photo-copiers.

Planning the office

There are numerous factors to be considered in planning the physical conditions of offices and deciding what types of offices should be provided. These range from objective, measurable items such as temperature and lighting to more subjective matters such as status. Some of the more important factors include:

☐ What work must be done? Is there a normal sequence or work flow?

☐ What communications are required? Internally? Externally?

☐ What equipment (and necessary services) is required? Is it noisy? Does it need to be separated?

☐ How can the existing space be best utilised?

☐ How can team work and co-operation be encouraged?

☐ How can movements, distractions etc. be reduced?

- [ ] How much supervision is required? How will this be provided?
- [ ] Are there privacy and security requirements?
- [ ] Will visitors/customers/clients need to be dealt with?
- [ ] What legal requirements must be met?
- [ ] Regardless of minimum legal standards, what physical working conditions (light, temperature, air etc.) are necessary to ensure good working conditions?
- [ ] What type of furniture and equipment best suits the staff and work to be done?

An important strategic decision relates to the types of offices provided. These can range from individual, private offices to open plan, landscaped offices. The characteristics of the main types of office are dealt with below.

Private offices

These are often provided for executives or for those who have to deal with confidential or high security work or who have numerous visitors. In many organisations the provision of private offices, often with individually chosen furniture, is more related to status and seniority than to the type of work carried out.

Departmental or cellular offices

These are larger offices designed to house a section or department carrying out related work. Such offices help to foster a team approach but may encourage an insular attitude to the rest of the organisation. In general, departmental offices are relatively expensive and use space inefficiently. However where there are security considerations (e.g. a computer room) their use may be justified.

Open plan offices

These are large offices, often housing several sections or departments, with staff of all grades in the one office i.e. clerks, supervisors and managers. Open plan offices have a number of advantages and disadvantages.

Advantages:

- ❑ Space saving: less space wasted by corridors, walls, doors etc.
- ❑ Less costly: less capital cost per employee and lower maintenance costs.
- ❑ More flexible: layouts and work-flows can be easily changed.
- ❑ Easier supervision: easier access and improved visibility means that fewer supervisors are required.
- ❑ Machine/equipment sharing becomes easier.
- ❑ Communications and work flow may be improved.

Disadvantages:

- ❑ Noise and distraction caused by movement, conversations, visitors, telephones.
- ❑ Less confidentiality and security.
- ❑ Loss of morale due to large numbers, change from small group offices etc.
- ❑ Perceived loss of status by managers and senior staff.

Whilst there are undoubtedly economic benefits from open plan offices, the loss of privacy and feelings of being a small cog in a large machine cause many clerical workers to dislike them. This was especially pronounced in the earlier open plan offices. These were regimented affairs with desks in straight lines where there was little or no attempt to demarcate particular work areas or teams. One way of over-coming some of the disadvantages of open plan offices is called the landscaped office.

The landscaped office

The idea of landscaped offices originated in Germany. They are an attempt to alle-viate the regimentation of the traditional open plan office, reduce noise and distrac-tion and to foster sectional or group identities. In a landscaped office desks and work areas are arranged either singly or in groups at different angles to one another. Boundaries between sections are subtly marked by low visual and acoustic screens, the liberal use of plants and the positioning of cabinets and equipment.

The general effect of landscaping is to soften and break up the formal appearance of a large office in order to tone down any regimented look. Great care is taken to make the office as attractive as possible with tasteful colour schemes, good lighting and coordinated furniture and equipment. The landscaped office uses space some-what less efficiently than an ordinary open plan one but the psychological benefits are generally thought to outweigh this disadvantage.

Legal requirements relating to offices

In addition to numerous statutes regarding employee rights, legislation relating to health and safety and working conditions is of particular importance to managers responsible for offices.

The main act which is relevant is the Health and Safety at Work Act (1974). This act reinforced earlier legislation including the Offices, Shops and Railway Premises Act of 1963, popularly known as the Offices Act. In general the Acts lay down that it is the duty of every employer to ensure, so far as is reasonably practicable, the health, safety and welfare at work of all employees. Specific issues covered include:

- ☐ The working environment must be clean with adequate lighting temperature, ventilation and toilet facilities.
- ☐ Gangways, corridors, entrances and exits must be kept in a safe condition.
- ☐ Management must develop a health and safety policy in writing which must be brought to the attention of employees.
- ☐ Employees must be insured against accidents at work.
- ☐ A fire safety certificate must be sought and the number of occupants must not exceed permitted numbers.
- ☐ First aid boxes and personnel trained in first aid should be provided.
- ☐ Staff operating machines must be trained.
- ☐ Noise and air pollution should be controlled and safety clothing and equipment supplied where necessary.

The Health and Safety at Work Act concerns the health and safety of all people at work. The Offices Act is more specifically directed at people in offices and shops and lays down more detailed standards of space, temperature, cleanliness, toilet facilities and so on. To an extent the requirements overlap those of the Health and Safety at Work Act. As examples of its detailed requirements the Offices Act specifies that the space provided per person must be at least 40 sq. feet (or 400 cubic feet if the ceiling is under 10 feet high) and that the temperature must reach 16°C within one hour of starting work.

Making offices more productive

Traditionally most efficiency and productivity studies dealt with the factory and production workers. This process started with the pioneering work of F.W. Taylor, the father of Scientific Management, and developed into what is known today as Work Study. The elimination of unnecessary operations and movements, better workplace and tool design, and other developments increased factory productivity enormously even before modern technology accelerated the rate of improvement. In earlier days relatively few people worked in administration so the efficiency and productivity of offices was largely ignored.

The position today is totally different. Far more people work in administration and offices than are directly employed in production. In most organisations administrative costs are a major element in their cost structure. Accordingly it is essential that office work is carried out as efficiently as possible and that the office is at least as productive as the factory. The temptation must be resisted to see productivity improvements as related solely to changes in the technology used. Of course, computers and IT enable gains in efficiency to be made but more fundamental questions need to be asked *before* the means of doing the work is considered.

Foremost among these are; is the work necessary? Can it be eliminated without loss of effectiveness? can the department or office be re-organised to cut out unnecessary operations? are the staff organised into suitable teams? are they motivated and well trained? and so on.

Because of the importance of studying and improving office work a special technique has developed for this purpose, known as *Organisation and Methods* (O & M).

Organisation & methods (O & M)

O & M provides a specialist service to management. Its main objective is to improve administrative, clerical and office procedures. To do this it is necessary to study not only methods of work but the way the organisation is structured and how work is sub-divided. This broader view is necessary because the various factors inter-relate and one cannot be studied without the others.

For example, assume that a study was being made of the production of Labour Cost Statistics in the Accounting Department. If the study was limited just to this, certain improvements may be found, perhaps by better form design or improved operations within the Accounting Department. However a broader review might show that greater overall improvement is possible if there was some re-organisation and the work was done elsewhere, say, as a by-product of the Wages Calculations in the Payroll section.

Underlying the O & M technique is a questioning, critical approach to every aspect of the work. The following questions are typical:

- ❏   WHY is the work/operation carried out? (i.e. its purpose)
- ❏   WHAT exactly is done?
- ❏   HOW is it done?
- ❏   WHEN is it done?
- ❏   WHERE is it done?
- ❏   WHO does it?

Each of the above questions is just the start of another series. For example , when the analyst finds out when something is done in the current system it is necessary to ask why is it done at that time, what would be the effect of doing it at some other time and so on. In this way in-depth understanding is gained which is vital in order to develop an improved system.

Steps in an O & M investigation

Experience shows that a systematic approach to O & M investigations produces the best results. Typically the stages in an investigation can be summarised as follows:

- ☐ Preliminary meetings in the department to explain investigation, gain co-operation etc.
- ☐ Decide sequence of investigation and/or areas to be studied.
- ☐ Record in detail the work, methods, forms, procedures etc. used at present. (Techniques include; interviewing, observing, flow-charting, etc.)
- ☐ Critically analyse current methods (i.e. why, what, who, when, where, how).
- ☐ Develop improved method (including work descriptions, work flows, new forms, staff requirements etc.)
- ☐ Obtain management approval.
- ☐ After agreement, install new methods (including, training and advice, printing, equipment ordering and installation, changeover etc.)
- ☐ Monitor operation of new system (including; minor amendments necessary, checking that expected results are obtained, learning from experience etc.)

The O & M analyst frequently records operations by means of charts. Two typical examples are Flow Process Charts and Procedure (or Forms) Flow Charts. Flow Process Charts are used to show the flow of work from one person or section to another and the type of work or action taken at various stages. Standard symbols are frequently used as shown in Figure 18.2

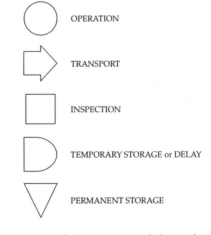

Note: on occasions the 'operation' symbol is made more specific. For example

Figure 18.2: Standard symbols used in O & M

Procedure or Forms Flow Charts shows the movement of various copies of a document from one section or department to another. Such charts provide a useful overview to complement the more detailed Flow Process Charts. Figure 18.3 shows the movement of the various copies of a Works Order through the five departments affected.

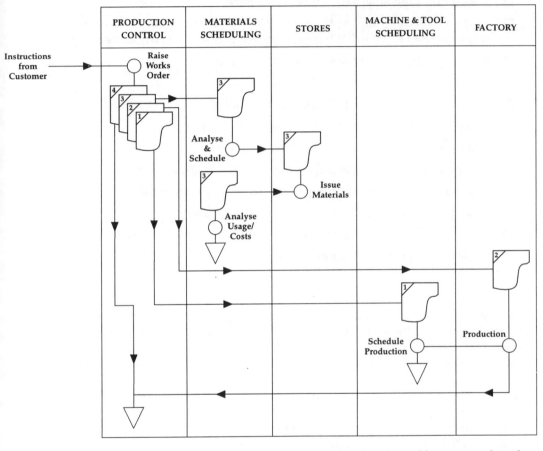

Figure 18.3: Procedure flowchart of four-part works order

Form design

Form design is an essential part of O & M. However a form cannot be designed in isolation. The procedures behind the form, its method of production, who initiates and uses the form, the purpose it is intended to serve and other factors all play their part in form design. Indeed the review of an important form can turn out to be a major task.

Forms are important tools used in clerical work. They are documents with fixed headings and often include standard questions. The general objective is to gather variable information and as such forms are an important means of communication and record. Before designing any form a number of questions must be asked, including;

- ☐ Is it necessary? Can it be eliminated?
- ☐ Does it duplicate information on another form?
- ☐ Who will have to complete the form? Will they be experienced/knowledge-able or unused to forms? What instructions/explanations will be necessary?
- ☐ Who needs the information? What will it be used for?
- ☐ Where will form be completed? In good or poor conditions?
- ☐ Will form need to be filed/stored? For how long?
- ☐ What size of form will best suit conditions of use, filing etc?
- ☐ Will form be produced manually or by computer?
- ☐ Are there any 'house' rules, regarding style, headings, titles etc?
- ☐ Will the use of colour assist use/understanding/communications?
- ☐ What quality of paper/card will best suit the conditions?
- ☐ Will the form be used as a source document for a computer system?
- ☐ Is it feasible to make it machine readable?

The answers to the above and other questions help to define the various requirements of the form. If the form has to be handled in bad conditions; for example, in the factory or in the cab of a lorry, care must be taken with the quality of the paper and it may be necessary to use card. If the form is to be completed by the general public clear, unambiguous instructions must be provided and adequate space given for replies. If the form has to promote a positive image for the organisation high quality paper, coloured printing, even embossed lettering may be considered worthwhile although costly. On the other hand, forms used internally will be produced more cheaply but they must still be designed to carry out their functions efficiently.

Typical stages in form design

Having obtained the outline requirements, operating conditions and objectives from the questions shown above, the design of the form can begin. The following are typical stages in the design process:

- Specify what must appear on the form (headings, instructions etc.)
- Determine the sequence which is best for; entering variable information, reading and using the form and referring to the form when filed. (It is likely that the sequences will vary).
- Determine the best compromise sequence.
- Decide the space necessary for each item
- Prepare and test several form layouts to obtain best overall compromise.

Any house style or common usage would normally be adopted. Examples could include: common positioning of routine information, use of colour coding to indicate destinations e.g. white copies to Stores, blue copies to Accounts, yellow copies to Production Control.

Forms should be as small as possible having regard to the amount of information and conditions of use. Unless there are exceptional reasons standard paper sizes should be used. Nowadays International Paper Sizes are used almost exclusively, as follows:

Code	Size (millimetres)
A3	297 x 420
A4	210 x 297 (most common)
A5	148 x 210
A6	105 x 148
A7	74 x 105

(NB. All sizes have dimensions in the relationships of 1:1.41).

Emphasis, heavy type and colour can all help to improve the appearance and effectiveness of forms. However they must be used with restraint, otherwise the effect is spoiled. A common fault in form design is to decide column width by the size of the column heading. The width of columns (and boxes) must be dependent on the amount of information to be entered, not the size of heading.

Forms control

Because of their importance in clerical work it is normal for there to be central control over the origination of new forms. Frequently this is the responsibility of the Clerical Services Manager or the O & M department. Such an arrangement ensures that the needs of the organisation as a whole are considered instead of the narrower requirements of a single department. There may, for example, already be an existing form which could be modified to meet any new requirements.

In addition to control over the design of new forms it is normal in larger organisations to maintain a central register of all existing forms. This enables usage to be monitored, stocks controlled and periodic reviews to be undertaken to eliminate unnecessary forms or to re-design forms not fulfilling their roles effectively.

Without some kind of central over-view it is inevitable that there will be a proliferation of badly designed, little used forms which would be wasteful and inefficient.

Key point summary

- ☐ Office work includes: originating, collecting and communicating information, controlling and safeguarding assets.

- ☐ The location of office work is changing because of better communications and IT.

- ☐ Centralisation allows greater efficiency and control, better utilisation of equipment but may be inflexible and unresponsive.

- ☐ Factors involved in planning offices include: what work is done, what equipment, how can the space be utilised, what security is required etc.

- ☐ The various types of offices include: private, departmental or cellular, open plan.

- ☐ Landscaped offices create a more informal atmosphere and help to foster group identities.

- ☐ The Health and Safety at Work Act states that it is the duty of every employer to ensure the health, safety and welfare at work of all employees.

- ☐ The Offices Act specifies detailed standards relating to space, temperature, cleanliness, ventilation etc.

- ☐ Organisation and Methods (O & M) is the systematic study of office procedures and organisation in order to improve efficiency.

- ☐ Underlying O & M is a questioning, critical approach i.e. why, what, how, when, where, who?

- ☐ Flow charts are widely used to record existing procedures.

- ☐ Form design is an essential part of O & M.

Self review questions

1. *What are the main functions of offices?*

2. *What is teleworking?*

3. *What are the advantages and disadvantages of centralisation?*

4. *What factors must be considered in planning offices?*

5. *Contrast private, departmental and open-plan offices.*

6. *What are the objectives of landscaping offices?*

7. *What are the main legal requirements regarding health and safety at work?*

8. *What is Organisation & Methods (O & M)?*

9. *What key questions underlie the O & M approach?*

10. *What are the steps in an O & M study?*

11. *What charts are used in O & M?*

12. *What questions must be asked before a form is designed?*

13. *What are the stages in form design?*

14. *How is the issue and design of forms controlled?*

Assessment and revision section

Assignments

1. Virtually all products sold in Supermarkets have a Bar Code recorded on them. Find out what the Codes are used for and the basis of the Code. Try to find out the complete system in which the Codes are used.

2. Select an item of office equipment (e.g. a photocopier or a word processor, or a fax machine etc.) and obtain details from various manufacturers about their machines. Do a comparative analysis of the key features offered by the various manufacturers. Which would you choose?

3. Find an application (not already computerised) that you think a spreadsheet package could be used on. What features make it a suitable application? What would be the advantages? What are the problems?

4. Prepare a report to management advocating why an organisation should consider using a Data Base and DBMS. (Use in your report features and details of one of the DBMS available commercially. You can obtain details from the suppliers.)

5. For a restaurant, a local authority and a paint manufacturer identify:
    (a) a strategic decision;
    (b) a tactical decision;
    (c) an operational decision.
    What information support is required for each of the decisions?

6. Find an example of a real multi-part form. Flowchart the movement of each of the copies.

Mini-Case 1 – Gratwoods Mail Order

Gratwoods is a large mail order business selling through a network of Agents. The Agents sell on commission and also receive a discount from the Catalogue price for personal purchases. Goods are normally paid for in 20 weekly installments and the Agents are responsible for collecting the amounts due and paying the money to Gratwoods through the bank giro system. The Agent sends the receipted paying in slip and an analysis of payments to Gratwoods weekly.

The Agent completes an order form for all goods required containing the quantity, catalogue code, price, customer name and delivery address. On receipt at Gratwoods the order form is checked and then used as direct data entry for the on-line order processing system. The system generates a multi part set which includes an acknowledgement to the Agent, Invoice copies, and a warehouse copy for despatch. Goods are supplied on a sale-or-return basis. If not required, the Agent returns the goods using a Returns Form which is input to credit the Agents account. Each week the computer system produces a payments schedule for each Agent. This shows payment due, balances, overdue accounts and so on.

Gratwoods use a multi-access computer with disks.

Task 1 *Flowchart the main information flows in the system.*

Task 2 *Draw a Systems Flowchart showing the computer system.*

Task 3 *Define the likely contents of the following files*
Agents file
Stock file
Suppliers file.

Task 4 *What information, additional to the items mentioned in the case, will the management of Gratwoods need to operate and control their business?*

Mini-Case 2 – Acme Mutual

Acme Mutual Life are a life assurance and pensions company based in Birmingham. There are 40 sales representatives housed in the company headquarters in the city centre. The company is concerned at the costs of operating from a city centre site and are contemplating a change in policy whereby the representatives work from their homes. Although the company recognises that there will be space and cost savings at Headquarters it is concerned about possible communication and control problems.

Task 1 *List the main communications with which the representatives will have to deal.*

Task 2 *Decide what equipment should be supplied to the representatives and give the functions which will be performed.*

Task 3 *Discuss what control problems might arise and how these could be overcome.*

Examination questions with answers

A1 Describe some of the professional skills and competences of written communication and written presentation. Why are these skills so important? Illustrate your answer using examples with which you are familiar.

ACCA – Effective Management

A2 The over-riding feature of information for decision making is that it should be relevant for the decision being taken. However, decision making varies considerably, at different levels within an organisation, thus posing particular difficulties for the management accountant.

You are required

(a) to describe the characteristics of decision making at different levels within an organisation;

(b) to explain how the management accountant must tailor the information provided for the various levels;

(c) to give an example of a typical management decision, state at what level this would normally be taken and what specific information should be supplied to the decision maker.

CIMA – Management Accounting Techniques

A3 (a) Distinguish between data and information.

(b) Why do organisations expend resources in the collection of information?

(c) What features should the output from a system possess to provide useful information?

IAM – Office Systems

A4 Draw up a draft outline guide to writing reports to management and clients. This draft is required for discussion and eventual use in your organisation as training material in the induction of newly employed graduates and part-qualified staff.

ACCA – Effective Management

A5 A 1992 survey by the National Computer Centre found that more than 1 in 8 firms now use some form of teleworking, and a third of these are planning to extend it.

(a) Define teleworking with reference to an example, and draw a simple diagram to illustrate the type of network which would be required.

(b) Explain the advantages of teleworking to:

(i) The employer

(ii) The employee

IAM – Telecommunications Management

A6 (a) Explain how the use of information technology can bring about improvements in productivity within a business organisation.

(b) Explain how the use of information technology may sometimes harm a business's performance.

CIMA – Business Environment & IT

A7 'The emphasis on change from cellular to open plan offices has perhaps slackened in recent years but there are still many advantages in the latter, i.e. open plan approach to office design'. (D.Greenaway).

Indicate some of the advantages, providing supporting evidence where possible.

IAM – Office Planning and Control

A8 What is spreadsheet software and why, in your opinion, is the spreadsheet the second most popular type of software package used on personal computers?

IAM – Information Technology

Examination questions without answers

B1 Distinguish between the meeting and the committee.
Describe some of the roles of the meeting and the committee in the communication and decision-making process within the enterprise.

ACCA – Effective Management

B2 Dr Bentley in Defining Management's Information Needs (CIMA MIS Series) says that the information systems designer should not
(i)   Just ask the manager what he wants.
(ii) Tell the manager what he needs.
(iii) Give the manager what is available
You are required
(a) to explain why the systems designer is recommended to avoid the three steps mentioned above;
(b) to describe how management's information needs could be defined;
(c) to describe the characteristics that information should possess for it to have value.

CIMA – Management Accounting Techniques

B3 Your new managing director has experience of quality control in manufacturing and suggests to you that similar techniques could be applied to the office. You are asked to prepare a report on the subject clearly indicating the major problems that may arise.

IAM – Office Planning & Control

B4 Describe the different types of written report, and comment on some of the techniques of report writing.

ACCA – Effective Management

B5 Your organisation is still beset with out-of-date and unnecessary forms despite many attempts at controlling them.
You have been given the task of dealing with this situation.
Prepare your preliminary report indicating where you think the principle problems lie and which problems you propose to tackle first.

IAM – Administration in the Office

B6 Indicate the advantages and disadvantages of centralising office systems, using a specific example to illustrate your points.

IAM – Office Systems

B7 Your manager has requested advice about electronic communications equipment which could be used to assist the administration of an organisation. In particular, she has asked for advice on the following terms: LAN, WAN, Teletext, Facsimile, Electronic Mail, Modem and Multiplexor. In a memorandum, define each of these and explain how it could be used to contribute to effective administrative management.

IAM – Information Technology

B8 'Teleworking is performed away from direct supervision of employers and delivered to, and received from, workers by IT based communications systems'. Review the reasons why an organisation might be attracted to teleworking.

IAM – Advanced Methods & Systems

Additional reading

Business Data Systems, H.D.Clifton, Prentice Hall.

Data Processing and Information Technology, C.French, DP Publications.

Information Systems: A Management Perspective, C.Martin and P.Powell, McGraw Hill.

Management Strategies for Information Technology, M.J.Earl, Prentice Hall.

Office Automation – Context, Experience and Future, A.Doswell, John Wiley.

Appendix: Outline answers to exam questions

Assessment and revision section – Chapters 1-3

A1 (a) *Legislation* is the body of rules enacted by statute in Acts of Parliament, private Acts, confirmation Acts and other provisions. It can be considered as a direct form of legislation.

Delegated legislation is that power of law making delegated to Ministers, Councils and other Statutory Bodies. Its legality is derived from the parent legislation. Because it is a form of indirect legislation it may be subject to legal scrutiny to ensure that it is within the enabling powers of the primary legislation.

(b) Key point is that the business is subject to two sets of law; the national laws of its home country and of the country in which it does business plus the laws of the European Union. The latter includes EU Directives on a range of matters including; consumer protection, corporate affairs, environmental matters, health and safety and so on.

A2 The aim of the Single European Market is to treat the existing 12 countries as one gigantic market with free movement of goods, capital and people. This means the eventual elimination of customs/frontier checks for EU nationals and, some time in the future, a common currency. The Single Market implies that eventually there would be harmonisation of excise duties, VAT and so on.

Although the above points are the objectives of the Single Market progress in many areas is slow or non-existent. For example there are still large variations in excise duties and VAT rates across the Union and progress towards a single currency has effectively been halted by the virtual collapse of the European Monetary System in 1992 when Britain and other countries withdrew from the system.

In spite of the slow progress in some areas the Single Market is becoming a reality. There is much more trade between the countries and harmonisation legislation regarding employees, consumers, health and safety, social affairs etc. is now in place and must be obeyed by both private and public sector organisations.

A3 Market conduct and performance includes such matters as; the efficiency with which goods are produced and distributed, pricing policies, growth, extent of differentiation and innovation and so on.

Dealing with the various points in the question:

Number and size of suppliers: These largely determine the amount and type of rivalry and competition e.g. large numbers of small sellers will lead to competitive pricing behaviour.

Entry barriers: these determine the ease of entry for new entrants and govern existing members of the market.

Potential Substitutes: these set a ceiling on prices and profits.

Power of suppliers and buyers: these greatly influence prices and profit margins. For example a virtual monopoly supplier can largely control prices (e.g. De Beers and

Diamonds) as can extremely powerful buyers e.g. the large retailing chains, Sainsburys, Tescos etc can exert strong influences on their suppliers.

A4 (a) A public company may be formed from a private limited company by following the statutory provisions of the Companies Acts regarding capital requirements, registration, incorporation and so on. The nominal value of the allotted share capital must be at least £50,000 of which not less than a quarter of the nominal share value plus any premium must be paid up. The company's Memorandum of Association must be altered to state it is a Public Company and the company re-registered. If a stock exchange listing is sought then the company must meet the detailed rules of the Stock Exchange, especially regarding disclosure of confidential information.

(b) In general the functions and duties of directors are more formalised especially with regard to audit and scrutiny obligations, more filing of documents, greater disclosure of financial information etc. Directors must avoid conflicts of interest and avoid self-dealing. If directors fail in their duties they may be made personally liable to make good any losses suffered.

A5 An important influence on local management is the extent of decentralised decision-making and the subsequent autonomy of the local unit. Assuming that there is a significant amount of local autonomy the following are important areas that will need to be considered.

❏ Sympathy/knowledge of the host country's culture: A major factor in ensuring success is to make sure operational styles, advertising, products,names etc. suit local conditions. In general local management will render assimilation much easier.

❏ Familiarity with language and customs.

❏ Knowledge of government procedures, regulations, laws etc.

❏ Access to and knowledge of communication systems, media.

❏ Carefully planned local organisational arrangements. These could include agencies, branch offices, subsidiaries, joint ventures, licensing, 'franchising' etc. Above all the arrangements must suit local conditions.

A6 (a) Although there may be some differences between the political parties the following would have general support as the objectives of government economic policy:

❏ full employment

❏ low or zero inflation

❏ maintaining or enhancing the standard of living

❏ economic growth.

(b) Monetary policy means using the banking and financial system to control the amount of money in the economy and hence (it is hoped) control inflation. Governments have a range of measures they can use (e.g. changes in taxation, physical directives etc.) of which monetary policy is only one. Economies are so complicated that reliance on one measure alone is unlikely to produce the desired effects hence governments tend to use a range of policies rather than say, rely on changes in interest rates alone.

Assessment and revision section – Chapters 4-6

A1 Centralisation/decentralisation refers to the extent that decision-making is delegated down the organisational hierarchy and not to physical locations.

Advantages of centralised decision making

- ❐ more control
- ❐ more uniformity of decision making and adherence to strategies
- ❐ less chance of sub-optimal decision-making

Disadvantages of centralisation

- ❐ slower response times
- ❐ stifles initiative
- ❐ possibility of information/decision-making overload
- ❐ lack of knowledge of local conditions may cause inappropriate decisions to be taken

Advantages of decentralisation

- ❐ may improve motivation and encourage initiative
- ❐ good training for junior management
- ❐ frees top management from routine matters
- ❐ ensures local conditions are considered.

Disadvantages of decentralisation

- ❐ lack of consistency
- ❐ problems of control and coordination
- ❐ more monitoring necessary
- ❐ may cause duplication and waste

A2   Vrooms Expectancy Theory of Motivation can be expressed thus:

$$\text{Valence} \times \text{Expectancy} = \text{Motivation}$$

where: Valence = strength of a person's preference for a situation or outcome
Expectancy = belief that the outcome will satisfy a person's needs.

In commonsense terms all this says is that a person will be motivated if he believes that effort will lead to better performance which will be rewarded in a way that suits the person.

It appears that Norman is currently motivated by: a good salary, pay increases, the type of work and high merit ratings.

The new job brings: more challenge, satisfaction from being in charge and recognition of past performance. The downside is that it is likely to be more demanding, may mean more travel and time away from home. Norman appears to have a fulfiling family and social life so it is difficult to draw firm conclusions. If he wishes to have even more recognition then the new job may be attractive. On the other hand he may feel that the possible intrusion into his family/social time may not be worthwhile.

A3   Main points

(a) Economic security, reputation/standing, recognition of achievements, social contacts, interesting work. In general although money is a motivator it appears not to be a lasting motivator. Factors associated with the work and self-esteem appear to be stronger motivators for most people.

(b) This is clearly an important part of every manager's job and a key to improving efficiency. Because motivation is a personal matter the conditions which motivate vary from person to person. However the following list provides the main factors.

- ❐ provide support and feedback

- ❐   make the job as complete and challenging as possible
- ❐   provide good training
- ❐   arrange for career development
- ❐   encourage group and team working
- ❐   good working conditions
- ❐   promote good communications
- ❐   be frank and fair
- ❐   provide adequate pay.

A4   A sole trader owns and manages the business. A partnership is a number of people who share ownership and, usually, the management of a business.

These types of organisation assist innovation and entrepreneurship in the following ways.

- ❐   *Flexibility, autonomy and independence*

   Sole traders and partnerships can take risks and quick actions in a flexible speedy fashion unhindered by committees and bureaucracy.

- ❐   *Local/market knowledge*

   This means that sole traders and partnerships can get to know their customers and markets and can react swiftly to exploit opportunities and market niches.

- ❐   *Ease of administration*

   Sole traders and partnerships are simple forms of organisations which means that little or no time is wasted on administration, communications and bureaucracy. This leaves more time for innovation and entrepreneurship.

Problems with sole trader/partnerships:

Unlimited liability. If there is a business failure the sole trader or partners are responsible for all debts.

Access to funds for exploiting new products and markets. There are severe limits to the amount that sole traders/partnerships may raise or borrow which may limit growth or the ability to exploit a new product or market.

Access to markets. Because of their small size and the amounts of funds available sole traders and partnerships may find it difficult to enter markets or to gain sufficient market share. Larger companies have national coverage, well known names and brands and existing distribution networks.

Note that small private limited companies are, for all practical purposes, in the same position as sole traders and partnerships.

A5   The main classical/traditional theorists include, F.W.Taylor, Fayol, Brech and others. They concentrated on structures and formal organisation with less emphasis on the people in organisations. The key emphasis was on finding formal principles of organisation which would enable the organisation to function effectively and achieve its objectives.

The humans relations theorists include, Mayo, Herzberg, Likert, McGregor and others. These theorists concentrated on people in the organisation, their social relationships, team working, personal growth, fulfilment and so on. The work was developed by Maslow and others in an attempt to discover what factors motivate, and de-motivate, people at work. The human relations approach was to an extent a reaction against the more impersonal classical approach.

Nowadays it is realised that no single approach can hope to explain all facets of organisations and the people who work in them.

A6 (a) The main principles and explanations can be taken from the text. The principles include: span of control, definition of objectives and duties, the scalar principle, specialisation and division of labour, and the principle of correspondence.

(b) The main criticisms of the Classical Approach are;

❏ there was undue emphasis on structures, formal authority and control.

❏ the behaviour and needs of the people in organisations was largely ignored.

❏ the approach was prescriptive with only limited analysis of actual behaviour.

The contributions of the classical theorists provided a foundation upon which later researchers could build and they made the study of management respectable in an intellectual sense.

Assessment and revision section – Chapters 7-10

A1 The main features of Theories X,Y and Z can be taken from the text. These include:

Theory X. Described by McGregor as based on the assumption that employees dislike work and avoid it whenever possible. This means that management must adopt a rigid, authoritarian approach to planning and control with centralised decision making.

Theory Y. Suggests that people find work as natural and desirable as leisure. In consequence management need to create conditions which foster this attitude and allow people to take responsibility and decisions. Self-supervision and initiative should be encouraged and people should be allowed to realise their personal potential.

Theory Z, developed by Ouchi extends Theory Y by seeking more consensus and trust among employees. Throughout the organisation teamwork and cooperation are encouraged and there is a more informal and democratic atmosphere. Central to Theory Z is long-term employment and progressive career paths for employees and mutual trust.

Some of the contingencies which help to determine management style are:

❏ type of organisation and technology used

❏ employee expectations

❏ traditions of the area/country/organisation

❏ culture and values of the organisation

❏ type of employees

❏ type of ownership.

A2 (a) Autocratic i.e. where the manager controls everything and takes all decisions. Common in traditional industries especially in owner/manager situations. Also necessary in risky or dangerous conditions e.g. airline pilot, surgeon.

(b) Missionary i.e. where the manager seeks to persuade workers and thus obtain their cooperation and thus increase motivation. Common where the staff are highly qualified and where teamwork essential.

(c) Consultative i.e. where manager consults staff before taking decision. Necessary in complex situations where it is difficult for one person to know of all the consequences of a decision.

(d) Democratic i.e. where staff are actively involved in the decision process and the decision represents a majority view. The style may increase motivation and is useful where teamwork is essential.

A3 The question considers leadership as having three possible meanings:

❐   related to personality. These have been called the 'trait theories'. The problem is that surveys have shown that few traits are found in common.

❐   characteristic of certain positions e.g. the Managing Director or Chief Executive of an organisation. Although some people in such position make good leaders others do not.

❐   as an aspect of behaviour i.e. what tasks and functions the leader performs and how he/she behaves.

Of the above three possibilities the behavioural approach seems to be the most accurate and considerable research has been undertaken in this area. This includes work by McGregor, Likert and Adair who developed a contingency view of leadership i.e. the leader adapts his behaviour to suit the circumstances.

A4 This can be taken directly from the text.

A5 There are two broad aspects to this question. Firstly the assessment of past performance (which should be relatively easy) and judgement about future potential which is naturally a more difficult task.

Typical of the detailed factors which would probably be considered are the following:

❐   Work/task performance and competence

❐   Evidence of commitment and willingness.

❐   Ability to work with others.

❐   Personal qualities e.g. communication skills, patience, humour, intelligence etc.

❐   Evidence of personal development e.g. further study, qualifications etc.

❐   Judgements on a person's identification with the organisational culture and value.

❐   Ability to take responsibility.

A6 For effective delegation managers should:

(a) set clear objectives and standards of performance expected

(b) define what authority is delegated

(c) provide what resources, training and guidance is necessary

(d) set up a control system to monitor results

(e) when the task is completed review performance with the subordinate.

In general the art of delegation is getting the trust/control ratio right. Having set up the system managers should not interfere.

A7 (a) Profit is a well known and accepted measure of performance. It can be used for all profit-seeking businesses and enables comparisons to be made easily. It provides a measure of how well funds are used within the business, especially when compared to the capital employed i.e. Return on Capital Employed.

(b) There are a number of limitations of using profit as a performance measure. These include:

❐   Profit figures can be manipulated and can be calculated in several ways.

❐   Concentration on profit encourages short-termism and ignores liquidity.

❐   Profit is an inadequate measure to monitor all the functions of a business.

(c) Non-financial performance measures (NFPMS) relating to matters such as quality, timing, satisfaction and so on have the advantage that they are an attempt to assess performance in a more comprehensive fashion. However there are problems with NFPM's. For example some have to be assessed subjectively e.g. satisfaction, various of the NFPMS may conflict with one another and a proliferation of measures may mean that less notice is taken of any one.

Assessment and revision section – Chapters 11-14

A1 Training and development needs may be identified in various ways,

- ❏ during staff and performance appraisal.
- ❏ from supervisors/managers reports.
- ❏ when undertaking manpower planning.
- ❏ during manpower reviews and audits.
- ❏ when compiling job descriptions.
- ❏ during re-organisations of methods, department and jobs.

Training and development have to be implemented in ways that meet objectives and are tailored to suit the individual's needs. Typical ways include: in-house methods of structured coaching, observation, progressive experiential learning based on increasingly difficult tasks and responsibilities, internal lectures and courses and so on. External methods include; college courses, professional trainers, secondments, conferences and so on.

Note that training programmes tend to be task/job oriented whereas development programmes concentrate on personal and self-development.

A2 From the details it is clear that there is low morale, poor team spirit, and a lack of motivation in the department. The company also appears to be in difficulties and is placing more demands upon staff which is not improving matters. It also appears that staff in the department are not fully trained and there are uneven work loads on individual staff members.

 The numerous problems will not be resolved immediately but typical of the steps that George could take are the following:

- ❏ Hold briefing meetings and keep staff fully informed about company and departmental developments.
- ❏ Invite suggestions and endeavour to get the staff to participate in making any necessary changes.
- ❏ Carry out detailed staff appraisals and establish agreed performance targets with all individuals.
- ❏ Analyse work loads and tasks and adjust loadings
- ❏ Establish what training is required and implement personal programmmes with clear objectives
- ❏ Encourage team work and cooperation
- ❏ Provide regular positive feedback and encouragement
- ❏ Make clear that good performance and cooperative attitudes will be properly rewarded.

A3 Can be taken directly from the text.

A4 Note: It is assumed that the question should read 'too low'. This is because it is beneficial for the firm for the ratio to be as high as possible.

(a) There are two ways that would help to decide whether the ratio is too low. Firstly compare it with previous internal stock turnover ratios for earlier years and see the trend. Secondly compare the ratio with ratios from similar firms. For this comparison to be valid it is necessary to check that the calculations have been carried out on the same basis and that the firms are similar in all respects.

(b) To improve the ratio i.e. increase it would require either stock levels to be reduced and/or sales to be increased.

A5 (a) Test marketing means marketing and selling the product in a small area prior to a national launch. Care is needed to ensure that the area chosen is reasonably representative.

   (i) Main benefits
      ❐ Provides information on consumer reactions, pricing policy,
      ❐ Packaging, distribution etc.
      ❐ May enable problems to be solved relatively easily
      ❐ Enables alternative promotional policies to be tested
      ❐ Helps to eliminate problems with the product/packaging/instructions etc.

   (ii) Possible alternatives
      ❐ Market research
      ❐ Consumer panels
      ❐ Free samples and response questionnaires
      ❐ Trade testing and assessment
      ❐ Buyer surveys

   (iii) Details of one of the above can be taken from the text.

(b) Any form of new product screening is risky and subject to major error. However because of the substantial amount of investment required to launch a new product on a national basis all manufacturers screen new products in order to eliminate ones that are likely to be unsuccessful. Normally several screening tests are made including:
   ❐ Consumer panels
   ❐ In-depth attitude surveys
   ❐ Specially commissioned market research
   ❐ Major customer consultation
   ❐ Test marketing.

However no screening method(s) can guarantee success and new product launches are always risky.

A6 (a) Pressure groups are people organised to change opinions and to bring pressure on large business, central and local government. By publicity, protests and sometimes direct action they bring to public attention what they perceive to be injustices, bad products, bad policies or incorrect decisions. Examples include; motorway protest groups, animal rights, the Consumers Association and many others.

(b) Detailed market research and analysis is necessary to establish the exact causes of the sales reduction. The cause may be some other factor (e.g. price, new competing product) not the activities of the pressure group.

   Assuming that the fall in sales is due to the way the firm tests its products then it will be necessary to consider changing its test methods. If this is done the change should be positively promoted and advertised, if possible with the endorsement of prominent people or even the pressure group itself. It is not likely that ABC could continue animal testing and mount a positive campaign that would restore sales. Since the success of 'Body Shop' with its policy of no testing on animals users of cosmetics have been very conscious of this procedure and would be unlikely to use products that could not make the claim.

A7 The newer manufacturing environment is characterised by such things as:

❑ small batches

❑ constant drive for improvement

❑ emphasis on quality

❑ little or no stocks

❑ considerable use of automation

❑ rapid change

and so on

Conventional management accounting measures e.g. absorption costing based on labour or machine hours, budgetary control and standard costing were developed in a more stable and unchanging environment where long, uninterrupted production runs were considered highly desirable.

The traditional measures concentrated mainly on costs and non-financial measures such as quality, lead times, efficiency and so on, received little attention. The result was a concentration on maximising output even though this resulted in increased stocks, poorer quality, and increased financial charges. There was an over-emphasis on direct labour, even though this typically only represents 10 – 20% of costs and labour was treated as a variable cost even though it is essentially fixed. Traditional reporting systems are examples of feedback control where, after some delay, a report on last period's performance is given to management so that they control current activities. This process might have some value if operations were exactly as previous but in the new environment this is not likely. The constant drive for improvement is at odds with the traditional standard with its idea of a target to be achieved and maintained.

In summary, traditional management accounting and control, which has essentially remained unchanged this century, is not able to deal with the new environment without major changes in emphasis.

(b) Typical ways in which management accounting is adapting to the new environment:

(i)   The use of Activity Based Costing and the notion of cost drivers rather than traditional absorption based on labour or machine hours.

(ii) Performance measures in non-financial terms emphasising quality, reliability, lead times, customer satisfaction and so on.

(iii) The replacement of standard costs by actual costs and monitoring the trends in actual cost in order to show improvements.

(iv) The use of feedforward control instead of delayed feedback control. The emphasis is on control at the point where costs are initiated. Production workers are encouraged to monitor and reduce set-up times, minimise scrap and defective production and so on.

A8 JIT systems apply to both Production and Purchasing.

JIT Production is a demand-pull system which is characterised by

❑ low or zero inventories

❑ emphasis on perfect quality

- ❐ constant improvement
- ❐ elimination of all waste and unnecessary movements

JIT Purchasing means that goods are delivered just in time to be used. This means that suppliers must deliver perfect quality parts and materials exactly to schedule.

There are numerous effects of JIT systems on organisation and management. These include:

- ❐ need to integrate and coordinate all activities
- ❐ need for employees to take more responsibility for quality and scheduling
- ❐ increased participation through quality circles, meetings, seminars etc.
- ❐ more training to increase worker flexibility
- ❐ emphasis on quality and getting it right first time for all levels
- ❐ need for more team work.

Assessment and revision section – Chapters 15-18

A1 The skills and competencies of written communication include:
- ❐ the ability to write clear, understandable English
- ❐ the ability to select language to suit the recipients
- ❐ choosing an appropriate channel of communication to suit the message and recipient e.g. reports, memos, E Mail, letter as appropriate
- ❐ choosing the style of presentation which suits the message and recipient
- ❐ checking on understanding of the recipient
- ❐ providing record and evidence, where necessary
- ❐ understanding the level of technical knowledge/jargon which suits the recipient.

A2 (a) & (b) The three levels of management can be described as STRATEGIC, TACTICAL and OPERATIONAL.

The following table summarises the decision and information characteristics at the various levels.

Management Level	Decision Characteristics	Information Characteristics
Strategic	Long time horizons, large scale resources, much creativity and judgement, usually unstructured, problems difficult to define, infrequent, much uncertainty	Largely external, informal sources important, forward looking, qualitative information important, precision unimportant, instant access not vital, wide ranging, incomplete
Tactical		
Operational	Repetitive, short time scale, small scale resources, usually structured, clear objectives and decision rules, often critical, narrow in scope, comprehensive	Largely internal, mainly historical detailed, often quantitative, high precision, instant availability
little or no discretion		

(c) Any realistic decision example would be accepted. Examples include:

Management Level	Decision Examples	Information Requirements
Strategic	Mergers and acquisitions, new product planning, capital investments, financial structuring	Market and economic forecasts, political and social trends, legislative, environmental and technological constraints and opportunities
Tactical	Pricing, capacity planning, budget preparation, purchasing contracts	Cost and sales analyses, performance measures, summaries of operations/production, budget/actual comparisons etc.
Operational	Production scheduling, maintenance, re-ordering, credit approval	Sales orders, production requirements, performance measures, customer credit status, deliveries, despatches etc.

A3 (a) Data are events, facts and results which have been recorded. They are the raw materials from which information is produced. Information is data that have been processed in such a way as to be useful to the recipient.

(b) Information properly used, adds value to planning, decision-making and control. Information does not have value in itself, its value derives from the changes in decision behaviour caused by the information being available. Without information most decision making would be simply guess work.

(c) Useful information has the following features
  - ❏ Relevance for problem/decision being considered
  - ❏ Communicated in time to the right person
  - ❏ Accurate and complete enough for the problem
  - ❏ Understandable by the user.

A4 Most of the answer can be taken from the text. Note particularly the need for; clarity, brevity, knowing the target audience, understanding the purpose of the report and tailoring the language and technical content to suit the recipients, not the writer.

A5 The answer can be taken from the text.

A6 Productivity is usually defined as the output per worker. Machinery of all types, materials handling, IT and various forms of capital equipment all contribute to improvements in productivity.

(a) The special features of IT that can improve productivity include:
  - ❏ faster access to information and records
  - ❏ automatic processing and decision-making
  - ❏ wider range of information availability through files and databases
  - ❏ electronic communications of all types
  - ❏ automatic monitoring of balances, stock levels, debtors etc. etc.
  - ❏ reduction of errors caused by human processing
  - ❏ ability to use simulations, modelling and operational techniques

(b)   The use of IT can harm performance in various ways

- ❐   where IT use is uncontrolled, files and data may be lost or corrupted
- ❐   competitors may be able to access confidential files through networks
- ❐   unauthorised amendments to programs and files may be made for fraudulent purposes
- ❐   computer viruses may cause disastrous problems.

A7   There are still a number of advantages in the open plan approach to office design. These include:

- ❐   space savings
- ❐   flexibility, which is especially important where conditions/operations change rapidly
- ❐   economy
- ❐   ease of supervision and control
- ❐   improved communications

With careful planning and appropriate landscaping, open plan offices are popular with staff and provide significant cost savings for the organisations. Proof of this is the continued existence of open plan offices in virtually every large organisation.

A8   In addition spreadsheets enable various options to be explored which would be difficult to deal with manually. For example assume that a spreadsheet was used to prepare a machine loading schedule for the various machines in the factory. A small change in a delivery date or hours available would require all the machine loadings to be re-calculated. This would be a massive task done manually but is a simple one using a spreadsheet package.

Details of spreadsheet facilities can be taken from the text.

Table A: Present value factors

Present value of £1 $(1 + r)^{-n}$

Periods (n)	Interest rates (r)%								
	1%	2%	4%	6%	8%	10%	12%	14%	15%
1	0.990	0.980	0.962	0.943	0.926	0.909	0.893	0.877	0.870
2	0.980	0.961	0.925	0.890	0.857	0.826	0.797	0.769	0.756
3	0.971	0.942	0.889	0.840	0.794	0.751	0.712	0.675	0.658
4	0.961	0.924	0.855	0.792	0.735	0.683	0.636	0.592	0.572
5	0.951	0.906	0.822	0.747	0.681	0.621	0.567	0.519	0.497
6	0.942	0.888	0.790	0.705	0.630	0.564	0.507	0.456	0.432
7	0.933	0.871	0.760	0.665	0.583	0.513	0.452	0.400	0.376
8	0.923	0.853	0.731	0.627	0.540	0.467	0.404	0.351	0.327
9	0.914	0.837	0.703	0.592	0.500	0.424	0.361	0.308	0.284
10	0.905	0.820	0.676	0.558	0.463	0.386	0.322	0.270	0.247
11	0.0896	0.804	0.650	0.527	0.429	0.350	0.287	0.237	0.215
12	0.887	0.788	0.625	0.497	0.397	0.319	0.257	0.208	0.187
13	0.879	0.773	0.601	0.469	0.368	0.290	0.229	0.182	0.163
14	0.870	0.758	0.577	0.442	0.340	0.263	0.205	0.160	0.141
15	0.861	0.743	0.555	0.417	0.315	0.239	0.183	0.140	0.123
16	0.853	0.728	0.534	0.394	0.292	0.218	0.163	0.123	0.107
17	0.855	0.714	0.513	0.371	0.270	0.198	0.146	0.108	0.093
18	0.836	0.700	0.494	0.350	0.250	0.180	0.130	0.095	0.081
19	0.828	0.686	0.475	0.331	0.232	0.164	0.116	0.083	0.070
20	0.820	0.675	0.456	0.312	0.215	0.149	0.104	0.073	0.061
21	0.811	0.660	0.439	0.294	0.199	0.135	0.093	0.064	0.053
22	0.803	0.647	0.422	0.278	0.184	0.123	0.083	0.056	0.046
23	0.795	0.634	0.406	0.262	0.170	0.112	0.074	0.049	0.040
24	0.788	0.622	0.390	0.247	0.158	0.102	0.066	0.043	0.035
25	0.780	0.610	0.375	0.233	0.146	0.092	0.059	0.038	0.030

Present value of £1 $(1 + r)^{-n}$

Periods (n)	Interest rates (r)%								
	16%	18%	20%	22%	24%	25%	26%	28%	30%
1	0.862	0.847	0.833	0.820	0.806	0.800	0.794	0.781	0.769
2	0.743	0.718	0.694	0.672	0.650	0.640	0.630	0.610	0.592
3	0.641	0.609	0.579	0.551	0.524	0.512	0.500	0.477	0.455
4	0.552	0.516	0.482	0.451	0.423	0.410	0.397	0.373	0.350
5	0.476	0.437	0.402	0.370	0.341	0.328	0.315	0.291	0.269
6	0.410	0.370	0.335	0.303	0.275	0.262	0.250	0.227	0.207
7	0.354	0.314	0.279	0.249	0.222	0.210	0.198	0.178	0.159
8	0.305	0.266	0.233	0.204	0.179	0.168	0.157	0.139	0.123
9	0.263	0.225	0.194	0.167	0.144	0.134	0.125	0.108	0.094
10	0.227	0.191	0.162	0.137	0.116	0.107	0.099	0.085	0.075
11	0.195	0.162	0.135	0.112	0.094	0.086	0.079	0.066	0.056
12	0.168	0.137	0.112	0.192	0.076	0.069	0.062	0.052	0.043
13	0.145	0.116	0.093	0.075	0.061	0.055	0.050	0.040	0.033
14	0.125	0.099	0.178	0.062	0.049	0.044	0.039	0.032	0.025
15	0.108	0.084	0.065	0.051	0.040	0.035	0.031	0.025	0.020
16	0.093	0.071	0.054	0.042	0.032	0.028	0.025	0.019	0.015
17	0.080	0.060	0.045	0.034	0.026	0.023	0.020	0.015	0.012
18	0.069	0.051	0.038	0.028	0.021	0.018	0.016	0.012	0.009
19	0.060	0.043	0.031	0.023	0.017	0.014	0.012	0.009	0.007
20	0.051	0.037	0.026	0.019	0.014	0.012	0.010	0.007	0.005
21	0.044	0.031	0.022	0.015	0.011	0.009	0.008	0.006	0.004
22	0.038	0.026	0.018	0.013	0.009	0.007	0.006	0.004	0.003
23	0.033	0.022	0.015	0.010	0.007	0.006	0.005	0.003	0.002
24	0.028	0.019	0.011	0.008	0.006	0.005	0.004	0.003	0.002
25	0.024	0.016	0.010	0.007	0.005	0.004	0.003	0.002	0.001

Index

Essential Elements

covering the core *of* modular courses

Essential Elements of **Management Accounting** *Jill & Roger Hussey*

Contents The role of management accounting; Cost classification and control; Total costing; Marginal costing; Capital investment and appraisal; Budgetary control; Standard costing; Appendices.

ISBN 1 85805 103 7

Essential Elements of **Financial Accounting** *Jill & Roger Hussey*

Contents The accounting framework; Users and uses of financial information; The cash flow forecast; The profit and loss account for a sole trader; The balance sheet for a sole trader; The financial statements of a limited company; Interpretation of financial statements.

ISBN 1 85805 091 X

Essential Elements of **Business Economics** *Mark Sutcliffe*

Contents: The UK economy – an overview; Resource allocation; Business costs; The structure of business and its conduct; Small firms and multinationals; Wages and the labour market; Investment, R & D and training; National economic change and business activity; Money, banking and inflation; Economic policy and the business environment; The international dimension; Europe and business.

ISBN 1 85805 095 2

Essential Elements of **Business Planning and Policy** *Jim Jones*

Contents The nature and importance of policy and planning; Organisation philosophy and objectives; Policy and levels of planning; Analysis for strategic planning; Choosing the strategy; Implementation of strategy; Evaluation of strategy; Framework of project planning; Project planning and control; Annual plans; Information systems for planning; Contingency planning.

ISBN 1 85805 100 2

Essential Elements of **Business Statistics** *Les Oakshott*

Contents Survey Methods, Presentation of data, Summarising data, Probability and decision making, The Normal Distribution, Analysis and interpretation of sample data, Testing a hypothesis, Correlation and regression.

ISBN 1 85805 103 7

Essential Elements of **Quantitative Methods** *Les Oakshott*

Contents: Index numbers, Investment appraisal, Time series analysis, Linear programming, Critical path analysis, Stock control methods, Simulation.

ISBN 1 85805 098 7

All titles in this series are approximately 128 pages long, and measure 275 x 215mm.

Management
Theory and Practice

G A Cole

This best-selling book provides, in one concise volume, the principal ideas and developments in the theory and practice of management required by university and college students whose courses include an element of Management Studies.

It is known to be used on the following courses: CIMA, ACCA, AAT, IComA, BTEC HNC/D, IM, BA Business Studies, BA Accounting, MSc Information Technology, BSc Software Engineering, Hotel and Catering Management courses, CIB, CIM, IAM, DMS, CIPFA, IPS, CBA, ICM, DMS, CBSI, ABE, IPM, IOM, NEBSM, DBA, MIOM, Dip. HSM, BTEC ND, Dip. in Administrative Management, BSc (Hons) Software Engineering, MSc Computing, HND IT, NVQ 5 in Management. It is also on the reading lists of ACCA, LCCI, ABE, AAT, AEB, IAM, ICM, IPS, CIMA and CIB.

Review comments

'Very accessible to students, and forms a useful basis for lectures.'
'Excellent book, good format and easily readable.'
'Excellent content, logically and well set out.' Lecturers

4th edition • 480 pp • 245 x 176 mm • 1993 • ISBN 1 85805 018 9

Personnel Management
Theory and Practice

G A Cole

This book is intended to meet the need of students and lecturers for an introductory textbook on personnel management.

It is known to be used on the following courses: IPM, ICSA, HNC/D Business and Finance, CNAA Diploma in Personnel Management, CNAA Degrees in Business Studies (Personnel Management Options), DMS, CIB, Institute of Training and Development, A Level Business Studies, CPP, HNC/D Human Resource Management, MIOM, IMS, BA Business Studies, IOH NEBSM, Association of Business Executives, CIPFA, Advanced GNVQ Business. It is also on the reading list of CIMA.

Review comments

'Clear, concise and comprehensive.'
'Good value all round text. Well researched and up-to-date.'   Lecturers

'Clearly presented and delightfully well written.'
Enterprise Magazine December 1993

3rd edition • 576 pp • 215 x 135 mm • 1993 • ISBN 1 85805 019 7

Strategic Management

G A Cole

This book provides a comprehensive introduction to the theory and practice of strategic management. It avoids the narrow focus and complexity of many other books written in this area, but enables the reader to identify and make connections between the key features of strategic management and the issues and choices that arise from them.

It is aimed at BA Business Studies but is expected to be used on ACCA (Management and Strategy) and CIMA (Strategic Management Accountancy and Marketing). It will also be suitable for students on postgraduate courses in Management or Business Studies, including the Diploma in Management Studies and introductory stages of MBA courses.

Contents: Part 1 Knowledge base Strategic management: an introduction; Defining mission and objectives; Assessing the environment; Formulating a strategy; Competitive advantage; International dimensions of strategy; Organisational culture.; Strategy implementation; Business planning; Forecasting the future; Managing change; Achieving excellence; Managing innovation; Managing quality; Role of marketing in strategic management; Role of personnel management in strategic management; Measuring performance and reviewing strategy; Managing success; Strategic management – a working model. Part 2 Strategic management in practice: case studies Multi-national organisations; Industrial/commercial organisations; Public sector organisations; Charitable/voluntary sector organisations; Small/medium sized enterprises. Workbook section – Exercises and questions (some with and some without answers) drawing together Part 1 and Part 2.

1st edition • 300 pp (approx) • 245 x 176 mm • *August 1994*
ISBN 1 85805 099 5

Tackling Coursework
Projects, Assignments, Reports & Presentations

D Parker

This book provides the student with practical guidance on how to approach the coursework requirement of a typical business studies course, i.e. projects, assignments, reports and presentations. The text makes clear the different approaches needed for the different types of coursework, with examples of each in an Appendix, and there is advice on how to conduct research, collect information and present results, in either written or verbal form. It is expected to be used on the following courses: any business studies course at undergraduate (e.g. BABS) or postgraduate (e.g. MBA) level. It would also be useful as a preparatory text for a research degree.

Contents: Introduction, Dissertations and projects, Essays and papers, Management reports, Seminars and presentations, Research methods Appendices: Further reading, Example of dissertation proposal, Example of citations, Dissertation contents, Example of an essay

1st edition • 96 pp • 215 x 135 mm • ISBN 1 85805 101 0